1595

The Mentally Ill in Contemporary Society

The Mentally Ill in Contemporary Society

A Sociological Introduction

AGNES MILES

MARTIN ROBERTSON · OXFORD

© Agnes Miles 1981

All rights reserved. No part of this publication
may be reproduced, stored in a retrieval system,
or transmitted in any form or by any
means, electronic, mechanical, photocopying,
recording, or otherwise, without the prior written
permission of the copyright holder.

First published in 1981 by Martin Robertson, Oxford.

British Library Cataloguing in Publication Data

Miles, Agnes
   The mentally ill in contemporary society.
   1.   Mental illness
   I.   Title
   301.5   RA790

ISBN 0 85520 376 5 (case)
ISBN 0 85520 377 3 (pbk)

Typeset by Pintail Studios, Ltd., Ringwood, Hampshire
Printed and bound in Great Britain by Book Plan Ltd., Worcester

Contents

Preface   *vii*

1: Who is Mentally Ill?   1
    Medical Critics   5
    The Labelling Theorists   12
    Some Consequences of the Anti-Psychiatric Approach   21

2: From Person to Patient   25
    Recognising the Problem   26
    Interpreting the Problem   33
    Consulting the Social Group   36
    Accommodation   43
    Decision to Seek Professional Help   49

3: The Social Role of the Mental Patient   54
    The Sick Role   55
    The Public Image of the Mentally Ill   60
    Stigma   69
    The Social Role of the Mentally Ill   72
    Assuming the Mental Patient Role   74

4: The Social Role of the Ex-Mental Patient   90
    The Climate of Public Opinion   93
    The Management of Stigma   102
    Performance of Social Roles   106

5: The Family of the Mentally Ill   115
    The Burden of Mental Illness   117
    The Social Position of the Family   128
    The Attitudes of Relatives   134

6: Men, Women and Mental Illness 143
Biological Factors 145
The Position of Men and Women in Society 146
The Responses of Men and Women to Illness 150
Defining Men and Women as Mentally Ill 155
Differential Use of Psychotropic Drugs 161

7: Social Class and Mental Illness 164
'Downward Drift' 167
Environmental Stress 171
Differential Labelling and Differential Treatment 188

8: The Expansion of Psychiatric Problems 192
The Expansion of Minor Psychiatric Symptoms 192
Disapproved Behaviour as Mental Disturbance 202

References 208

Index 221

Preface

In the twentieth century, and particularly from the 1950s onwards, a voluminous English language literature has appeared concerning diverse social aspects of psychiatric disorders. This still-growing number of books and articles reflects the interest of both social scientists and health professionals in the social causes and consequences of mental illness. Very many research programmes have been undertaken, resulting in a proliferation of research findings, some of great importance, others less so; some confirming previous findings, others contradictory. Much of the literature consists of reports on individual research projects, dealing with social factors as causes of mental disturbance and as influencing its course and outcome, the social distribution of these disorders, their effects on family life, public attitudes to mental disturbance and other allied topics (frequently, as in this volume, terms such as 'mental illness', 'mental disturbance', 'psychiatric disorders', etc., are used generically). As the interest of professionals became more pronounced many different teaching programmes were developed to include courses on the sociological and psychological aspects of psychiatric illness. Now, students of the health professions, as well as those of the social sciences, find themselves directed to an accumulation of research findings in the mental health field, which are relevant to their studies.

However, certain difficulties confront the student seeking to gather information from books and research articles. The latter are scattered among a variety of different journals and the processes of selecting and of tracking down the required information can be daunting. Once located, research findings are by no means easy to interpret; individual studies, even when concerned only with a narrow area of research, have particular aims, use different samples and methods, with the consequence of seemingly contradictory findings. Perhaps the biggest problem facing students is that many research projects carried out during the last three decades have been undertaken by researchers of different disciplines; sociologists, psychologists, epidemiologists, psychiatrists, social workers and physicians have all been active in researching the subject of mental illness from their own standpoints. Some of these researchers were concerned with the advancement of knowledge in their disciplines, others with treatment methods for psychiatric conditions and others again with the improvement of services. Besides these researchers, planners, practitioners, ex-patients and members of their families have contributed their views on aspects of psychiatric services and treatments and on their beliefs and notions concerning mental illness.

The available reading material is rich and stimulating as a consequence of the multiplicity of approaches, and the interested and experienced reader has a fine opportunity to examine particular issues from widely different angles. However, readers with less experience of this field may find the variety of arguments and perspectives initially confusing and it is hoped that an introduction from the perspective of a single discipline will prove useful.

The purpose of this book is to introduce students to some of the literature and to acquaint them with arguments and problems relating to the situation of mentally ill people in contemporary Western society, and to do so from the perspective of medical sociology. It is intended for the use of those studying to become health professionals and for students of the social sciences. Those who trian to become health professionals, for example students of medicine, nursing, social work and health administration, increasingly find the sociology of health and illness included in their training programmes, and for some the field of mental health is to be their special concern. Heightened social awareness, brought about by educational advances, political maturity and the popularisation by the media of previously not-talked-about subjects such as venereal disease, homosexuality and mental abnormality has led to large number of undergraduates entering social science courses. Many of today's students become interested in the study of medical sociology (especially those who intend later to work in the health field) and it is the intention to develop their interest by considering some selected topics in the sociology of mental health and mental illness.

Sociologists try to understand and explain the ways people act in particular social situations, through an understanding of how the persons themselves see their situation and the world about them. Sociologists argue that the actions of individuals can be understood only by reference to the social world, the cultural milieu, in which they are performed. Thus, the actions of those who become, or who have been, mentally ill can be usefully viewed within their social setting as can the actions not only of persons who unexpectedly find themselves dealing with a disturbed individual but also of those whose professional business it is.

The focus of the book is the consideration of sociological issues surrounding the situation of mentally ill people, rather than the sociology of mental illness. Even with this restriction, the topics which could be included are too numerous for an introductory volume and the subjects discussed here are selective. There were two bases for selection: one, to consider subjects on which research findings are available for discussion but not elsewhere presented for the use of students in a coherent form; the other, a personal interest in the subject, in the belief that one can only teach, and write with enthusiasm, on topics which one finds stimulating.

The first chapter serves as an introduction to the rest of the book. Although it deals with issues which have been presented for students and the general reader before, it is a necessary starting point for those unfamiliar with this field. It considers the question 'Who is mentally ill?', and looks at medical sociology's concern with the problems of mental illness.

The next three chapters have to do with the social role of the mentally ill; with the social processes involved in a person's becoming known in his social group as a mental patient; with the nature of the social role of the patient and with the situation of ex-patients. The focus of these chapters is the thinking, beliefs and attitudes of lay people.

Chapter 5 concentrates on the families of the mentally ill

rather than on the patients: the effects of having a mentally disturbed husband, wife or child, on the rest of the family, are considered. Chapters 6 and 7 are concerned with whether particular social groups have a greater incidence of mental disturbance than others and if so, why? In particular, the relationship between mental illness and social class, and the question of whether women are more prone than men to mental disturbance, are explored. The last chapter looks at what has been termed the 'medicalisation' of problems; the view that people are turning increasingly to psychiatric interpretations of their problems and to medical solutions for them.

The chapters are designed to be read independently of each other, one at a time, according to the interest of the reader, or to accompany appropriate lectures of teachers. The literature, for most of the topics discussed, is far too extensive for a complete review to be attempted. The books and articles referred to are selected to illustrate particular points under discussion and to give the reader an idea of some of the important research which has been carried out. The text of the book does not require any previous knowledge on the part of the reader either of sociology or of psychiatric disorders. The sociological terms used in the book are explained and lack of familiarity with psychiatric terminology should not interfere with understanding, as the book is concerned with sociological issues. However, the assumption throughout has been that it will be of interest to those who, from their studies or from their work, have an interest in either the mental health field or sociology. Indeed, it is hoped that this book will encourage readers to combine those interests.

CHAPTER 1

Who is Mentally Ill?

Who is mentally ill? This has proved an exasperatingly difficult question to answer. There is no consensus of opinion on the subject, in spite of the voluminous literature. The purpose of this chapter is to discuss briefly some controversial issues surrounding the concept of mental illness from the perspective of medical sociology.

Much controversy is centred around the notion of illness. There have always been individuals in society whose behaviour seemed odd, unusual or bizarre to their fellows and who were called by them 'mad', 'crazy', 'lunatic', or a variety of similar terms; are they 'ill' in the same sense that someone suffering from pneumonia, heart disease or arthritis is ill? The issue is confusing because the term illness has more than one meaning. Thus, the American sociologist, Eliot Freidson, makes a distinction between illness as a 'bio-physical state' and illness as a 'social state' (Freidson, 1973). The former, to which the term disease is also applied, refers to abnormalities in the biological functioning of the human body. Such abnormalities can be said to have an objective, biological reality, independent of how people think of them, and are subject to laws which apply to man, mouse or monkey. A fractured bone (or pneumonia or arthritis) is a biological state, it is 'there' whether the individual notices it or not, names it 'illness' or not, considers it a good thing or a bad.

By contrast, illness as a social state is bound up with people's beliefs, evaluations and actions.

> In human society, naming something an illness has consequences independent of the biological state of the organism. Consider two men in different societies, both with the same debilitating infection: in one case, the man is said to be ill, put to bed, and taken care of by others; in the other case, he is said to be lazy, and he is abused by others. The course and outcome of the disease may be the same biologically in both cases, but the social interplay between the sick man and others is significantly different. And consider the social consequences of diagnosis behaviour: one diagnosis may lead to 'cure', another diagnosis may lead to death. While disease may be 'there', it is what we, as social beings, think and do about it that determines the content of our lives. (Freidson, 1973, p. 208)

Illness as a social state is of particular interest to sociologists, as it is bound up with social evaluations and actions. Central to the notion of illness is the existence of a set of norms representing health, normality and the way things should be. Illness is seen then as a difference, or deviation, from such norms. Arthritis or a fractured bone exist independently of this normative element, but the evaluation of these conditions as some sort of deviation from a desirable state of things is connected to notions of what is desirable. Moreover, the norms of health and deviation are social and cultural norms, in the sense that in particular societies, at given times, general agreement exists among its members as to what is health and what is ill-health. A condition may be regarded as healthy in one society and not in another.

Most people would agree that a healthy person is able to walk out of his house, unaided by crutches, or that he is able to pick up a knife and fork preparatory to eating. If a person is not able to do these things, his fellows (and himself) will say that something is 'wrong' with him, that he deviates from the normal, healthy state. In contemporary industrial societies Western medicine has been established for many years as the authority on matters relating to ill-health. In these societies the person who cannot walk out of the house or lift a knife and fork will consult a doctor, because that is the culturally appropriate, accepted action. On examination the doctor will pronounce that person's deviation from normal functioning as being due to a fractured bone, or to a certain biological malfunctioning of the body. By giving a medical name to the condition (i.e. assigning it to a diagnostic category), the doctor confirms, or 'validates', the tentative lay definition of the deviation as illness. The person will be called 'ill' and a number of social consequences will follow, such as relieving that person from normal duties, looking after him, etc. If the illness is prolonged, if it is accompanied by unpleasant or repulsive sights or smells, then stigma will be attached.

The beliefs and action surrounding the illness are culturally and historically specific. In another society the person seen as deviating from the normal may be taken to a different kind of medicine man, a magician or herbalist, who may ascribe the deviation to evil spirits or to the ill will of an enemy. Treatment and social consequences, possibly quite different from those in a Western society, would then follow.

At the centre of the illness notion in all societies is an agreement as to what is normal functioning, and an evaluation of the abnormal as undesirable, something which should be changed into normal. But what of the person who is unable to walk out of his house, not because he needs crutches to support his body, but because he is terrified of the space outside and feels sure that something terrible will happen to him there? What of the person who cannot lift the knife and fork because a voice, speaking to him clearly from the centre of his head, forbids him to do so? People in many different societies would agree that such a person deviates from the normal. Not all deviations however are regarded as illness; some are regarded as criminality, wickedness, bad manners, sin, betrayal or madness.

Madness has a long tradition in the history of Western societies. Since biblical times there have been records of people who seemed odd: who said that they could hear voices which no one else could hear, or see things which no one else could see, or fly through the air. At various times such people have been regarded as witches, saints, persons possessed by the devil or suffering from black bile or from mental derangement. Researchers of the records of biblical times and of ancient Greece and Rome have attempted to reconstruct the case-histories of madmen and the criteria that led to their being regarded as such (Rosen, 1968). Although 'divine madness' in prophets and oracles was accorded high prestige, more commonly those labelled insane became objects of abuse, scorn and ridicule. Some of the physicians of the time regarded mental disorder as being closely related to physical illness, but popular concepts were negative, the mad person being deprived of rights (e.g. under Roman law the insane could not marry or dispose of property), restrained or, in extreme cases, driven out of society. The Middle Ages brought belief in witches and possession by evil spirits, and people turned to the priests to exorcise the evil spirits and so cure the affliction. The concepts of the harmless fool and the insane coexisted with these beliefs, and there were medieval physicians who looked for physical causes of madness.

Over the ages, physical illness and mental disturbance were variably seen as similar or as different types of problems by individual physicians. Sedgwick argues that certain societies readily view mental disturbance and physical complaints as one. 'Ceremonies of ritual purgation and demon-expulsion, along with primitive "medical" methods of a herbal or surgical type, are used indifferently by traditional healers on patients with a mental or bodily disfunction. Fever and madness, the broken limb or broken spirit are situated within the same normative frame, within the same explanatory and therapeutic system' (Sedgwick, 1973, p. 35). A unitary perspective on deviations which are now called physical and mental illness also seemed natural to seventeenth century physicians in Western Europe: both types could be attributed to 'the vapours', 'the fluid', 'the humours' or 'the spleen'.

Whether a particular deviation is classified as illness in a society largely depends on it being seen by people as a deviation from health, and as such in the domain of expert healers, and on the healers' acceptance of it as belonging to their province. Classification of deviations in society is an ongoing process, many types being reclassified from time to time according to changing notions of their nature. For example, in western societies regular and heavy consumption of alcohol by an individual has recently changed from a 'bad habit' to an illness called 'alcoholism', for which doctors are the relevant experts. Similarly, certain types of anti-social behaviour are increasingly reclassified as deviations from a health norm and belonging therefore to the province of doctors. Indeed, there has been a general shift towards regarding an increasing number of deviant conditions as illness, especially as twentieth century pharmacological development has encouraged medical intervention in many conditions.

Thus, it can be argued that the person who cannot walk out of the house because of fear of the outside, or who cannot lift the knife and fork because a voice forbids it (to use the previous examples), is certainly regarded as deviating from norms, and in Western societies during the nineteenth and twentieth centuries, such deviations have increasingly become regarded as illness and as such in the province of medicine. Doctors have been increasingly willing to regard certain types of behaviour, traditionally thought 'odd' by people generally, as indicating illness, and, similar to the social process that takes place in respect of a sprained ankle or arthritis, they validate a tentative lay definition by according a medical diagnosis to the condition.

The main contemporary controversy surrounding the question as to who should be regarded as mentally ill, was started by some psychiatrists and social scientists arguing that the trend of regarding more and more deviations as mental illness had gone far enough (this will be discussed in a later chapter). Some critics of Western psychiatric practice then went on to question the very notions of deviations and illness, and indeed the practice of psychiatry itself. These critics became very outspoken during the 1960s and 1970s, expressing views based on different theoretical perspectives and many of their arguments and recommendations were contradictory. They share one thing however: the critical stance they have adopted towards psychiatric theory and practice; and for that reason they have jointly become known as the school of 'anti-psychiatry' – a misleading term as it implies some unity of perspective that is not the case.

MEDICAL CRITICS

One widely read and influential medical critic is Thomas Szasz, a professor of psychiatry in the United States. He writes in an easy style and his books reach not only professionals but also many people who have not previously considered the issues raised by him; thus his influence is considerable. His pronouncement that 'there is no such thing as mental illness' has been much quoted (Szasz, 1961; Szasz, 1971). The central argument in the writings of Szasz is that the various conditions that western psychiatrists currently call mental illness are not 'illness' in the same sense as is physical illness. He argues that in the case of physical illness it is possible to state in terms of anatomy and physiology how the human body functions when healthy and to show illness as a deviation from that normal functioning. For example, it is possible to state, in terms of physiology, how the respiratory system works when healthy and to demonstrate what goes wrong in the case of malfunctioning. Therefore, doctors concerned with physical illness are dealing with objective, biological, value-free categories: a broken bone is a broken bone everywhere.

By contrast, when it comes to what is generally called 'mental illness', Szasz holds that it is not possible to state in terms of anatomy and physiology how the mind functions when 'normal', nor to show what goes wrong in cases of apparent malfunctioning. It is only possible to state that the way a person behaves, or feels, seems abnormal to him or to his fellows and this statement is a social and ethical, not a medical, judgement. For example, the bizarre conduct of some people can only be stated in behavioural terms: not in such a fashion do people behave in society.

> We speak of mental symptoms, on the other hand, when we refer to the patient's communications about himself, others and the world about him. He might state that he is Napoleon or that he is being persecuted by the Communists. These would be considered mental symptoms only if the observer believed that the patient was not Napoleon or that he was not being persecuted by the Communists. This makes it apparent that the statement that 'X is a mental symptom' involves rendering a judgement. The judgement entails, moreover, a covert comparison or matching of the patient's ideas, concepts or beliefs with those of the observer and the society in which they live. The notion of mental symptoms is therefore inextricably tied to the social (including ethical) context in

which it is made in much the same way as the notion of bodily symptoms is tied to an anatomical and genetic context. (Szasz, 1960, p. 114)

Szasz agrees that brain dysfunction can cause disorders in behaviour and thinking, but allows this only where some disease of, or injury to, the brain is discernible and in any case states that sufferers from such conditions are physically, not mentally ill. In respect of the much larger number of persons diagnosed as mentally ill, where no organic cause has been satisfactorily demonstrated, Szasz contends that the term 'mental illness' is entirely inappropriate. He does not say that everything is fine with such people, but that they have 'problems of living' and not illness conditions (Szasz, 1961).

Two important points have been made by subsequent writers. The first is a challenge to Szasz's argument that it is not possible to demonstrate how the mind functions either when healthy or apparently sick. If someone wishes to walk out of a house or to lift a knife, actions of which human beings are capable in any society, but finds that he is unable to do so, then some malfunctioning is demonstrated. Anthony Flew argued that the concept of normal capability, of what we can or cannot do if we try, is central to the notion of health and illness, both physical and mental. 'There is a difference between on the one hand the case of – say – my liver, which however hard I try I cannot move at all except by shifting my whole torso; and on the other hand my little fingers, which I can wriggle around whenever and however the fancy takes me' (Flew, 1973, p. 38). When someone cannot wriggle his little finger or do any of the things which normally functioning people can do at will, that is malfunctioning. '. . . the function of whatever is normally subject to our wills precisely is to be in this normal way thus subject' (p. 39); and further, 'If he or she is unable to move the paralysed member or, as the case may be, unable to stop the compulsive performances . . . it is necessarily authentically incapacitating. There is therefore no reason for denying that here is a case of disease' (Flew, 1973, p. 62).

The second point is that Szasz mistakenly regards physical illness and the work of physicians as value-free and independent of social beliefs and judgements. To use Freidson's terminology, Szasz concentrates on illness as a biophysical state and ignores illness as a social state, and yet the diagnosis and the treatment of physical illness are inherently social actions. Notions of health and normal functioning are cultural and medical knowledge itself is specific to particular societies and times. The history of medicine shows that today's medical conceptions are not the same as the 'modern' notions of yesterday, and some, at least, of tomorrow's conceptions will contradict the notions of today. In a criticism of the notions of Szasz, Martin Roth pointed out that 'Microorganisms such as the streptococcus or tubercle bacillus cause fatal infections in some individuals and live harmlessly in others. As the latter do not suffer pain or incapacity, we do not diagnose disease or regard them as ill' (Roth, 1976, p. 318).

The whole medical enterprise is concerned with judgements and evaluations, based on current knowledge. Some very apt comments are made by Sedgwick: 'The attribution of illness always proceeds from the computation of a gap between presented behaviour (or feeling) and some social norm. In practice of course we take the norm for granted, so that the broken arm or the elevated temperature is seen alone as the illness. But the broken arm would be no more of an illness than a broken fingernail unless it stopped us from achieving certain socially constructed goals; just as, if we could all function according to approved social requirements within any range of body temperature, thermometers would disappear from the household medical kit'. (Sedgwick, 1973, p. 34); and, further, 'The blight that strikes at corn or at potato is a human invention, for if man wished to cultivate parasites (rather than potatoes or corn) there would be no "blight", but simply the necessary foddering of the parasite crop' (Sedgwick, 1973, p. 30).

Thus, Szasz's argument that physical illness is free of social evaluations can be challenged just as much as his notion that mental illness cannot be adequately stated in terms of malfunctioning.

Of all the writings of Szasz, perhaps most often quoted is his accusation of western psychiatrists as agents of an oppressive society. His view of mental illness as a set of value-laden judgements of human behaviour leads him to question who is making the judgements and why; his answer is that individuals who do not conform to social rules but behave differently from the accepted norms, and in ways which upset others, are called mentally ill by psychiatrists and are oppressed in the interest of the powerful sections in society. These non-conforming persons are then locked up, put away and coerced, by so called 'treatments', until they conform. In very strong words Szasz calls psychiatrists 'professional hirelings', 'jailers' and 'torturers', the psychiatric hospitals 'prisons' and psychiatric practice a 'conspiracy' (Szasz, 1961). These are words which make stirring speeches, but are not easily translated into propositions for or against which evidence can be produced. Clearly Szasz is very angry about the injustices that he believes are done to psychiatric patients, and he is certainly right in that there many things to be angry about. The lot of the mentally ill is not easy; they are stigmatised, placed into inferior social positions and are given inadequate help – as will be shown in later chapters. He is also right in that psychiatry can be over-expanded and abused. But while fighting for the rights of the mentally ill, Szasz also denies their suffering and their need for help. He sees the psychiatric hospitals as symbols of oppression; but, as Martin Roth put it, Szasz shuts his eyes to some facts about patients: '. . . that their troubles are desperate, their sufferings extreme; that, indeed, they feel, and are, very ill; that the psychiatrists who care for them are not guilty conspirators but earnest and compassionate men and women, trying to do what they can to help the sufferer in each individual case' (Roth, 1976, p. 324).

To the question 'Who is mentally ill?' Szasz would answer that no one is, that some people are called that in order to suppress their behaviour which displeases others. In this opinion he is joined by Ronald Laing.

Laing, like Szasz, built on his own experiences as a psychiatrist and, also like Szasz, came to criticise in strong terms the concept of mental illness and psychiatric practice (Laing, 1959, 1961, 1967). He is most concerned with schizophrenia and his central argument is that the behaviour and the communications of those identified as schizophrenic are not 'irrational' but makes sense when viewed from the position in which the patient finds himself. The delusions and hallucinations of the schizophrenic can all be understood, according to Laing's argument, if the particular psychological and social pressures on him are revealed, it being especially important to understand the patient's family setting and the web of relationships that surround him. Laing and his colleague Esterson described what they regarded as some typical features of a 'schizophrenic family' in their book *Sanity, Madness and the Family* (1964). Based on a study of eleven families in which one member was diagnosed as schizophrenic, the material presented consists of case histories and extracts from long interviews with the various family members. Laing argues that the dynamics of such families as these manoeuvre the patients into situations in which it is impossible to behave otherwise than in a seemingly irrational manner; that in particular, impossible and destructive demands have been made by the families on the patients. In analysing the early experiences of the schizophrenics, Laing made extensive use of the notion of 'double-bind', developed by Bateson and furthered by Lidz (Bateson *et al.*, 1956; Lidz *et al.*, 1965). According to this notion, in certain families a child is subjected to contradictory demands to which it is impossible to respond satisfactorily. Contradictory demands may come from one parent or from both. An illustration of the former is the mother, who stiffens and expresses displeasure by her posture and facial expression when her son puts his arms around her; when the son responds to this by withdrawing, the mother says 'Don't you love me any more?' Thus, contradictory and mystifying messages reach the son, who finds that it is not possible to respond satisfactorily to the mother's demands: she wishes to be loved and not to be loved at the same time. In the second type of double-bind situation, the mother and the father make demands which are incompatible with each other and, at the same time, they demand a response from their child which is acceptable to both. According to Laing, the essence of the double-bind family situation is that there is no 'rational' way to make satisfactory sense of it, no 'rational' way to respond and survive; only 'irrational' behaviour makes sense.

Building on the notion of double-bind Laing developed his

theme of a certain type of family as a 'pathogenic institution', in which the child is surrounded by overwhelming psychological and social stresses. Laing suggests that the parents in such families are extremely rigid in their discipline (for example in early toilet training and in limiting activities) and prevent the child from becoming a person in his own right. The experience and behaviour that is called schizophrenic is, according to this argument, a special strategy by which a person can live in an unliveable situation. The parents destroy the individual by mystifying him and he responds by counter-mystifying them, i.e. by irrational behaviour.

Thus, Laing's position is that the only difference between the persons called schizophrenic and everybody else is that impossible demands were laid on the former, who, in turn, responded by appropriate, though irrational-seeming behaviour. Any of us might have responded in similar ways, or in even more devastating fashion.

But this is exactly the question which Laing's assertions raise: would all of us respond in similar ways? Schizophrenic patients have been reared in families with other siblings who did not become mentally ill. It is possible of course, as Laing suggests, that one person in a 'schizophrenic family' becomes the scapegoat on whom all the stresses are concentrated, but then it has to be explained why that person, rather than the others, plays that role and why that person responded to the family situation in just such a way: i.e. by hallucinations, persecutory delusions, obsessive rituals or other symptoms. Is there any evidence to show that Laing is right and that certain family dynamics result in one member's irrational schizophrenic behaviour?

Laing himself does not answer these questions and produces no evidence on the basis of which others may find answers. He is against systematic investigations aimed to provide evidence and is opposed to controls and comparisons. In a discussion, Wing says that

> The study falls into that large group of uncontrolled investigations in which an enormous mass of information is collected in an unstandardised and unsystematic manner about a very small number of people. From this material a personal selection is made in order to illustrate a highly complex theoretical

interpretation. The extracts from the interviews are included as demonstrations of a theory whose truth is regarded as revealed. (Wing, 1977, p. 160)

Laing's insights are certainly very thought-provoking and he may well be right in many of the things he says, but it is impossible to be sure without further evidence, one way or another. There have been attempts to study some of the Laingian notions; for example Hirsch and Leff (1975) looked into the possibility that double-bind situations may be particularly common among families of schizophrenics, but found no convincing evidence for this. They did find that parents of schizophrenic patients have more psychiatric disturbances themselves than is found among a random selection of the general population, and that there are more conflicts in such families, but this is equally consistent with a genetic explanation of the disorder.

Laing's position regarding psychiatric practice is that it is coercive and repressive, that diagnosis and treatment are used as means of controlling people who make nuisances of themselves. He feels that by calling a person schizophrenic, the psychiatrist is colluding with the family in blaming the patient for the faults of the parents and that much damage is done by consigning the patient to a mental hospital. As Laing does not accept schizophrenia as a pathological state he views such a diagnosis by doctors as 'ascribing stigma' in order to suppress. Thus, Laing, like Szasz, argues that the concept of mental illness in general is misleading and that no one is mentally ill. As one of his colleagues, Cooper, puts it: 'Madness, that is to say, is not "in" a person, but in a system of relationships in which the labelled "patient" participates: schizophrenia, if it means anything, is a more or less characteristic mode of disturbed group behaviour. There are no schizophrenics' (Cooper, 1970, p. 43).

THE LABELLING THEORISTS

During the last three decades sociologists also have become increasingly interested in the theoretical and practical issues surrounding mental illness and, like Szasz and Laing, some of them have become highly critical of a medical approach to the subject. The most cohesive and elaborate statement comes from Thomas Scheff, who formulated what he called a 'sociological theory' of mental illness, in his book *Being Mentally Ill* (Scheff, 1966).

In developing his propositions about mental illness Scheff built on a theoretical perspective known as the labelling theory. This was originally developed as an approach to the study of deviance in society by Lemert (1951 and 1964) and subsequently by Becker (1963). The relevant argument is that deviance is a function of the responses of others to a particular action. For example, singing in the street after a famous victory is not deviant, everyone else is singing too, but the drunkard singing late at night in a quiet neighbourhood is something else, and the beggar singing for alms, something else again, resented by some and pitied by others. And what of the man singing for no discernible reason? Clearly, then, singing in the street is an action which only becomes deviant when people view it as such. The characteristics of the singer and his action are of less importance in producing deviance than are the social responses to them.

This approach to the study of deviance was developed by critics of the more traditional 'clinical' approach, in which much attention is given to the deviant's motivation and characteristics. The important question in a clinical framework is to determine how someone becomes a thief, a bank-robber or a killer, i.e. what psychological and social characteristics in upbringing, cultural milieu or emotional life make a person into a deviant? This approach can be called clinical, because the task of those studying deviance is seen to be the determination of the causes (or aetiology) of a certain type of behaviour and the finding of the appropriate management or treatment for it.

Critics of the clinical approach say that instead of focusing attention exclusively on the deviants themselves, sociologists should concentrate on the social processes by which certain actions come to be labelled deviant in a particular society and should consider why any particular action is considered to be one kind of deviance rather than another. Advocates of this approach became known as the labelling (or societal reaction) theorists.

The more moderate adherents of this approach argue that both the deviants and the labellers (those who impute deviance) require studying, and that the study of the interplay between the characteristics of deviants and the social reaction or labelling is a most promising approach. The more extreme proponents of the labelling theory, however, argue that the characteristics and motivation of individual deviants are unimportant in producing deviance in society, that it is labelling an action and a person deviant that creates deviance. Therefore the most important, if not the only important, questions are those which concern labellers and the process of labelling.

Scheff applied the labelling perspective to mental illness: he argued that the behaviour exhibited by psychiatric patients can be viewed essentially as 'rule-breaking' behaviour, i.e., behaviour which violates the agreed-upon rules of society. In other words, persons who are called mentally ill deviate from certain standards or norms of behaviour. But which norms are being violated? Scheff argues that there are some social norms which are so much taken for granted, so much accepted by everyone in a society, that breaking them seems a bizarre action.

> A host of such norms surround even the simplest conversation: a person engaged in conversation is expected to face his partner, he is expected to look toward the other's eyes, rather than, say, toward his forehead; to stand at a proper conversational distance, neither one inch away nor across the room, and so on. A person who regularly violated these expectations probably would not be thought to be merely ill-bred, but as strange, bizarre and frightening, because his behaviour violates the assumptive world of the group, the world that is construed to be the only one that is natural, decent and possible. (Scheff, 1966, p. 32)

Violation of such taken-for-granted rules is, then, a special kind of rule-breaking; Scheff says that when the culture of the group categorises the various violations as crime, bad manners, sin, etc., there is a residue of diverse kinds of violation, for which the culture provides no explicit label. This he calls 'residual rule-breaking', part of which are symptoms such as hallucinations, withdrawal, continual muttering, etc.

The Labelling Theorists

According to Scheff, residual rule-breaking arises from many diverse sources: organic, psychological, external stress and deliberate acts of innovation or defiance. Thus, genetic or biochemical conditions may cause odd behaviour (organic source) and so may peculiarities of upbringing and training (psychological source); or it can happen that external stress such as sustained hardship, fear, lack of sleep, combat conditions in war, can result in rule-breaking. There are also deliberate acts of defiance and rebellion and, finally, innovation: Scheff illustrates this by examples from art-history: the early reactions of people to French impressionist painting was dismay, the pictures were thought of as so unreal as to be evidence of madness. These diverse types of source can all produce rule-breaking behaviour.

Scheff further argues that a great deal of diverse residual rule-breaking goes on unrecorded and unacknowledged, without public identification of the persons involved as violators of rules, and he pays much attention to the question of why some, but not other, such rule-breakers become identified as mentally ill. His answer is that most rule-breaking is denied or minimised by the social group: it is accepted that people may go through a 'bad phase' and behave in an unusual manner for a time, or that some people are eccentric or idiosyncratic in certain ways. The denied or minimised rule-breaking is transitory and often not repeated. In a small proportion of cases however, he argues that the reaction of society is the opposite: the violation of rules is exaggerated, its extent and degree magnified, and the individuals are labelled mentally ill by their families, by doctors, or by other social agencies. Mental illness, or madness, has a cultural stereotype, and once labelled this way a certain 'mad' behaviour is expected from the person concerned.

> In a crisis, when the deviance of an individual becomes a public issue, the traditional stereotype of insanity becomes the guiding imagery for action, both for those reacting to the deviant, and at times, for the deviant himself. When societal agents and persons around the deviant react to him uniformly in terms of the traditional stereotypes of insanity, his amorphous and unstructured rule-breaking tends to crystallize

in conformity to these expectations, thus becoming similar to the behaviour of other deviants classified as mentally ill, and stable over time. (Scheff, 1966, p. 82)

For Scheff the act of being labelled as mentally ill is the most important thing that happens to the individual concerned; at that point the person's residual rule-breaking behaviour stabilises and he goes on to behave, according to expectations, in ways that are more odd, more bizarre, than the symptoms that gave rise to the original label. Scheff suggests that once labelled the person will be rewarded by others around him for accepting the label and for playing the ascribed role; acceptance is facilitated by the rule-breaker being highly suggestible in a crisis situation. If everybody tells you that you are mad, you come to accept it. It is especially likely that the label will be accepted when a person of authority and influence, such as a judge or psychiatrist, applies it.

Thus, Scheff's answer to the question of 'Who is mentally ill?' is that those labelled as such, are.

Scheff's mode of applying the labelling theory of deviance to mental illness raises some important issues. It is possible to accept the importance of societal reaction and labelling without being in full agreement with the position of the more extreme statements of the labelling theorists. It was said earlier that calling something illness has important social consequences, which are independent of the clinical condition: when a person is labelled 'ill', certain social responses follow, just as much as when a person is labelled 'criminal' or 'traitor'. Certainly, to call someone mentally ill has considerable and far-reaching consequences affecting that person's social standing, acceptability, self-image and many other aspects of his life, as will be discussed in subsequent chapters. The labelling theorists, however, go beyond this: they argue that the act of labelling someone mentally ill creates the mentally ill behaviour; that the original symptoms are unimportant and without labelling would go unnoticed. The implication of this argument is that persons labelled mentally ill would be quite all right if it were not for the act of labelling.

This is very different from pointing out the social consequences of being identified as mentally ill. To minimise the importance of the original psychiatric symptoms to that extent is, essentially, to agree with Szasz that 'mental disorder' is not recognisable in any specific form before the label is applied to it.

Scheff supports his propositions from his own research carried out in a Midwestern state of the United States in 1962: he studied patterns of admissions and discharges in three state mental hospitals. His experience was that psychiatrists applied diagnostic categories to patients carelessly, after short, superficial examinations.

> The behaviour or 'condition' of the person alleged to be mentally ill is not usually an important factor in the decision of officials to retain or release new patients from the mental hospital. The marginal nature of the majority of the cases, the peremptoriness and inadequacy of most of the examinations, when considered in light of the fact that virtually every patient is recommended for commitment, would appear to demonstrate this proposition. (Scheff, 1966, p. 154)

Scheff concluded that the psychiatrists in the study were not concerned with the proper medical work of finding out what illness, if any, the patient suffered from but with the attachment of a medical label to those rule-breakers who had been taken to them by families or courts; and that psychiatrists acted as agents of social and legal control. The implication is that the rule-breakers brought to the psychiatrists exhibited symptoms that were in fact widespread in the normal population and that these symptoms were used as pretexts for labelling them mad. This is, indeed, a very strong criticism of both the concept of mental illness and the work of psychiatrists, and the special importance of the criticism for Scheff's theoretical propositions lies in his argument that once a person is labelled mentally ill he will continue to play the role of the mental patient and behave in the ways expected of such a person. If diagnosis by psychiatrists is careless and based on uncertainties and ignorance then many patients really suffer from nothing more than labelling. This is also the view of another, very influential sociologist, Erving Goffman. In his analysis of the 'moral career' of the mental patient Goffman says that such patients suffer from 'contingencies' rather than from anything else; such contingencies being the hazards of labelling by families and professionals (Goffman, 1961).

Whether Scheff's experiences in the Midwestern hospitals of the early 1960s are applicable to the situation of today and to psychiatric practice elsewhere, is questionable. At that time most psychiatric patients in the United States were compulsorily detained but the legal position has changed since, while in Britain the vast majority of psychiatric patients have been, for a long time, 'voluntary' admissions to hospitals. It has also been pointed out that the chance of being diagnosed as schizophrenic is between two and three times greater in America than it is in Britain and that therefore generalisations may be unsafe (Office of Health Economics, 1979). But perhaps more important is the point that if Scheff is right in saying that psychiatrists diagnosed without adequate skill and due care and took too little time, then this shows the need for more care and attention and above all for better diagnostic skills. To conclude from the existence of bad psychiatric practice that no good practice is possible, and moreover that mental illness is not meaningful, is unwarranted. To give an illustration from the field of physical illness: if it is demonstrated that a good many physicians diagnose venereal diseases wrongly, the conclusion would not be that it is not possible to diagnose these conditions accurately, nor indeed that such diseases do not exist, but that physicians should be better trained and more careful. This conclusion would be reached even though the label of having a venereal disease is socially damaging to the individual.

Scheff's formulation of the labelling theory of mental illness is not without its opponents, who represent varied medical and sociological perspectives. One of the most vocal of these is the sociologist Walter Gove who argues that Scheff's propositions are wrong and are unsupported by evidence (Gove, 1970). Gove maintains that the vast majority of persons who become psychiatric patients suffer from a serious mental disturbance which exists before, and independently of, any label that may be applied to individual sufferers. The debate between Scheff and Gove is often acrimonious and the reader gains the impression that they provoke each other into taking rigidly fixed positions.

On the whole, there is far more debate than systematic research regarding the labelling theory of mental illness. Scheff's argument is supported by a much publicised study of Rosenhan that describes how investigators pretended to be mentally ill by falsely professing to have certain psychiatric symptoms; and how psychiatrists were fooled and accepted the investigators as genuine patients (Rosenhan, 1973). This study is both methodologically and ethically dubious; but if it shows anything it is that labelling is important: once mistakenly diagnosed, the false patients were treated as genuine by all hospital staff. In support of the opposite position, Gove produced evidence that the act of labelling is less important than labelling theorists believe (Gove and Fain, 1973); and in a rather rare systematic investigation concerning the application of diagnostic labels, Bean (1979) found that practising psychiatrists are not lacking in care and skill, nor do they endorse lay labelling as easily as Scheff suggested. (This and other studies will be discussed in later chapters.)

Other aspects of Scheff's propositions have also been criticised by subsequent writers. Thus, to say that rule-breakers easily accept the verdict of labellers and then convincingly play the part of the disturbed patient, appears a doubtful proposition to many. Coulter questions Scheff's assumption that those who believe quite bizarre things and act in very odd ways are not genuinely insane. 'Instead, we are urged to think of them as acting uncritically on the basis of a stigmatised role imputed to them by hostile audiences to minor social gaffes ... the victim is supposed to internalise without question the audience's imputation of mental derangement' (Coulter, 1973, p. 64). If this were so, says Coulter, then mental hospitals would be populated by frauds. Another critic, John Wing, points out that it is difficult to see how societal reaction would force a person 'to adopt the central schizophrenic syndrome since this would need special coaching from an expert'. (Wing, 1973).

The various critics of the 'illness' approach to mental disorder write from different perspectives and pursue different lines of argument, but there is a curiously common theme in their writings: an assumption that people become psychiatric patients through the ill-will and victimisation of others around them. In Laing's writings it appears that the schizophrenic patient is the victim of his family's particular dynamics and scape-goating; and Szasz emphasises that psychiatrists carry out the wishes of a hostile group when they call innocent, but non-conforming, persons 'mentally disturbed'. Scheff, without spelling it out, implies that psychiatrists' endorsement of lay labelling means a medical approval of incompetent or malicious lay verdicts: according to him some rule-breakers meet with hostile responses from people who 'exaggerate' and 'distort' their behaviour and 'seek out signs of abnormality in the deviant's history to show that he was always essentially a deviant' (Scheff, 1966, p. 81). Likewise Goffman argues that mental patients are 'discredited' and 'betrayed' by hostile family and hospital staff (Goffman, 1961). This assumption of hostility towards certain individuals is sometimes called the 'conspiratorial' approach to mental illness: a perspective in which society is seen to conspire against certain individuals and to manoeuvre them into a position of appearing mad. What is not crystallised in the various writings is why society, or certain groups in it, should exhibit such hostility towards some, especially as the victims appear to be a diverse set of people, different in terms of family background, social class and personality. Neither is any evidence given to show that the hostility exists; rather the assumption of it is offered as an explanation of why some individuals, whom the writers assume to be perfectly sane, are still regarded as mentally disturbed by those in contact with them. But there is no convincing reason to assume that all lay and professional labellers are hostile, any more than to assume, as Scheff appears to, that lay verdicts are most likely to be wrong. On the contrary, there is considerable research evidence to show that family members and other lay associates of prospective patients apply the mental illness label with great reluctance and as a last resort. Neither is it likely that lay labelling is invariably mistaken. On the contrary, it is more likely, as Coulter says that any responsible member of a community, with no more than a control over the logic of his moral, social order, can discriminate grossly between insanity and sanity; indeed, given the onus of having to furnish some reasons for an ascription, it is doubtful if that onus does not operate as an important motive for ensuring adequacy of recognition or an effort to assure oneself that one does possess sufficiently convincing evidence, not the least to avoid the charge of malice. (Coulter, 1973, p. 66)

SOME CONSEQUENCES OF THE ANTI-PSYCHIATRIC APPROACH

The writings of some of the critics of mental illness as a concept of psychiatric practice, have reached a wide readership: the books of Laing, Szasz and Goffman especially have been read in both Britain and the United States by many lay people as well as by those with a professional interest in the subject. The advantage of this lies in lay readers having become more knowledgeable and more sophisticated in matters surrounding mental illness; and in both lay and professional readers having been made aware of the controversial nature of the issues. The important achievement of these critics was that they revealed the existence of social processes in diagnosis and treatment, and acquainted a wide readership with the argument of social scientists – that mental illness is a social construction and psychiatry a social institution that incorporates the values and demands of its surrounding society. Readers became aware, as Sedgwick put it, that 'to say that somebody is mentally ill, or to announce oneself as mentally ill, is to attach complex social meanings to acts and behaviours that in other societies, or in different contingencies within our own society, would be interpreted in the light of quite different concepts' (Sedgwick, 1973, p. 27). The problem is that sociologists also argue that physical as well as mental illness has a similar social dimension and to limit the notion of social construction to mental illness alone, as Szasz, Laing and Goffman for example have done, is incorrectly to imply that physical illness is somehow different in this respect.

There are other important problems, however, with the popular success of the anti-psychiatric critics. These writers attacked the illness approach to mental disorders and the practice of psychiatry; they put forward the 'conspiracy' approach in which psychiatrists, and indeed all psychiatric hospital personnel, are seen as agents of an oppressive society, whose motives and methods of treatment are, at best, doubtful. As a result, psychiatry has become thoroughly unpopular with some sections of the reading public interested in social and health matters. Consequently such people do not press for better psychiatric services, nor for more resources to be allocated to treating disturbed patients and researching into psychiatric disorders. If it is questionable whether mental illness exists at all and whether psychiatrists do any good, then potential pressure groups remain doubtful and silent. Likewise, potential helpers of disturbed patients and their families lack certainty as to the relative merits of the arguments and tend to withdraw from any helping action. By focusing attention on the labellers rather than the labelled the notion has gained acceptance that if only people in society became more tolerant of aberrant behaviour and did not apply derogatory labels, the problem of mental disorder would disappear. In a discussion of the illness model of mental disorder, Sedgwick says:

> In trying to remove and reduce the concepts of mental illness, the revisionist theorists have made it that much harder for a powerful campaign of reform in the mental-health services to get off the ground. The revisionists have thought themselves, and their public, into a state of complete inertia: they can expose the hypocrisies and annotate the tragedies of official psychiatry, but the concepts which they have developed enable them to engage in no public action which is grander than that of wringing their hands ... (they are) in the battle, on the wrong side: the side of those who want to close down intensive psychiatric units and throw the victims of mental illness on to the streets. (Sedgwick, 1973, p. 39)

Meanwhile, what happens to the mentally disturbed, to those who are unable to leave the house because of a phobia, or to carry out simple actions because they feel themselves forbidden to do so (to return to previous examples); or to those who suffer from many other incapacitating fears, threats, compulsions or distresses? The most serious charge that can be levelled against the advocates of anti-psychiatry is that they leave suffering, helpless individuals without assistance and expose them, and their families and associates, to potential harm. While the critics of psychiatric practice advocate more tolerance, an end to labelling and the cessation of treatment, one patient sinks into melancholic gloom and kills himself, another kills his much-loved wife because of a delusion and a third screams and bites all who go near him. (For personal accounts of mental disturbance see, for example, Balt, 1972; Barnes and Berke, 1971; and Wing ed., 1975.) Not many of those who work in hospitals, clinics and treatment centres are converted to anti-psychiatry. 'They find it difficult to believe that all patients whom they are seeing and treating are victims of a myth and are merely playing some reciprocal game with the authorities of society. The patients do not go away' writes a psychiatrist (Arthur, 1971, p. 28).

The critics of the concept of mental illness question the motives and efforts not only of professionals but also of the families of disturbed patients. What emerges from the writings of Laing and his colleagues is that it is the family who has driven the patient mad, that the patient's mother, or nuclear family, or parents' marriage is to blame, that the family's conduct is destructive. Goffman wrote movingly about patients' feelings of having been betrayed by their nearest and dearest who abandoned them to the mental hospital. Laing and Goffman may well be right in many of their insights; there may well be families that have a disastrous effect on one of their number and many patients may well feel abandoned. What is more, their writings serve as a healthy counterbalance to the assumption that everything a family does to its members is good and should not be questioned. However, they have also shifted the blame and by discrediting families who may be struggling with the disorder of one of their members and making huge efforts and sacrifices, have ensured that they receive less help and less acknowledgement than they might otherwise have done. Wing aptly described this as another form of scapegoating and labelling: 'This scapegoat tendency is one of the least attractive aspects of the new doctrines and illustrates the harmful effects of labelling quite as well as the misuse of diagnosis does' (Wing, 1973).

A further point to be considered is that if the disturbed individual is not regarded as ill, but as a deviant of another sort, the social consequences may be more, rather than less, severe. For example, alternatives might be the label of criminal, with the consequence of prosecution and a prison sentence; or 'tramp' or 'down-and-out' leading to poor provision in some night shelter. In less severe cases, the consequence of rule-breaking might be contempt or derision. There have been no systematic studies regarding the relative social consequences of applying different deviance-labels.

Who is mentally ill then? In the preceding discussion some of the difficulties involved in trying to answer this question were considered. Different writers would answer this question in different ways, some by saying that no one is, because mental disturbance does not exist; others by saying that the mentally ill are those to whom the disease theory can be usefully applied. Sociologists have been divided on these issues. In a critical note, Keith Hope wrote that sociologists who turn their attention to fields such as psychiatry often lack the experience and knowledge that would enable them to employ psychiatric concepts and terminology and that they therefore seek to forbid their use.

> But we do not have to be intimidated by their strictures. If we compare a psychiatric term such as 'psychotic depression' with a sociological term such as 'labelling' we find that textbooks exist which give guidance on the circumstances in which 'psychotic depression' may and may not be applied whereas 'labelling' appears to have no bounds set to its explanatory competence. Labelling theory is an ace which has only to be played to trump every other card. But science knows no trumps, and labelling need be taken seriously as an explanation only where, and to the extent that, empirical studies have demonstrated the existence of differences in treatment accorded to people who differ only with respect to their labels. (Hope, 1976, p. 322)

CHAPTER 2

From Person to Patient

The debate about the concept and nature of mental illness, conducted by medical and social scientists and appearing in the pages of books and learned journals, is remote from the daily practice of professionals and even more so from the everyday lives of laymen. Despite the lack of accepted definitions lay people make frequent use of the term mental illness, or one of its many substitutes, (such as 'crazy', 'mental' or 'mad') and have their own ideas as to what these mean.

For the sociologist, there is much interest in the question of how people get into the situation of being regarded, or regarding themselves, as mentally ill. What types of problem are perceived by laymen to indicate mental disturbance and what actions do they take in respect of the problems thus perceived? Are there any systematic variations between social groups in their recognition of, and actions in response to, mental disturbance?

An individual living in contemporary western society, performing customary social roles and pursuing customary social activities, would find himself in the position of being a mental patient only after a complex and usually lengthy social process. There follows, in this chapter, an exploration of the stages of this process, in the course of which a number of relevant research studies concerning lay perceptions and actions will be reviewed.

RECOGNISING THE PROBLEM

For an individual, the social process of becoming a mental patient generally begins when there is observed in him a departure from what was, until then, regarded as his normal condition. Such a change is first likely to be noticed by one or more of his close associates, such as a member of his family, a friend, workmate or employer, who will discern differences in behaviour, or in physical appearance, a deterioration in work performance, incoherences of speech or the telling of bizarre experiences. Alternatively, it may be the individual who is first to recognise in himself one or other such difference. So, the problem may, in the first instance, be self-recognised and self-defined or recognised and defined by others.

Either way, recognising and evaluating a change in a person is far from straightforward. The difficulties arise partly because the manifestations of mental disturbance are extremely varied and many different types of change, some minor and easily ignored, others major and disturbing, are capable of being regarded as problematic. Moreover, behavioural changes occur in specific social settings (family, work, etc.) and may not always be evaluated similarly by different observers.

Many studies concerned with lay recognition and definition of mental illness have endeavoured to determine the sort of changes in the condition of an individual that first evoke the thought that he may be disturbed, and in general have tried to describe the signs by which laymen recognise mental disturbance. These studies employed a variety of methodological approaches. Some researchers asked members of the general public how they would recognise mental illness and in this connection presented respondents with a series of verbal sketches of persons displaying various forms of aberrant behaviour, for example, a violent, threatening man having the characteristics of paranoia, a withdrawn schizophrenic who isolates herself, a young truant from school who lies and steals, an alcoholic and so on, this technique having been developed by Star in the early 1950s. (Most of Star's original work is unpublished.) In some cases respondents were asked whether anything was wrong with the individuals described and, if so, what was wrong; in others, respondents were asked directly whether they thought the aberrations depicted were indicative of mental illness (for a review of the literature see Rabkin, 1974). One thing came through clearly from the studies using this kind of approach: that there exists among members of the public a high level of agreement regarding behaviour of the type that these researches described as violent and threatening – most respondents thought of mental disturbance when presented with the sketch of a violent paranoid. Regarding the other sketches there was uncertainty and disagreement among the respondents, most of whom recognised in the characters portrayed the presence of a problem but not necessarily one of mental disturbance. Star herself had found that only extremely disturbed behaviour was recognised as such by the majority of respondents who generally tended to resist applying to anyone the term 'mentally ill' which they used only as a last resort.

It can be objected that a disadvantage of approaching members of the general public must be that to put questions to people who may never have come into contact with, or had occasion to recognise, a mentally disturbed person runs the risk of their answers reflecting some 'popular' image of mental illness and that faced with the reality they would use quite other criteria. Some researchers preferred to go direct to identified psychiatric patients or members of their families, asking them how they had, in fact, first recognised disturbance. This course, however, runs the risk of distortions, omissions and systematic bias in the accounts of respondents who may well have re-evaluated their experiences in the light of subsequent events, so that what they report with hindsight may differ from what they would have said initially. Even so, this approach is of value as can be seen from an early and very influential study conducted by Yarrow, Schwartz, Clausen and others and reported in a series of papers in the 1950s (Yarrow *et al.*, 1955a; Yarrow *et al.*, 1955b; Schwartz, 1957).

The study by Yarrow and her colleagues illustrates the difficulties experienced by lay people when trying to interpret behavioural or other changes in someone close to them. Only in a minority of cases does mental disturbance manifest itself in threatening or violent behaviour and, as shown by the responses to other sorts of aberrant behaviour mentioned above, recognition of the problem as being one of mental disturbance is not something that necessarily suggests itself to ordinary people. The Yarrow study group interviewed in great depth thirty-three wives whose husbands had entered a mental hospital, diagnosed as psychotics and psycho-neurotics, and they based their data on these women's reconstructions of their earlier experiences. The wives were asked about the 'problem behaviour' of their husbands which first caused concern. Table 2.1 shows the categories of such behaviour.

The most often reported problem was that the husband had appeared nervous, irritable, worried: this category included such things as inability to sleep and loss of appetite; the second most often reported problem was deviation from routine behaviour. Much further down the list is the category

TABLE 2.1 Reported Problem Behaviour at Time of the Wife's Initial Concern

Problem behaviour	Psychotics	Psycho-neurotics
Physical problems complaints, worries	12	5
Deviations from routines of behaviour	17	9
Expressions of inadequacy or hopelessness	4	1
Nervous, irritable, worried	19	10
Withdrawal (verbal, physical)	5	1
Changes or accentuations in personality 'traits' (slovenly, deceptive, forgetful)	5	6
Aggressive or assaultive and suicidal behaviour	6	3
Strange or bizarre thoughts, delusions, hallucinations and strange behaviour	11	1
Excessive drinking	4	7
Violation of codes of 'decency'	3	1
Number of respondents	23	10

Source: Yarrow *et al.* (1955a).

of aggressive, assaultive or suicidal behaviour, which, as mentioned, Star and others found to be more easily recognised and evaluated.

Thus, most of the symptoms with which the wives were confronted were not of a type generally associated in the public mind with mental disturbance, a finding that indicates the dilemma of lay people struggling to make sense of many kinds of non-violent behaviour.

Another important research finding of the Yarrow study resulted from asking the wives how and when they first noticed in their husbands the changes which subsequently proved to be indicators of mental illness. For most of them, it emerged that they could not pinpoint any specific single instance of problem behaviour by their husbands that, with hindsight, they could identify as the first indication of the disorder. Indeed, for the wives the beginning of the illness could not, in retrospect, be localised in time; the suspicion of mental disturbance in their husbands arose out of an accumulation of many inexplicable actions and communications of 'strange' feelings occurring over a period of time. They mentioned their husbands staying out late, not sleeping, expressing obscene thoughts, striking them and talking continuously. Particular incidents recalled by the wives, turned out to be significant only as part of an accumulation of troubles and were usually situationally specific. In general, that which alerts someone to a problem is the recognition in another of some deviation from that person's accepted standard of personal functioning, some failure to make the expected response in a given social situation. For example, one wife began to realise the presence of a problem when her husband went shopping with her (although he had never done that before) and expressed his great worry that he might physically lose her.

In the case of self-recognised problems, the range of manifestations that can cause initial concern is also broad. In a study concerned with patients of psychiatric clinics in New York, Kadushin asked respondents for a general description of the problem or problems which they first noticed (Kadushin, 1968). The majority of the patients described at least two and their replies were classified by the researcher. Most of the problems mentioned he classified either as 'inner-emotional' or 'social' problems, the former category including complaints of thought processes such as inability to concentrate or to make decisions, depression, anxiety and specific fears as of the dark or of confined spaces; the latter, 'social' complaint category including problems relating to work, and to particular persons. A smaller, but still considerable, proportion of respondents described their problems in bio-social terms, complaining of somatic difficulties such as insomnia, fatigue, appetite disturbances, 'bad health' and alcoholism.

In recent years several personal accounts have been published by sufferers from mental illness about their experiences (Balt, 1972; Barnes and Berke, 1971; and a collection edited by Wing, 1975) and it seems clear that there exists a wide variety of problems that may cause initial concern to persons experiencing them. The following illustrations are from the account of schizophrenic patients looking back on their early experiences.

> My parents tell me that they noticed I was not my usual self about one year before I had my breakdown. I had had the flu in the January and gone back to work after having a fortnight off. It was soon afterwards that very occasionally I came out with some rather peculiar sayings. My mother tells me that I started complaining to her that people were talking about me behind my back. My mother did say to me on several occasions that she thought I was imagining it and if they were talking about me they might be complimentary things but I always insisted they were all against me and were saying detrimental things about me. (Wing, 1975, p. 26)
>
> In retrospect my schizophrenic experiences started when I was about eleven. I had a few brief incidents of thoughts like a tape-recording being played in my head. . . . Then at sixteen years my academic performance fell off but this was not apparent to anyone but myself and I felt very guilty about it. (Wing, 1975, p. 45)

Thus, whether self-recognised or recognised by others these first signs of a problem often appear disconcerting or even fearful to the observer.

Early and Late Recognition

Individuals may be aware of a change in themselves or in another but the translation of this awareness into concern, initially or some time later, will depend on how serious the change appears to be to the observer. Some experiences, communications and behaviour changes may seem trivial or unimportant and in no way threatening. Recognition of the existence of a problem and the attribution of seriousness to it depend on a number of factors.

Early recognition is likely when aberrations persist and accumulate whereas strange behaviour which occurs only intermittently, with spells of normality between, is less likely to be recognised as problematic, even if inexplicable at the times of its happening. As Yarrow and her colleagues reported: 'The husband's behaviour itself is a fluctuating stimulus. He is not worried and complaining all the time. His delusions and hallucinations may not persist. His hostility toward the wife may be followed by warm attentiveness. She has, then, the problem of deciding whether his "strange" behaviour is significant' (Yarrow *et al.*, 1955a, p. 21). Such fluctuations of behaviour not only delay the process of recognition, but make it more difficult.

Recognition is also affected by social visibility. If the onset of the disturbance takes the form of behaviour which offends or disrupts the activities of others, causing them to complain, recognition will follow more quickly than it would in the case of behaviour which is secretive. Socially embarrassing conduct in public is quickly noticed. If a person shouts on the streets or is noisy at nights, disturbing the sleep of neighbours, if he adopts odd postures or peculiar facial expressions in public places, his conduct will soon attract attention. Conversely, behaviour involving withdrawal from social contacts and isolation may for some time go unnoticed by the world at large because it is less visible socially. Drunkenness in the street has more immediate consequences, than it has in the home. Another factor influencing early recognition has to do with disruption of the individual's important social roles, usually those connected with work and family life: roles as mother, wife, wage-earner and work-mate being especially important since others, as well as the person concerned, depend on their satisfactory performance. Disruption of these roles, whether by physical illness or unusual behaviour, is quickly noticed. Thus a physical symptom, such as backache, is more important for a young mother, who thereby becomes unable to lift or bend down to her baby, than for an office worker for whom lifting and bending are not central to his function. Backache of mother or nurse is likely to be seen as problematic much sooner than it would be in the case of someone of more sedentary occupation. Recognition of unusual behaviour as problematic will likewise follow upon the disruptions of major social roles. A fear of open spaces may not prevent the mother of a young baby from caring adequately for her child within the walls of her home: but if it later interferes with being a good mother to school-age children the phobia will be regarded as more serious because more disruptive.

A related point has regard to the individual's position in his intimate social unit, the importance of which was highlighted by a study of Muriel Hammer (1968). She interviewed patients of a psychiatric hospital in Manhattan about their experiences before they started treatment in hospital. Her findings indicate that the problems of those occupying a critical position in the social unit, whose performance is crucial for the unit's maintenance, were the most likely to be noticed early and thought of as serious. The woman whose problems disrupt the performance of her important social role as mother of young children, occupies a more critical position where no older woman (e.g., her mother or mother-in-law) is there to take over her function than is the case where such assistance is available. In the latter situation the problems may go comparatively unnoticed or be regarded as not serious.

The home setting and interpersonal relationships may also influence early recognition of the problem in a family member. The single, the separated and the widowed, who live alone, are less likely to have their problems identified early by others than are those living within a family: quite simply there may not be anyone around to notice any changes. However, there may be family constellations in which early recognition is equally unlikely, as was illustrated by research carried out by Sampson and his colleagues (Sampson *et al.*, 1968) who studied families of which the wife had been admitted to a mental hospital for the first time. The researchers described a type of family situation in which early recognition of mental disturbance was particularly difficult, as in a marital relationship characterised by mutual withdrawal, that is in which the spouses had drawn apart, each being absorbed in his or her separate concerns. In such a climate of alienation, involving a mutual emotional inaccessibility, changed behaviour, distress or strangeness in one partner might go unnoticed by the other for a considerable length of time. Sampson gives this illustrative case:

> For two years prior to hospitalization, Mrs. Rand was troubled by various somatic complaints, persistent tension, difficulty in sleeping, a vague but disturbing conviction that she was a sinner and intermittent states of acute panic. Mr. Rand was minimally aware of her distress. He worked up to fourteen hours a day, including weekends, in his store and eventually a second job took him out of home three evenings a week. On those infrequent occasions when his wife's worries forced themselves on his attention, he dismissed them curtly as absurd, and turned once again to his own affairs. (Sampson *et al.*, 1968, p. 206)

A marital relationship of this type would much hinder recognition of mental disturbance because the person best placed to notice the changed behaviour had become isolated from the other and hence that other's problem.

INTERPRETING THE PROBLEM

Observing a change in oneself, or in another, and recognising it as a problem are first steps only in the social process of becoming a mental patient. The observer then has to evaluate the problem, i.e., decide what kind of problem it is. Such early evaluations very rarely attribute the problem to mental disturbance.

In a further study of wives' recognition of their husbands'

behaviour-changes, Schwartz (1957) showed that the wives interpreted these changes within three general frameworks: characterological, somatic and psychological. In the first of these, wives viewed the problems as those of the husband's characters which were seen as weak, spoiled, aggressive or lazy. For example, one wife said: 'He is irresponsible. He's always been a problem to everyone who's ever known him. He could have gotten some place, but something is lacking, just not there' (Schwartz, 1957, p. 283). Thus, the wife notices her husband's deviation from the acceptable, but attributes this to his character. Other wives commented: 'He has been spoiled rotten'; 'He is just a baby'; or used such expressions as 'stubborn and self-centred'.

In the second framework the husband was viewed as someone with a somatic illness or physical impairment. The problematic behaviour was interpreted as physical illness for which medical (physical) treatment was appropriate. For example, one woman attributed her husband's problems to trouble with his teeth and talked about a remarkable improvement since they were extracted.

Even when the problems were viewed in the third, psychological framework, they were not necessarily interpreted as those of mental illness, but were sometimes defined as 'slight upsets'. As one wife explained: 'I say he is upset. A person who is crazy would do different things than he did. . . . They would be violent and hollering and do funny things. He never did anything funny. . . . I know he is disturbed, but he talks rational. He reads the papers' (Schwartz, 1957, p. 285).

Thus, early interpretations may vary, but problems are seldom seen straight away as mental illness. Several researchers found, in fact, that families were very reluctant to admit mental disturbance in one of their members. This is understandable as such disturbance may be personally threatening to others in the family, and interpreting problems in this light leads to consideration of future changes in relationships and in social roles. A wife for example, as Yarrow explains, has to contemplate giving up 'modes of relating to her husband that may have had satisfaction for her and to see a future as the wife of a mental patient' (Yarrow, 1955a, p. 22). The stigma of mental illness, which will be discussed in the next chapter, would also add greatly to families' reluctance to consider that possibility.

In the case of a self-recognised problem, its interpretation within a psychiatric framework may be even more threatening. It would mean someone having to interpret his actions or experiences as evidence that he may be 'losing his mind', a frightening conclusion. Goffman, for example, considered this eventuality as the 'most pervasively threatening thing that can happen to the self in our society' (Goffman, 1961). When the suggestion of such an interpretation occurs to an individual, or is put to him by others, often his first inclination is to reject it (Mills, 1962).

Not only self and relatives but other members of a social group (workmates, neighbours, etc.) may note, and try to interpret, the behaviour of the disturbed individual. Laymen, confronted with unacceptable behaviour, first try to understand it. To use the language of Mead, they attempt to empathise, to take the role of the other. If this approach is successful in that they feel able to understand why the person concerned is behaving that way then an explanation of the unacceptable behaviour will be given in terms of character, which will be defined as bad, weak, delinquent, etc. If, however, there is failure to empathise, an inability to comprehend the motivation behind the unacceptable behaviour, then the explanation is likely to be given in terms of mental disturbance. For example, if a middle-aged woman becomes known as a shoplifter and it transpires that she stole food or blouses, then the motivation can be seen by others in the social group as weakness or dishonesty. People are able to feel that they understand why she acted as she did: presumably she wanted the goods. But if the woman steals teddy bears from toy shops, with no children to give them to, then the motivation is not easy to understand and the stealing is likely to be explained as disturbed behaviour.

Usually, initial interpretations of the recognised problem, whether by relatives or strangers, are made with caution and may undergo several changes. Yarrow and her colleagues found that people's interpretations typically tend to shift backwards and forwards, defining the problem within different frameworks as they struggle to attach meaning to it.

Wives were inclined to wait, sometimes for lengthy periods, for additional clues which either confirmed their definitions or led to new ones. To quote: 'Initial interpretations, whatever their content, are seldom held with great confidence by the wives. Many recall their early reactions to their husbands' behaviour as full of puzzling confusion and uncertainty. Something is wrong, they know, but in general, they stop short of a firm explanation' (Yarrow *et al.*, 1955a, p. 19).

The way that people make sense of their daily lives is of the greatest interest to sociologists. So far in this chapter lay recognition and interpretation of mental disturbance have been examined and an understanding of this process is necessary for the next stage of this analysis: the actions taken by laymen to deal with the problems of unusual or aberrant behaviour.

CONSULTING THE SOCIAL GROUP

The tentative interpretation of a problem confronts the layman with two difficult, but related, questions: am I right in my thinking and, if so, what should be done about the problem? For the majority, the first appropriate step will be to consult the immediate social group.

Direct experience of anxiety, depression or hallucinations is intensely personal; similarly, the experience of one's husband, or wife, becoming a stranger is, again, very personal. But when someone tries to attach a meaning to his experiences, to explain, understand and decide what to do, he will make use of the meanings and explanations provided by his culture and in this he will be helped by others who share the same culture. The individual, struggling to make sense of his problems, will draw on the cultural experiences of his social group by discussing with his relatives and friends the things that are troubling him. In this way, a great deal of advice-seeking and advice-giving goes on in health matters generally; people solicit advice about the way they feel or about the way their spouses or children seem to feel, in order to decide whether they are ill or not. Sometimes advice is volunteered rather than sought: someone might say 'Your husband looks quite poorly, don't you think something is wrong with him?' Thus, in a case of mental disturbance, lay discussions are likely to include talking over the particular behaviour-changes and new experiences that indicate the problem and lead on to some definite advice being given about the meaning and explanation of the problem and what to do about it. The advice might be to do nothing as the problem will pass or solve itself; to make changes in the life-style, or to consult the physician, priest or other appropriate expert.

In an influential book, sociologist Freidson lays much stress on the importance of lay consultations in the process of decision-making about illness. He argues:

> Such advice contains an implicit diagnosis of the problem. As important, it tends to constitute a referral to some agent or agency thought competent to deal with the problem, thereby moving the complainant towards care. Even if the advice is solely diagnostic in its content, a diagnosis carries with it a prescription that one seeks help from that class of people which deals with the problem specified by the diagnosis. In this sense, we may consider advice-seeking and advice-giving in health affairs among laymen to organise the direction of behaviour by referral to one or another consultant. And so we can speak of a lay referral system which is defined by 1. the particular culture or knowledge people have about health and health agents, and 2. the interrelationships of the laymen from whom advice and referral are sought. There is, then, a cultural content in the system, whether of ethnic or socioeconomic origin, and a network or structure. (Freidson, 1973, p. 290)

Consultation within the social group (or the lay-referral system, to use Freidson's terminology) is a very important social mechanism. It not only helps the individual to make sense of his experiences, but also indicates to him the 'right' and 'proper' ways of thinking and acting in a given situation, according to the social norms of his group. In other words, the advice-giving process provides the individual with knowledge of the socially approved ways of behaviour in that particular situation. It also reinforces the tendency of members of the social group to act in similar ways.

Although lay consultations are widespread some people are

more active than others in this respect. For example, women are more likely than men to talk about their problems (see Chapter 6). Marital relationships also influence the extent of help-seeking, as a study by Horwitz has shown. He interviewed 120 patients of a community mental health centre in New Haven and asked them about their experiences before treatment (Horwitz, 1978). He distinguished four types of husband–wife relationship: the uninvolved, the mutual, the conflict and the separated and found systematic variations in lay advice-seeking according to type of relationship. The most active help-seekers were those who had conflict relationships with their spouses; this was also the most common type, characterised by hostility between husband and wife who quarrelled frequently and considered separation. Most quarrels were about household duties, drinking problems, money and other domestic matters, i.e. problems for which lay advice-seeking seemed most appropriate. The problems that eventually led to psychiatric treatment were usually first interpreted as marital difficulties and relatives and friends were often approached by prospective patients to help to resolve these conflicts.

The other type of persons most likely to seek lay advice were those separated from their spouses; they, too, relied on relatives and friends for informal help and opinions regarding their problems, which were interpreted as being the natural results of separation. By contrast, those enjoying mutual marital relations relied much less on the advice of friends and relatives; spouses supported each other and attempted to resolve problems together. Finally, the uninvolved relationship between husband and wife was characterised by a lack of communication, emotional distance and isolation (a setting similar to that described by Sampson). Those in this situation tended not to seek advice from the lay group in spite of the lack of marital support, perhaps because of an inability to maintain relationships, whether with spouse or other. Also, Horwitz found that the patients in this category consisted mostly of men, who are, in any case, less active help-seekers.

Thus, people turn to their lay-referral system for advice with their problems; the important question is whether certain types of lay-referral system are more likely than others to define these problems as psychiatric and to guide the help-seekers towards the psychiatric services.

The Cultural Content of the Lay-Referral System

Few studies have investigated the systematic variations between social groups in their norms of behaviour relating to the interpretation of mental disturbance, and thus, in this connection, little is known as yet about what Freidson calls the 'cultural content of the lay-referral system'. Does lay interpretation of behaviour-changes and strange actions vary according to the education, social class or ethnic origin of different sets of people? Do these variations affect definitions of problems and subsequent decisions? Freidson argues that 'within modern Western societies, those members of the population who are most like the members of the medical profession in attitude and knowledge manifest a culture or subculture that is more likely to lead them to demonstrate medically approved conceptions of illness than are those least like the profession' (Freidson, 1973, p. 287). This would indicate that people whose social class origin, educational background and occupation are on a similar level to those of medical practitioners, that is members of the middle classes with higher educational attainments, would define mental disturbance in terms approximating to those of doctors. In fact, studies confirm that middle class people are more likely than working class people to identify symptoms of mental illness in accordance with current psychiatric views, as well as to hold more favourable opinions about psychiatry; the latter are less informed about existing psychiatric services, and know less how to locate them.

Kadushin, in his study of patients of New York psychotherapy clinics, argues that more important than social class and education is the type of social circle a person moves in (Kadushin, 1968). He defines 'social circle' as being certain sets of friends and acquaintances who are linked by their participation in cultural and social activities. According to Kadushin, the level of cultural and psychiatric sophistication of a person's social circle is the best predictor of how he would define mental disturbance and of whether he would apply to a psychiatric clinic for treatment. Members of the more sophisticated social circles are likely to come into contact with others who are able to recognise psychiatric problems and who know where to find psychiatric agencies. He found that although this 'sophistication' is often closely related to educational levels and social class, this is not invariably so, and that occupation is a better guide – the type of occupation rather than its social prestige is what seems to matter. Thus, Kadushin finds that even within the middle class, those who work, for example, in the health occupations, teaching, the arts and showbusiness, advertising and communications are more likely to be psychiatrically sophisticated than are businessmen, lawyers or engineers.

Other researchers also stress the importance of the cultural and social milieu of the immediate group for the interpretation of problems as psychiatric or otherwise. For example, Scheff, investigating student applicants for psychiatric help in comparison to a random sample of the population that had free access to the same clinic, found that a certain type of applicant was over-represented: those with college-trained parents, not involved in religious activities and of urban professional background were most ready to define their problems as needing psychiatric help. Scheff, like Kadushin, emphasises the importance of sophistication in entertainment and general interests for the definition of problems as psychiatric or otherwise:

> Of particular significance, they (i.e. the over-represented group) probably are exposed to the same kind of educational and mass media influences: sophisticated fiction and political commentary, new and special features. . . . By the same token, the majority are not psychiatrically sophisticated. For them, personal problems are not defined as psychiatric until they are overwhelming. (Scheff 1966, p. 120)

Studies like those of Scheff and Kadushin have also shown that those deeply involved in religion are less likely than others to turn to psychiatric clinics with their problems. This seems to be the case whatever the particular religion may be, and researchers have speculated that people with strong religious participation may turn to the priest or the minister rather than to medical men and try to solve their problems within a religious framework.

An interesting example of cultural differences in this respect is that of the Hutterite communities of Canada. The Hutterites are a religious sect living in several small agricultural communities; they are pacifists, believers in communal ownership and the renunciation of worldly pleasures, and constitute a very cohesive, close-knit group, whose members look after and support each other. For some time it was thought that mental illness was unknown among them as they never appeared as patients in mental hospitals. But when researchers investigated the population of these communities they found the incidence of mental disturbance to be much the same as for the population of Canada in general, but that their culture did not encourage psychiatric help-seeking (Eaton and Weil, 1968). Hutterites with problems of a psychiatric nature did not seek help beyond the lay group and were maintained within the communities. Possibly their very strong religious affiliation, their reluctance to have much to do with the world outside the community (marriage to a non-Hutterite is forbidden) and their willingness to look after the afflicted all combine to influence them against the interpretation of symptoms as needing professional psychiatric help.

Social Networks

An individual's lay referral system, has not only a cultural content but also a structure (see Freidson above) and this, too, has an important bearing on the advice given among laymen.

Much relevant sociological work in recent years has made use of a conceptual tool, called the 'social network'. Elizabeth Bott, whose early research much influenced thinking on this subject, has argued that small, nuclear families, typical in contemporary industrial societies, are connected, through their members, with a lot of individuals, groups and institutions (Bott, 1957). These individuals, groups and institutions may be, but are not necessarily, linked with each other. Thus the contemporary family lives in, and forms part of, a 'network', consisting of kin-group, friends, neighbours, colleagues, etc. (see Figure 2.1), and this network has both 'formal' and 'informal' constituents.

Bott distinguished two types of network, the close-knit and the loose-knit. The former is characterised by its cohesiveness and strongly localised nature; in such a structure people are likely to have lived in the same locality all their lives, working in the same place of employment as their friends and relatives, with little experience outside the area and with a lot of mutually reinforcing interaction. This close-knit network is marked by its highly 'connected' nature; such networks tend to be found in areas where people grow up and stay in close association with each other for economic reasons: long-established rural communities, and fishing villages are good examples of this type of network as are those parts of industrial towns where generations of workers have found employment in the same factory and lived in its vicinity.

Quite different is the type of network called loose-knit. In this, people would have friends and relatives in different parts of the country, in different types of occupations, and typically all would be residentially mobile. Few members of an individual's network would be likely to know each other as there would be few connecting links.

Network studies have shown that the type of network an individual has is related to the seeking and giving of advice for psychiatric problems in two important ways. First, networks differ in the amount of social support and help their members receive. People in close-knit networks of kin and friends readily turn to them for advice and receive much emotional

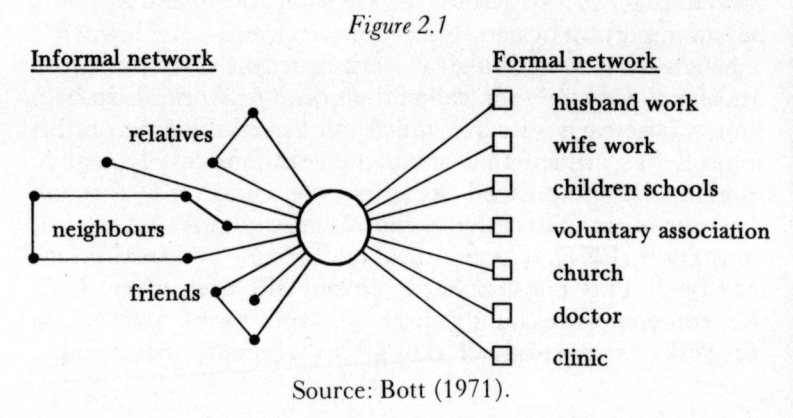

Figure 2.1

Informal network	Formal network
relatives	husband work
neighbours	wife work
friends	children schools
	voluntary association
	church
	doctor
	clinic

Source: Bott (1971).

support and practical help; kin and friends live near, are well-known and in a position to help. Consequently the individual with psychiatric problems is likely to rely much on the lay social group and not turn to professional helpers until the problems become very severe. By contrast, members of loose-knit networks receive less support and assistance and rely more on professionals whom they consult at an earlier stage (Horwitz, 1977; McKinlay, 1973).

Second, people in a close-knit network receive lay advice from members of one cohesive local set who are likely to have limited prior experience of the range of manifestations of mental disturbance and limited knowledge of psychiatric services, as they largely rely on the experiences of each other. By contrast, persons knowing a number of people not connected with each other, (i.e. loose-knit networks) gain more diverse information; they themselves have experiences in a number of localities and their contacts are among different sets of people with varied personal experiences. Thus, in loose-knit networks, advice is more likely to include interpretations of problems within a psychiatric framework and information about psychiatric services. Members of these loose-knit networks are likely to be advised by their social group to seek help for symptoms before they become severe and to be able to locate such help efficiently. Horwitz found that patients from loose-knit networks entering treatment had less severe problems, of shorter duration, than had those from close-knit networks (Horwitz, 1977).

Interestingly, Horwitz also reports that friends are more likely than kin to suggest that persons with problems should visit a professional for assistance. Possibly, friends are not as committed as relatives and are less willing to devote much time and effort to assisting the individual help-seeker and so suggest professional help in order to avoid involvement. Friends are also less afraid than kin of the stigma attaching to psychiatric treatment.

ACCOMMODATION

Having recognised a problem, defined it tentatively as being of a certain type and sought the lay-referral group's advice, the individual has two available choices. He may decide on 'non-action' i.e. to do nothing, to wait, to ignore the problem (except possibly for some attempt at self-treatment); or he may decide to consult a professional with the appropriate expertise. It is very tempting to opt for the the first course and many people do so in the hope that the problem will prove to be insignificant and temporary. There are several reasons for favouring non-action.

The thought of mental illness in oneself or in a close relative is very disturbing. It was mentioned earlier that the first interpretation of a problem is seldom made within a mental illness framework, partly because of the threat such interpretation would pose to personal identity, to relationships and to the future in general.

Even with such common and comparatively trivial conditions as toothache there is a tendency to ignore the early signs in the hope that it is nothing serious and that a visit to the dentist can be avoided. So, faced with the possibility of mental illness, the individual and those close to him may minimise the problem, or pretend not to notice it, rather than face up to its implications.

There is also much reluctance to report the disturbed behaviour of a close relative to a professional helper. A wife, for example, may feel that she rejects and betrays her disturbed husband by talking to strangers about him; or feel that doing so may seem like betrayal and rejection to him or to others in the social group. Writing about relatives of schizophrenics, Creer and Wing described this feeling:

> One patient's sister, for example, said, 'I don't like saying anything about him – I feel like I'm betraying him. After all, blood is thicker than water.' Other relatives felt guilty at complaining and said 'I'm painting a very black picture', or, 'Don't write that down. It makes him sound so awful'. Even when relatives found the patient's behaviour hard to tolerate, they sometimes felt that to complain of it was in some sense to reject the patient. (Creer and Wing, 1974, p. 68)

Also, to many people, calling on an outside expert to intervene in what they may regard as a family problem, seems an acceptance of failure to cope, a last resort, to be employed only when everything else has been tried. For them, seeking such advice about mental disturbance means that the matter is to be taken out of their control, that the drawing of professional-authoritarian attention to their problems constitutes an irreversible action. The strong stigma attaching to mental illness (which will be discussed in the next chapter) makes people reluctant to take decisive action which, they fear, will bring about their stigmatisation.

Thus, there are several reasons why people avoid taking action; instead, they normalise, minimise and accommodate the mental disturbance. 'Normalisation' is a very usual response to the problem of mental illness in the self or in a close relative. For example, Yarrow and her colleagues described how wives tried to normalise their husbands' strange behaviour, often over long periods. They reported that the wives explained and justified their husbands' actions by pointing out similarities of behaviour in people who were 'normal'. One wife explained her husband's hallucinations by remembering that she herself heard voices when she went through the menopause; another wife normalised her husband's delusions and nightmares by pointing out that 'a lot of normal people think there is something wrong when there isn't. I think men are that way; his father is that way' (Yarrow *et al.*, 1955a, p. 22). Some of the wives stretched the range of normality in their efforts to understand and explain the odd behaviour and communications of their husbands. Similarly Mills, who interviewed relatives of patients admitted to a mental hospital in East London described how members of the family tried to explain away disturbed behaviour by stretching the limits of plausibility (Mills, 1962). There is a tendency to balance odd behaviour with the normal and to stress those instances when the relative was kind and loving as well as those when he was hostile and threatening.

This kind of response to disturbed behaviour may, for some, prove to be the right one as the problem may turn out to be temporary and disappear after a time. There are people who, in situations of personal conflict, stress or fatigue, experience temporary disturbance which passes without any action being taken. Such temporary problems are illustrated by the experiences of army psychiatrists, who described how soldiers show many symptoms of mental disturbance under stress on the battlefield, but later revert to normal without psychiatric treatment (Mechanic, 1968).

However, for many the symptoms of mental disturbance do not disappear regardless of attempts to ignore or to normalise them. It is one of the most remarkable features of lay behaviour that a great deal of mental disturbance is 'accommodated', in the sense that those involved learn to live with it, often for remarkably long periods.

Accommodation of disturbed behaviour within the family unit is managed by making adjustments to it: relationships, activities and expectations are modified. If normalisation is carried on for a long time, relatives get used to the problems and come to regard them as, indeed, 'normal' features of everyday life. The customary expectations of behaviour in another will be adjusted to the disturbed person's behaviour and the relatives will learn how to deal with the practical problems created by the illness. If a disturbed wife or mother cannot cope with her household functions, her mother may move in to help; if someone exhibits unacceptable, embarrassing behaviour in public, he, and often the whole family, may stay at home. For example, Hammer, in her retrospective study of patients in a Manhattan psychiatric hospital, found that most family units had been reorganised; relatives avoided situations which were likely to disturb the individual with psychiatric problems and made fewer demands on that person than they did on others. Relatives also tended to exclude the patient from tasks and interaction and to maintain him in a marginal position (Hammer, 1968).

Accommodation of symptoms occurs a great deal in respect of physical illness also; much pain, discomfort and disability can be accommodated by modifying daily activities and reducing expectations. Routines can be adjusted to such an extent that the symptoms are hardly noticed; it takes a sudden change in symptoms or circumstances to redirect attention to the illness. If, for example, a man becomes breathless or develops a limp, his subsequent daily activities can be adjusted to his capacity: he will not run or climb stairs, his work rate will be reduced. Once the routine is established, the symptoms will excite little notice and neither the afflicted person nor his family will think it worth reporting the condition and seeking help for it. Likewise, someone may exhibit symptoms of mental disturbance, for example withdrawal from social contacts, or fear of leaving the house, which are accommodated in the family and after a time accepted, as 'part of the person', and not as something requiring attention. Only a change in the disturbed person or in the family situation will redirect attention to the symptoms.

In certain types of family, disturbed behaviour may even be accommodated without adjustments having to be made. For example, Sampson and his colleagues said of families in which the 'uninvolved' marital partners had grown apart from each other, pursuing their own, largely separate lives:

> In these families the patterned responses to distress, withdrawal or illness in the wife was further withdrawal by the husband, resulting in increasing distance between, and disengagement of, the marital partners. These developments were neither abrupt nor entirely consistent, but the trend of interaction in these families was toward mutual alienation and inaccessibility of each partner to the other. In this situation, early involvement of the wife in a professional treatment situation was limited by her own withdrawal and difficulty in taking the initiative for any sustained course of action in the real world, as well as by the husband's detachment. (Sampson et al., 1968, p. 206)

In such families one partner's mental illness will, at least for a time, fit into, without disturbing, the evolved pattern of family life.

Thus, much mental disturbance is normalised, minimised and accommodated without the seeking of professional help. These responses are sometimes coupled with another: self-treatment, in the sense that the disturbed individual or someone close to him attempts some form of medication or therapy not based on professional advice. One example of this self-treatment is the taking of over-the-counter medicines.

The results of numerous social surveys show that medicine-taking has become part of daily life for people in modern Western societies. For example, one survey in Britain found that 80 per cent of the respondents had taken some medicine during the fortnight prior to being interviewed (Dunnell and

Cartwright, 1972); a result confirmed by others. A great deal of such medication is taken without having been prescribed by doctors: in another study in London it was found that for every prescribed medicine taken by respondents during a two-week period, two non-prescribed items were taken (Wadsworth *et al.*, 1971). It seems therefore, that a common response to discomforts and problems of many types is to buy medicines. Of course, the great majority of the relevant and effective drugs for the treatment of mental disturbance are obtainable on prescription only and there is little information about the number of people who turn to unprescribed medicines in an attempt to treat problems they have classified as depression, anxiety or 'nerves'.

Another form of self-treatment is the attempt to make changes in life-styles; some may think that conditions they recognise as problems would improve if they took more exercise, acquired new interests or changed employment. Efforts along these lines are sometimes made not by the individual experiencing the difficulties but by others on his behalf. An illustration of such an approach by others comes from the account of a schizophrenic man:

> ... my behaviour was certainly altered. I became very introverted and found it impossible to communicate with my friends. I suffered from loss of concentration – I could not take notes at lectures – I read one page of a book two or three times before moving onto the next page. I couldn't write essays and was compelled to copy them out of books. My memory was hopeless. My friends realised that something was wrong and tried to help me by taking me out to parties etc. – their cure for my "depression".... I wanted to resign from being secretary of the cricket club, but was persuaded to continue in office. (Wing, 1975, p. 12)

Yet another possible form of self-treatment consists of attempting to bring about changes in personal relationships: to be more loving, to take greater interest in the activities of others, to show greater pliability or firmness. In the studies of Yarrow (1955a) and Schwartz (1957), wives who interpreted their husbands' problems within a psychological framework saw such attempted changes as being appropriate. For example, where the problem was perceived as due to being 'spoilt' or of 'never having grown up' a change in relational response was accepted as the best way of dealing with it.

DECISION TO SEEK PROFESSIONAL HELP

Measures taken to adjust to symptoms become woven into the fabric of daily life in many families, a finding confirmed by research studies. So, if people are able to accommodate disturbed behaviour in the family, who goes to the doctor and when?

The American sociologist, Zola, has argued convincingly that accommodative patterns can break down, not necessarily because the symptoms get worse, but for a number of social reasons (Zola, 1973). The studies carried out by him and his colleagues were primarily concerned with the behaviour which surrounds physical illness but their conclusions are applicable to people coping with mental illness, as several specific researchers have demonstrated. Zola was especially interested in the timing of the decision to seek aid; he argued that often the decision to seek medical aid was taken because some event in the social setting triggered off that action. In fact he described a number of 'triggers': a crisis drawing attention to the symptoms (e.g. family quarrels, moving into a new neighbourhood, the need to look for a new job); the sudden interference of symptoms with specific relationships or activities (e.g. wife's complaint that husband is always tired and is not interested in her draws attention to husband's condition); interpersonal sanctioning (e.g. someone in the social group advises or insists on medical attention); new light being shed on the symptoms by experience within the social group (e.g. someone else developing similar problems with disturbing results). Thus Zola's argument is that the decision to seek medical aid is inextricably bound up with events in a person's social and emotional environment.

Not only changes within the family group, but, also, changes in the wider social group may disturb previous accommodative patterns. During stress situations the vulnerability of social groups increases, prompting action that may not otherwise have been taken, as during periods of economic crisis, unemployment or threat of war. However, to stress the importance of social factors in the decision to seek professional help is not to minimise the significance of the symptoms: action is often taken when the symptoms become more frequently manifested, more visible, or in other ways indicate a worsening of the disturbance.

When the individual or his social group decide to seek expert advice, the appropriate professional has to be selected. This selection will depend on how the problem is defined. Of course, this is so with any problem; someone feeling a pain in the jaw might put it down to trouble with teeth and decide to visit the dentist, whereas another might suspect sinus trouble in which case a professional with the expertise applicable to that condition would be sought. Similarly, if the problem were defined as being due to a character defect or to marital difficulty, the relevant expert might be a psychologist, priest or social worker. Lay definition of a problem as illness leads to consultation with another sort of expert, the doctor. Thus, the many social factors discussed before, which influence the recognition and definition of a problem as psychiatric or otherwise, combine to steer the person concerned towards a certain type of helper, usually through his lay-referral system.

The choice of expert, however, is also influenced by considerations that are unconnected with the definition of the problem. An important influencing factor is the relative accessibility of the helpers: the one regarded as the most relevant may be out of reach and in such cases reference may be made to someone else. For example, there is much evidence to show that people in Britain turn to the medical practitioner with a great variety of problems other than physical or mental illness; marital difficulties, problems with children, personal worries and housing problems being some of them. One reason for this is that the probably more relevant professional is not easily located: many people in Britain would not know how to find a social worker, a psychologist or a marriage guidance counsellor, but would know the location of the doctor's surgery. Those who are able to find the social worker or psychologist, perhaps because of previous contact or more knowledge of the system, may turn to that adviser with the same problem that someone else would take to the doctor. Also, one type of helper may be more accessible than another because of financial considerations: visits to physicians in the United States can be related to the financial status of the patient: those lacking means may choose a cheaper alternative helper; in Britain the private psychoanalyst is financially out of the reach of the vast majority.

Perceived usefulness of the expert also influences the choice. A problem may be defined as a character or an environmental problem, but the expert dealing with such troubles be perceived as of little use in the situation, leading to a doctor being consulted instead. Thus, a woman may decide that her depression or anxious irritability is due to marital problems but regard the marriage guidance counsellor as of little use in her particular situation. She may then turn to the doctor instead, who would not solve her marital difficulties but would prescribe some medicine to help her depression or irritability.

Whether someone chooses the medical practitioner or an alternative helper is also influenced by previous experiences with doctors. By the time an adult in Western society contemplates medical help for problems of mental disturbance, he and members of his family are likely to have had a measure of contact with the medical profession, either in the framework of an ongoing relationship with the family doctor or by way of isolated meetings with different medical practitioners. In any case, the patient's past experience of interaction as well as the treatment received will influence his future decisions. If the past experience was unpleasant or disconcerting, for example, if the doctor seemed impatient or did not give enough information (common complaints of patients in the UK, see Cartwright, 1967) the patient will be reluctant to put himself in the same position again. Conversely, satisfactory past interaction will incline him to repeat the experience. In fact there is some research evidence to show that when people feel that their general practitioner is too busy or seems uninterested in their problems they are less likely to seek his help (Cartwright *et al.* 1973), and various studies have described how people have left the consulting room without having been able to tell the doctor their main worries (Korsch *et al.*, 1968; Stimson and Webb, 1975). Although much more research is needed to provide information on the ways doctor–patient relationships influence willingness to seek medical help, and especially help with mental disturbance, it is certainly probable that past experiences are influential in this respect.

In a social survey carried out in Britain, Dunnel and Cartwright (1972) asked over 1,400 adults to try to imagine what they would do in certain illness situations, among them 'a constant feeling of depression for about three weeks' and 'difficulty in sleeping for about a week'.

Answers to hypothetical questions of this type indicate the respondents' general frame of mind; they do not necessarily predict their actual behaviour. It is interesting to note, however, that quite a high proportion of the respondents (more than a quarter in the case of depression and nearly half in the case of sleeplessness) said that they would not consult a doctor. Of course, the 72 per cent who answered that they would go to the doctor for a constant feeling of depression might not actually do so if the occasion arose, because of the many influences affecting their behaviour. But the evidence from the authors of this study is that a person who says that he would consult the doctor in a hypothetical situation is in fact more likely to do so than one who says that he would not.

In this chapter some responses of laymen to symptoms of mental disturbance were examined. The stages of a process from first recognition of a change to the decision to consult a doctor, have been discussed. It is not suggested that these stages occur in an inevitable chronological order; on the contrary, people would move back and forth between them. Thus,

TABLE 2.2   Predicted Actions

	Depression (%)	Sleeplessness (%)
Proportion who would		
consult the doctor	72	53
do something themselves	7	17
do nothing	12	25
other	9	5

Source: Dunnell and Cartwright, (1972).

in the light of discussions with the lay group early interpretations of a problem may well change, the re-interpretation may lead to different decisions about appropriate actions and so on. In general, as with physical illness, for a person to seek medical help for himself or for another, a problem has to be perceived, evaluated and acted upon. Social factors influence each stage of this process, as people struggle to make sense of their experiences.

CHAPTER 3

The Social Role of the Mental Patient

Consulting a doctor is not the inevitable sequel to having psychiatric problems: this was shown in the previous chapter, where the social processes involved in recognition and help-seeking were discussed. A social selection operates in the process of becoming a patient in the doctor's waiting room: some get there, and others, with similar symptoms, do not. This social selection continues beyond the patient's arrival at the consulting room; of those diagnosed by the doctor as suffering from psychiatric disturbance only a minority will assume the social role of the mental patient. There are many reasons for this: some are connected with the attitudes and treatment decisions of the particular doctor whom the patient meets; others concern the meaning attached to the 'mental patient role' by social groups and the readiness with which such a role is accorded to individuals, and assumed by them.

It is important to distinguish between persons with recognised psychiatric problems, for which they may or may not receive treatment, but who continue their usual activities and perform their customary social roles, and those who, as a consequence of these problems, discontinue their usual activities and roles and instead assume a new role; that of the mental patient. To understand this distinction it is useful to explore the theoretical concept of the 'sick role' (as it applies to physical illness) and its applicability to mental illness.

THE SICK ROLE

An adult in contemporary industrial society performs many roles simultaneously as spouse, parent, employee, neighbour, churchgoer, club-member etc. Sociologists consider these to be 'social roles' because within each society there are commonly shared notions, or expectations, as to how a person assuming these functions should behave. Similarly, there are shared expectations concerning the ways others in society should behave towards the performer of a social role.

The activities attaching to each role, taken together, make up the daily life of the individual. A physical illness, especially one that involves remaining at home in bed or going to hospital, disrupts the performance of customary roles; the person concerned takes time off from work or is obliged to hand over the care of her baby to somebody else; in other words ceases to function as employee or mother and becomes a sick person. This, also, is a social role in that people in a society have shared notions about the ways that sick persons should behave and about the ways that others should behave towards them.

Talcott Parsons was the first important sociological theorist to turn his attention to the analysis of health and sickness in society from a distinctly sociological perspective and his work in this field, although criticised later, became well known and influential. In a series of papers between 1951 and 1958 (Parsons, 1951; Parsons, 1958; Parsons and Fox, 1968), Parsons developed his concept of the 'sick role' and described certain institutionalised expectations and associated sanctions affecting the sick, which, he argued, exist in contemporary industrial societies. According to Parsons, there are four essential aspects of the sick role:

1. The sick person is exempted from some or all of his social role responsibilities. This means that others around him accept that he is unable to carry out his usual activities and to fulfil his obligations because of the illness. The degree to which this is accepted depends on the nature and severity of the illness.

2. The sick person is also exempted from responsibility for his condition. Two notions are inherent in this: it is accepted

that people cannot help becoming sick and also that they cannot get well by willpower alone but need to be taken care of and helped. In other words, the sick person is not blamed.

3. The individual concerned is expected to define his sick condition as undesirable and to want to get well. He is expected not to resign himself to being sick nor to take advantage of it.

4. The sick person is expected to seek appropriate help, usually the physician, and to co-operate with that help toward the goal of getting well. Thus, as with other social roles, the sick role implies certain privileges (or rights) and certain obligations: the two rights of the sick role, namely exemption from responsibilities and from blame are dependent on the fulfilment of the two obligations, i.e. the wish to get well and co-operation with medical help to that end.

There are a number of important points which have to be noted about Parsons' notion of the sick role. What he had in mind were serious and acute illness conditions. In his model, the typical experience of a sick person would be to notice that he had some symptoms, consider the possibility of illness and then go to the doctor. The doctor would examine him, indicate the diagnosis and specify the treatment. The patient would discontinue his work and other activities and follow the treatment; he would be helped by others and would not be blamed for difficulites caused by his illness. The patient would get better after a time and resume his usual social roles. Thus, the sick role is essentially a temporary one which the person concerned will eventually leave. It is also a dominant role during the period of illness, central to the person's identity and replacing customary social roles which will be resumed only when the patient gets well.

Parsons gave much attention to the process whereby someone assumes the sick role. He pointed out that it is not enough just to claim to be ill; not enough to announce 'I am sick' and thereupon to discontinue activities and obligations and stay in bed, to be waited upon. Crucial, for a person seeking to assume the sick role, is the acceptance of his claim by the immediate social group, i.e. members of the family, workmates and friends. If they do not accept that he is genuinely ill then he will receive not help, kindness and exemption from obligations but sanctions such as blame and the label of malingerer, lazy or workshy. For the social group, too, there are problems; although in some cases it is quite easy to decide when someone is sick (for example, following an operation or a road accident) the condition is not always obvious and lay people can have very real difficulties in deciding whether complaints of ill-health should be accepted as genuine. It is important for people to be able to refer to some measure, some yardstick, by which sickness claims can be sifted.

The widely held belief in contemporary societies is that modern medicine is able to provide such a measure. It is the consequence of this belief (whether grounded in reality or not is irrelevant here) that members of the medical profession function as legitimising agents. Usually a person is legitimately sick (i.e. is accepted by the social group as legitimately occupying the sick role) if a medical practitioner affirms that he really is ill. The doctor usually does this by informing the patient of his diagnosis, that is by giving a name to the condition.

Parsons emphasised the importance of the legitimising process for society as a whole. In his theoretical works he was interested in considering the actions and interactions of individuals from the point of view of the broad social system. From this perspective he pointed out that the adequate health of most group members for most of the time is necessary for the functioning of society. Inherent in being sick is the possibility of abandoning normal role responsibilities and obligations without social disapproval. If too many people assumed the sick role at the same time, a severe strain would be imposed on the workings of society: therefore it is important for society to control not only the incidence of disease but also the means of access to the sick role. Parsons argued that the legitimising process is an important mechanism which controls the definition and adoption of the sick role.

Of course, in many illnesses the condition is sufficiently dreadful for the social group to think that a person is hardly likely to choose it in preference to health. But in other cases an individual may well prefer to assume the sick role and temporarily abandon responsibilities and obligations which have become too burdensome and difficult. Illness provides the possibility of a socially acceptable way of not meeting expectations and of abandoning responsibilities; most other ways of doing so would be met with disapproval and sanctions.

In certain circumstances the sick role may be imposed on a person by the group and be regarded by it as a duty. An individual may be reluctant to assume the sick role because he wants to continue his much valued normal activities but the group may insist on his withdrawal from them in certain cases, for example where infection may spread or where long-term damage to the person's health may result from denying the condition.

It is important to note that not everyone with symptoms will claim the sick role: if the condition is minor, such as a cold, backache or headache, the sufferer will normally continue his usual role-obligations without recourse to the sick role (Butler, 1970), expecting the symptoms to cease after a time. Even where the minor condition is more or less permanent (as for example a backache can be) the person's normal activities can be modified without his entering upon the sick role. Thus, there is an important difference between adjusting everyday role-performances in order to allow for certain symptoms and assuming the special role of the sick person. In the former case, there is what may be called a 'primary' development in the person's life, i.e. the presence of symptoms; in the latter case, there is also the 'secondary' development of an organised social role.

This terminology follows the classic work of Edwin Lemert; he was concerned with variations in human attributes and behaviour, especially those which appear to be deviant, that is, which deviate from a norm of society. Lemert made an important distinction between primary deviations, (for instance, getting drunk on Saturday evenings or having the occasional epileptic fit) which are transitory, occasional or hidden aberrations of individuals who otherwise play normal social roles; and secondary deviations (for instance, assuming the role of the 'alcoholic' or the 'epileptic'), which constitute their major social roles with concomitant social expectations.

Primary deviations or differences have no social importance unless they are 'organised subjectively and transformed into active roles and become the social criteria for assigning status' (Lemert, 1951, p. 75).

The sick role is, in this sense, a secondary or organised role. It carries low social status, as the person performing it is essentially in a dependent position; he is sick, by definition unable to perform normal activities and in need of help from others. The sick person is not a fully functioning and equal member of society, but, for the period of his sickness, takes a lower status as weak, helpless or unfortunate. As Parsons points out, the sick role is negatively achieved (through getting sick) and negatively evaluated.

The sick role formulation of Parsons has received both praise and criticism. Perhaps the most important criticism is that in his analysis he did not allow for such factors as social class, sex and ethnic origin which considerably influence people's illness-experiences and behaviour; and that by focusing attention on shared expectations in society and on the interest of the social system as a whole, he directed attention away from the differences which exist between the elements of a complex contemporary society. (The differences in illness-experiences and behaviour between one such element and another will be discussed in Chapters 6 and 7.)

It has also been pointed out that Parsons viewed the social role of the sick person as temporary and dominant, although these features do not apply to chronic conditions: such illnesses (for example a heart condition or diabetes) though long lasting or permanent, do not necessarily 'dominate' the sufferers' lives. This is a valid comment on the nature of the sick role model, which was developed for temporary, acute illnesses; but it is hardly a criticism, as Parsons never denied the possibility of other social roles, for example those of the permanently disabled or of the dying.

As mentioned, the sick role notion also received praise; it was the first genuinely sociological approach to illness and many researchers found it a useful conceptual tool. It is also useful as a model against which related social roles can be mapped out. Thus, the expectations and behaviour surrounding mental illness may be outlined and better understood by a comparison with Parsons' sick role model.

The position of the mentally ill differs, in some important respects, from that of the physically sick person. Mental illness, or 'madness', has a distinct public image unlike that accorded to physical illness, and it is this public image that shapes the role of the mental patient.

THE PUBLIC IMAGE OF THE MENTALLY ILL

The concepts of 'mental illness' and 'the mental patient' have an unfavourable public image: this has been the evidence of numerous surveys designed to elicit public opinions and attitudes. Studies have consistently shown that people evaluate mental illness negatively, reject and discriminate against mental patients and base their views on traditional stereotypes.

These findings have to be considered in the perspective of evaluations of health and illness in general. Health is one of the most important social values: most people would agree that good health is desirable and valuable and that it represents a condition for the enjoyment of the good things in life. Ill-health, by contrast, is negatively evaluated; there is agreement in society that it represents undesirable things such as suffering and the lack of ability to achieve success and to enjoy life. Thus, to find that mental illness has an unfavourable image is not by itself particularly startling: all illnesses share that. However, the surveys show that public opinion goes further in that mental illness seems to elicit special responses of fear and rejection far exceeding in intensity responses evoked by physical illness.

Although the surveys all came up with the result of negative public views, the particular findings of each do not add up to a clear and unified picture. One difficulty is that the researchers had specific, often different, aims: some wished to investigate attitudes to mental illness, others attitudes to mental patients; certain studies focused on changes over time or on specific demographic variables; some researchers were interested in opinions, others in behaviour. Nevertheless, there emerged from the studies conducted during the last three decades considerable information concerning the public image of the characteristics of the mentally ill, and of the causes and outcome of mental illness.

Three characteristics are commonly attributed to the mentally ill: they are assumed to be easily recognisable, potentially dangerous and very unpredictable. Mental illness is thought to be caused, at least partly, by character defects and its outcome is viewed pessimistically.

One research into the attitudes and feelings of the public towards the mentally ill was carried out in the Netherlands (Swarte, 1969). In it, respondents were asked to express their views about statements made to them concerning the characteristics of mental patients and the causes of mental illness and these views were then compared to those expressed by psychiatrists. The results showed that lay respondents tended to agree that mental patients are 'easily distinguishable from normal people' and that they have a 'strange expression in their eyes'. Many were of the opinion that such patients laugh more and devote less attention to their appearance than do normal people. They viewed mental patients as potentially dangerous and the majority agreed that 'young girls must always be particularly careful of them'. There was a tendency to associate mental patients with crime, especially with crime against the person; indeed, their agreement that young girls should be careful indicates that they viewed mental patients as potential sexual offenders. Moreover, respondents said that the incidence of rape would be reduced if mental patients were more closely confined. Mental patients tended to be associated much more with sexual crimes, crime against children and violence in general than with property offences. Another important finding was that the mentally ill are regarded as unpredictable and inexplicable.

When these responses were compared to answers given to the same questions by psychiatrists, a wide difference was revealed as between the views of laymen and specialists; the psychiatrists disagreed with most of what the lay people said concerning the characteristics of mental patients. For example, the psychiatrists estimated that only 2–3 per cent of psychiatric patients are dangerous.

The findings of this research matched those of several American surveys which also showed negative characteristics being attributed by the public to the mentally ill. One extensive study, carried out by Nunally (1961), based on 400 respondents, revealed that the mentally ill were regarded with fear, distrust and dislike by the general public while several researchers confirmed Swarte's finding that people regarded the mentally ill as being violent and unpredictable.

Concerning the causes of mental illness, people generally tend to think that character plays an important part. Swarte showed that people considered lack of moral strength, a worrying disposition and disappointments in life as factors leading to mental illness and Nunally found that low intelligence, insincerity and 'worthlessness' were regarded as contributory factors. Lay respondents of various studies were reported as thinking that, unlike physical illness, mental disturbance does not strike people indiscriminately, only those have it who were probably not terribly worthwhile to begin with (Rabkin, 1974).

Attributing mental disturbance to character defects may in some cases be the consequence of certain particular manifestations of the disturbance: what is noticed by the social group is often the violation of some rule of conduct or social norm. The person concerned appears to act in 'wrong' or offensive ways and people may easily come to feel that the 'wrong' behaviour is due to viciousness, maliciousness or weakness of character.

The public also rates the chances of recovery as slight: this adds to the generally gloomy and pessimistic view of mental illness.

It seems then that the image of the mental patient is considerably less favourable than that of a person suffering from physical illness and in certain respects it appears to be more like the public image of the criminal. This was the finding of Swarte's study and also that of Tringo (1970) who attempted to establish a hierarchy of lay preferences regarding the sufferers from different types of illness, disability and social problem. He asked 500 respondents to rate various categories of sufferers on a scale; extreme items on the scale included 'would marry' and 'would put to death'.

Respondents ranked the physically sick and disabled categories highest, followed by those suffering from sensory disorders (blind, deaf, dumb) and last came the mentally retarded, ex-prisoners and alcoholics with the mentally ill as often the lowest category. In another study (Elinson *et al.*, 1967) three-quarters of a New York sample agreed with this statement: 'Unlike physical illness, which makes most people sympathetic, mental illness tends to repel most people.'

The conclusion from all these studies is that there exists a stereotype of mental illness and of the mental patient which is negative and which is widely held by the lay public. How did this situation come about? Scheff (1966) has argued that a stereotype of 'madness' is learned in childhood and is constantly reaffirmed throughout the life of the adult in Western societies. According to Scheff, children probably learn the stereotype of 'crazy' and 'mad' from their peers and from adults during their early years in the same way as, for example, they learn of racial stereotypes. These images survive into adulthood because they are reaffirmed by the mass media and by everyday discourse.

Certainly the mass media plays an important part; in radio and television programmes, alongside the more serious documentaries in which experts and informed laymen voice their opinions, there are programmes which reinforce traditional images of madness. It can commonly be read in newspapers that a murderer, a rapist or an escaped prisoner had been treated for mental illness, thereby reaffirming an image of dangerousness, criminal tendencies and unpredictability. Headlines, such as 'ex-mental patient sought by police' are common. The reader is left to draw his own conclusions, and it can be argued that reporting, in order to catch the reader's interest, is highly biased. Scheff argued that

> Even if the coverage of these acts of violence was highly accurate, it would still give the reader a misleading impression because negative information is seldom offset by positive reports. An item like the following is almost inconceivable: Mrs. Ralph Jones, an ex-mental patient, was elected president of the Fairview Home and Garden Society at their meeting on Thursday. (Scheff, 1966, p. 72)

This view of bias in press reporting receives support from research results. Swarte and his colleagues analysed the content of press references in 1955 to the mentally ill in the Netherlands. The analysis showed that press reports much emphasised the connection of mental illness with crime: more than half of all reports and articles which contained references to mentally disturbed persons were dealing with crime. Violence was especially emphasised: half of the items referring to crimes by mentally disturbed people related to crimes of violence with the illustrated weeklies devoting more space than newspapers to 'sexual offences'.

It is further argued by Scheff that the negative stereotype of mental illness is constantly confirmed in daily life by jokes involving mental patients and by expressions commonly used in conversation.

> Such phrases as 'are you crazy?' or 'it would be a madhouse' or 'it's driving me out of my mind' or 'we were chatting like crazy' or 'he was running like mad' and literally hundreds of others occur frequently in informal conversations, and the discussants do not mean to refer to the topic of insanity and are usually unaware that they are doing so. (Scheff, 1966, p. 74)

Other factors also contribute to the existence of the negative stereotype. Lack of familiarity and general ignorance on the part of the public can be cited. Indeed, stereotyping is classically reserved for persons who are strangers to us. Especially in the past, before mental hospitals practised an open door policy, few lay people came into contact with the mentally ill and even today most laymen have no occasion to become familiar with the problem. Nunally reported that respondents were not so much 'misinformed' as 'uninformed' about mental illness.

The past management of the mentally ill (or the 'lunatics' of earlier times) is another very likely contributor to the stereotype: till the mid-1950s the mental hospitals in Britain and the United States were crowded with in-patients, many of whom were long-stay (i.e. in the hospital for many years, even for the rest of their lives) and very little was done in the way of effective treatment for them. The general impression of poor prognosis was reinforced in those visiting the hospitals, who saw patients being compulsorily detained (especially in the American State Hospitals) in crowded, gloomy and carefully locked wards which did nothing to change preconceived notions of the hoplessness of the condition.

Changes in the Public Image

Public opinion is not static, it changes over time. Lay views of mental disturbance may well be undergoing changes, especially as treatment and management of psychiatric patients have dramatically altered. A high proportion of sufferers are now treated as out-patients, or admitted to hospital for a short stay only; few are compulsorily detained; medication is prescribed in the same way as it is to sufferers from physical illness; many hospitals are open and wards unlocked. Moreover, during the second half of this century lay thinking has been much exposed to the view that mental disturbance should be regarded as an 'illness', like any other, that can strike anyone and that can be conquered. There have been campaigns to promote this view (Cumming and Cumming, 1957) and also less formal efforts by psychiatric personnel to lessen ignorance and to influence public opinion through educational programmes. All this has been done on the assumption that if people know more about mental disturbance and if they accept it as 'illness' then more favourable views of the mentally ill and less fear and distrust of them will follow.

Several studies investigated the possibility of changes in public opinion but the findings are contradictory. Some researchers during the 1960s found that lay respondents were considerably better informed about mental illness than earlier studies had indicated and that many people accepted the proposition that mental disturbance was an illness. In a study of laymen's knowledge and opinions in Baltimore, Lemkau and Crocetti (1962) found that a very high proportion of respondents replied in the affirmative to the question 'Do you think people who are mentally ill require a doctor's care as much as people who have any other sort of illness?' They also found that their respondents were quite well informed about psychiatric conditions.

The findings of Lemkau and Crocetti were confirmed by other researchers (Elinson *et al.*, 1967; Dohrenwend and Chin-Song, 1967) but in contrast others detected only minor changes, if any, in public opinion finding, in the main, that people continue to regard mental illness with the same fear and aversion traditionally exhibited.

These differing research results are not quite as contradictory as they first appear. The view that mental disturbance is an illness, like any other, appears to have gained acceptance, by some sections of the public at least, in the United States where most studies have been carried out and it is likely that this holds good in Britain also. But people may have come to feel that the view advocated by psychiatric personnel represents 'progressive' and 'modern' thinking, and that it is 'correct' to answer interview questions accordingly, without however being convinced of its validity and rightness. In the New York survey mentioned earlier, (Elinson *et al.*, 1967) where three-quarters of the respondents agreed that, unlike physical illness, mental illness tends to repel people, only 16 per cent admitted to being repelled themselves, the rest indicating that only others reacted in this way, another pointer to a possible tendency on the part of respondents to subscribe to the medical view of mental illness without necessarily feeling it right and applicable.

A general conclusion of the many studies must be that people in Western societies appear to be moving towards greater acceptance of mental disturbance as another illness, and towards a lessening of the traditional fear, dislike and mistrust it implies. However, there is no knowledge of how slow this movement might be and certainly there still exists today a large proportion of the lay public that continues to hold the traditional notions.

Variations in Public Opinion

Although negative evaluations of the mentally ill are widespread in Western societies, variations exist between different sections of the population in the extent to which they hold to the traditional stereotype of mental illness or are influenced by it. Among the variables investigated in this connection are education, age, social class and previous familiarity with the condition. One of the most consistent findings in this area is of a strong association between the level of education of individuals and their evaluations of the mentally ill: the better educated people are the less likely are they to base their views on the traditional stereotypes and to hold negative attitudes (Rabkin, 1974; Halpert, 1969; Swarte, 1969).

The age of respondents is a variable consistently associated with opinions about mental illness. Younger people are more positive and sympathetic than older ones. Education may play a part in this too in that the younger generation in Western societies receives longer formal education, and, moreover, that contemporary education is more attuned to modern notions of illness than was that of former times. It is also possible that younger people are less conservative in their thinking and habits, more open to new ideas and more tolerant of deviant behaviour of many types.

The various researches show that each of the two variables – education and age – can influence opinions independently of the other; the association with attitudes to mental illness holds even when one of the variables is controlled. More research is needed, however, to establish whether the younger people of the present day will become less tolerant, less open to new ideas and less sympathetic to the mentally ill as they grow older, or whether in the future the whole of public opinion really will move towards more positive evaluations.

Somewhat more problematic is the influence that social class may have on opinions about mental illness and on attitudes to the mentally ill. In the Netherlands Swarte found little connection between the social class of an individual and his opinions about the mentally ill. However, in an early study carried out in the United States, Hollingshead and Redlich (1958) found a social class difference in people's views: lower class Americans showed more fear and resentment of the mentally ill than did middle class ones. More recent studies in America have also tended to show that high and low status groups view mental disturbance differently from each other: higher status groups, perhaps because of their more extensive formal education, see mental illness in less traditional and less negative stereotypes than do lower status groups (Dohrenwend and Chin-Song, 1967).

It is also likely that there exists a section of the population (possibly quite small) which possesses a 'psychiatric sophistication', attributable partly to education and social class but, more importantly, to belonging to certain types of urban circle. This was the opinion of Kadushin and Scheff, discussed in the previous chapter, who both said that such psychiatric sophistication is probably connected with occupations such as show business, the arts, higher education and health-care, and with reading certain types of book and watching certain television programmes all of which influence these people away from traditional popular views and towards those held by psychiatrists.

Considerable interest has been shown in the question of whether contact with psychiatric patients and familiarity with disturbed behaviour influences opinions to any great extent. It is often argued that stereotyping is applied by people to strangers but that as they come to know persons belonging to a stereotyped category, understanding, sympathy and a realistic assessment of personal qualities takes place. Thus, contact with psychiatric patients may result in a moving away from traditional stereotyping by lay people. If so, then public participation of volunteer programmes, hospital visiting and other activities which bring patients and public together, may serve to increase the number of people holding more positive attitudes to mental illness. However, research findings indicate that contact by itself has little influence on opinions. For example, Holmes (1968) investigated changes in the attitudes of the staff of community recreational centres in New York after their experience with psychiatric patients. Patients were brought from nearby hospitals to these centres to participate in recreational activities and Holmes found that exposure to psychiatric patients had a negligible effect on the attitudes of those running the centres. It is likely that the nature of the contact matters more than the frequency of it: patients brought to recreational centres may seem to be very obviously 'mental patients' if only because they come from the hospital, and so existing stereotypes are applied to them.

There is also some evidence to show that people with mentally disturbed relatives or friends show no more acceptance than do those without such relatives or friends. In a study which will be discussed further in this chapter, Phillips measured rejection of the mentally ill by the public on a social distance scale. Rejection rates for respondents who had a relative or a friend seeking help for mental disturbance from a psychiatrist or from a mental hospital, were only very slightly lower than the rejection rates for those who knew no one seeking such help (see Table 3.2).

STIGMA

It has been shown that there is considerable evidence that mental illness has a negative image, based on traditional stereotyping, which is resistant to change. It can be further argued that there is a 'stigma' attaching to mental illness.

Following Goffman's important discussion (Goffman, 1963), the term stigma is used to refer to an attribute which is deeply discrediting. According to Goffman:

> Society establishes the means of categorising persons and the complement of attributes felt to be ordinary and natural of each of these categories. Social settings establish the categories of persons likely to be encountered there. The routines of social intercourse in established settings allow us to deal with anticipated others without special attention or thought. When a stranger comes into our presence, then, first appearances are likely to enable us to anticipate his category and attributes, his 'social identity'.... While the stranger is present before us, evidence can arise of his possessing an attribute that makes him different from others in the category of persons available for him to be, and of a less desirable kind – in the extreme, a person who is quite thoroughly bad, or dangerous, or weak. He is thus reduced in our minds from a whole and usual person to a tainted, discounted one. Such an attribute is a stigma, especially when its discrediting effect is very extensive; sometimes it is also called a failing, a shortcoming, a handicap. It constitutes a special discrepancy between virtual and actual social identity. (Goffman, 1963, p. 2)

Stigma, then, is a societal reaction which singles out certain attributes, evaluates them as undesirable and devalues the persons who possess them. There are many types of stigma: physical deformities and disfigurements which affect the appearance of a person (the cripple, the hunchback, the dwarf, the badly burned, the amputee, for example, would come into this category): and blemishes of character and personality (the known criminals, prostitutes, drug addicts for instance). There are other types of stigma, e.g. the tribal, or that of a particular ethnic minority, but these are not the concern of the present discussion. It must be stressed that what matters is society's evaluation of some characteristics as stigmatising and that this evaluation is specific to place and time. In different societies, at different times, an epileptic or a homosexual might or might not be stigmatised.

There are certain sociological features common to all types of stigma. The individual concerned tends to be defined in terms of his or her stigmatised attribute; for example, a twenty-year old, blind, pretty, music-loving social science student would be constantly referred to as the 'blind girl'. The stigma tends to become all-important and to override other characteristics; consequently, possessing an attribute which is stigmatising means that the whole person becomes stigmatised. In Goffman's words, the person's identity becomes 'spoiled'.

The social consequences of stigma are very severe: the victim's life chances are often much reduced, he is discriminated against in many different ways, and is typically rejected by his fellows. The stigmatised is considered to be a less desirable companion, workmate, employee or tenant.

The concept of stigma, as Goffman developed it, is helpful to the understanding of the social role of the mentally ill: the traditional image of the mental patient as someone strange in appearance, dangerous and inexplicable, someone to be feared and mistrusted, is deeply discrediting and stigmatising.

A most important feature of stigma is that it undermines social expectations, a statement which touches the very core of sociological concerns; the explanation of how people interact with each other in specific situations. Of crucial importance for smooth interaction in society is that people have expectations as to how others will behave in given situations. These expectations enable people to orientate their own behaviour towards the anticipated actions of others. Social expectations are built up slowly and are based on accumulated past experience; without them, routines of daily life in society would not be possible. For example, a man entering a shop has a set of expectations: that the shopkeeper will be willing to sell his goods, that he will accept money in return, etc., and the shopper will have these expectations even if he has never entered that particular shop, nor met that particular shopkeeper. Social expectations form the basis of social roles: persons playing the roles of shopper and shopkeeper are both expected to behave in certain ways.

Possessing a stigma, which in Goffman's term is an undesirable differentness, implies that a person has an attribute which makes him different from others and that the usual social expectations are not applicable. People become unsure of what to expect and this disrupts ordinary interaction in society. If the shopper is uncertain as to what to expect from a particular shopkeeper he will refrain from entering the shop. An individual who is known to be mentally disturbed is thereby thought to be different; his other characteristics, e.g. that he is middle-aged, male and a town dweller become relatively unimportant as do his social roles as shopkeeper, father and husband. He is now identified as the mentally disturbed man and social expectations as to how he will behave are undermined.

When people say that the mentally ill are unpredictable and inexplicable, they typically express their feelings of uncertainty concerning social expectations.

In a sense, all types of illness are stigmatising. If the term stigma is accepted to mean an 'undesirable differentness', that is, an attribute evaluated as something bad and discrediting, then any physical illness comes into this category: serious, long-standing and disabling diseases being more undesirable than slight, short-term and self-limiting conditions. It is helpful to think in terms of a continuum of stigmatising illnesses, with conditions like backaches, headaches and colds as least stigmatising and diseases such as multiple sclerosis or paralytic polio as very stigmatising. Colds and backaches are accepted as something most people get and are therefore part of life, even compatible with overall good health, while disabling diseases such as multiple sclerosis or polio are considered as rare, singling out the sufferers as unfortunates, who are different from everybody else.

Mental illness is at the most stigmatising end of the continuum; as the studies discussed earlier show, it is consistently ranked by people as more undesirable and fearful than physical illness. It is popularly thought of as a serious condition, with little chance of full recovery, which hits people of not very admirable character. Moreover, the trouble is located in the 'mind' of the sick person and people tend to think that thereby the most essential part of the human being becomes questionable or discredited. As Goffman aptly phrased it, the stigmatised is regarded as less than human.

THE SOCIAL ROLE OF THE MENTALLY ILL

Thus, in modern Western societies mental disturbance is viewed differently from physical illness: what, then, is the role of the mentally ill and how does it compare to the sick role?

The role of the mentally ill is very much a social role in that definite social expectations, sanctions and responses surround it. It has a number of similarities to the sick role. A seriously disturbed person will discontinue normal, customary social roles as employee, parent, club-member, etc., and instead will assume the role of the mentally ill. Thus, an aspect of the sick role, exemption from obligations and activities, is an important feature of the role of the mentally ill too. As is the case with physical illness, not everyone with symptoms discontinues normal social obligations, exemption being dependent on the severity of the condition. The acceptance of the social group is essential for the mentally ill to be exempted from obligations and in this, too, the role is similar to that of the physically sick.

Another feature of the sick role is exemption from responsibility and blame: it is accepted by society that the sick individual could not help becoming sick and cannot get well by willpower alone. At this point there is a difference between the roles of the mentally and the physically ill. The view is widely held by the public that physical illness hits people indiscriminately and it is accepted, albeit grudgingly, that anyone may become ill. Illness is usually seen as something a person gets, or 'catches', through an external agent and therefore no blame is imputed to the sick person. Even when someone is thought to be responsible for his condition, by breaking his leg through reckless riding, for example, it is accepted that he cannot get better by willpower alone.

Mental disturbance, on the other hand, is seen by the public in a different light: the studies reviewed earlier have shown that people often attribute psychiatric problems to character weaknesses and defects. Consequently, responsibility is imputed to the individual for the condition. Likewise, the feeling is often present that all would be well if the person 'pulled himself together', 'mended his ways' and tried harder to overcome his problems.

The sick role is essentially a temporary one, accorded most easily to those whose condition is amenable to treatment and who may consequently be expected to return to health and to pre-illness roles. Mental illness, however, is seen by the laymen as a condition where the chances of recovery are slight and which, therefore, is not temporary. The role of the mentally ill is fundamentally different from the sick role in this respect: there is no similar assumption that the patient will return to normal social roles. In fact for many psychiatric patients today treatment involves either a short stay in a mental hospital or attendance merely as an out-patient: withdrawal from normal social roles is a temporary necessity similar, in many ways, to that occasioned by acute physical illness. But nevertheless, inherent in the public image of mental illness is pessimism regarding the outcome of it.

There is also a difference in the degree of willingness with which individuals claim the sick role as against the role of the mentally ill. The physically sick person usually claims the sick role himself by pointing out his symptoms and professing inability to carry out normal activities. Mental disturbance is often identified by the social group, while the individual concerned may not feel that anything is wrong with him nor feel the need to modify his activities. Moreover, a person may well be reluctant to claim a social role which is deeply stigmatising, even if he recognises his symptoms. Indeed, the prospective patient and members of his family may be equally reluctant to seek medical help because of the frightening nature of the stigma.

When one decides to claim a social role, whether it is the role of club member, teacher, patient or whatever, one has to weigh the expected benefits against the costs of such a step. Entry into the sick role, at the cost of withdrawal from normal activities, dependency on others and co-operation in treatment regimes, is undertaken in the expectation of obtaining the 'reward' or benefit of becoming healthy. However, to assume the role of the mentally ill or to assign it to a member of the family, has the additional cost of stigma while the reward of a return to mental health, or sanity, although highly desirable, seems to be uncertain. The price to be paid for an uncertain reward may be thought too high.

There is, however, another consideration. Not to claim the role of the mentally ill may result not in avoiding stigma, but in replacing one type of stigma with another. If a person has socially unacceptable habits or exhibits unacceptable behaviour, and mental illness is not imputed by the social group, stigma and social sanctions of various types can still follow; the behaviour can then be considered as a deliberate violation of social norms, i.e. as 'bad' rather than disturbed. For example, someone permanently out of work and withdrawn from social contacts may be called lazy, workshy and spoilt, instead of being regarded as mentally disturbed; loud, violent, threatening behaviour may be regarded as vicious, or malicious rather than a sign of mental disturbance. The stigma of mental illness is then replaced by stigma and social disapproval of another kind: that meted out to workshy, unreliable, vicious or malicious individuals.

Thus, claiming the role of the mentally ill presents a complex problem, and may be decided upon with more reluctance than a claim to the sick role would involve.

ASSUMING THE MENTAL PATIENT ROLE

One person diagnosed as having a psychiatric illness will assume the mental patient role; another, so diagnosed, will not. Becoming a mental patient is a socially structured event and for this to come about, the doctor not only has to make a diagnosis but has to communicate it to the patient or family; the social group has to learn of the diagnosis and has to define the person as mentally ill. With each step, the person is moved nearer to assuming the role of the mental patient. Thus the patient, the doctor and the social group each play a part in a social selection process, i.e. selection for the role of the mental patient.

Selection by General Practitioners

In the British National Health Service the usual first medical contact of people with problems of mental disturbance is the general practitioner to whom are customarily taken all problems that appear to be of a medical nature. In the United States some would similarly turn first to a general practitioner while others may go directly to a psychiatrist.

Diagnosis of the problem by a general practitioner as being of a psychiatric nature and, in some cases, the referral of the patient by him to a psychiatrist, constitute steps moving the mentally disturbed individual nearer to assuming the social role of the mental patient. But such diagnosis and referral are not the inevitable outcome of consulting the general practitioner in the first instance.

It has frequently been argued that general practitioners tend to 'under-diagnose' and 'under-report' psychiatric problems. By this is meant that of those patients whose complaints could be interpreted as being due to psychiatric problems, only some are so diagnosed by their general practitioners. There may be several reasons for this: the general practitioner may fail to identify psychiatric problems during a very short consultation time (in the National Health Service the average consultation time is only five to six minutes) unless the disturbance is serious. This is especially a difficulty as patients often present their problems as being physical ones. Other factors, however, are also involved in under-reporting.

Michael Balint (1957) has pointed out that general practitioners have a tendency to exclude the possibility of organic diseases before considering a psychiatric diagnosis. When a complaint is not easily diagnosed the doctor prefers to send the patient for physical tests, and only when these prove negative does he turn to the possibility of psychiatric explanation; Balint called this 'elimination by appropriate physical examination'. This tendency is partly explained by the doctors' training, which makes them feel on firmer ground when dealing with physical diseases, and by their anxiety not to overlook an organic disease by considering too readily the possibility of a psychiatric solution. Balint argued that for general practitioners, diseases are arranged in a kind of 'ranking order' where physical diseases and their diagnosis rank higher in importance than psychiatric illnesses, thinking which results in the under-diagnosing of the latter.

Even when the diagnosis is one of psychiatric illness, the doctor may decide not to acknowledge this to the patient and not to start a treatment; a decision which may seem right if medical intervention appears unpromising. Thus, there are a (necessarily unknown) number of patients with psychiatric problems who reach the medical practitioner but who do not move nearer towards becoming socially acknowledged mentally ill people.

Of those patients who are diagnosed as suffering from a psychiatric condition and in need of treatment, a high proportion is treated by the general practitioner without recourse to a psychiatrist. This was a finding of a survey carried out by Shepherd *et al.* (1966) in England into psychiatric illness in general practice. They found that of the new cases diagnosed as psychiatric, only 3.5 per cent were referred to a psychiatrist. A higher proportion of the very serious than of the less serious cases were referred, but the bulk of all types of patient was managed by the general practitioner. This finding has been confirmed by other investigations (Goldberg and Blackwell, 1970).

Shepherd's survey quoted a variety of reasons given by general practitioners for not referring appropriate cases to a psychiatrist. Underlying the most frequently cited reason was that stigma is attached to psychiatric care: practitioners were reluctant to suggest psychiatric treatment, knowing that this would frequently prove unacceptable to patients and their

TABLE 3.1 Factors Influencing the General Practitioners Against Psychiatric Referral

Factors influencing against psychiatric referral	Percentage[a]
The patient's dislike of being referred to a psychiatrist	60.0
A feeling that the treatment of neurotic patients is the job of the general practitioner	45.3
Delay involved between making the appointment and the consultation	40.0
The disadvantage to patients of being labelled as mental cases	26.7
The unsatisfactory way in which patients are dealt with in the psychiatric clinic	17.3
The lack of readily available psychiatric facilities	13.3
Consideration for the psychiatrists, knowing how busy they are	10.7
Lack of satisfactory rapport between G.P. and psychiatrist	10.7
Psychiatrist's delay in sending reports on patients referred to him	5.3
Others	10.7
Number of doctors: 75	

[a] Percentages add to more than 100% since doctors often gave more than one factor.
Source: M. Shepherd *et al.*, (1966), p. 160.

families. Practitioners also believed that the stigma which would be bound to follow contact with psychiatric services could be detrimental to the patient.

Most doctors were also influenced in their decisions as to referral by their own professional interests and by the orientation of the local psychiatrists: some general practitioners thought specialist treatment appropriate but disapproved of the type of psychiatry practised in the area, while others were interested enough in psychiatric illness to treat patients themselves: others again were cool or hostile to psychiatry and doubted its usefulness in most cases of disturbance. Frequency of consultation could also influence referral: a few doctors said that they referred to specialists certain 'regulars' with psychiatric problems in order to give themselves a respite:

But for many general practitioners it was the anticipated success or otherwise of therapeutic intervention that was of primary importance, influencing both their classification of illness and their referral decision.

> As an example, the perception of asthma as a psychosomatic affection is of no pragmatic value if such a formulation makes no difference to the management and treatment of this condition; if, however, a consultant psychiatrist in one area takes a particular interest in cases of asthma, and proves more successful therapeutically than his physician colleagues, then his results may well induce local practitioners to reappraise this disorder. Increasing numbers of asthmatic patients may then be assessed as psychosomatic problems, and as such referred to the psychiatric out-patient department. (Shepherd et al., 1966, p. 57)

The conclusion from this and other studies must be that whether or not a patient is referred to a psychiatrist depends a great deal on the views, interests and available time of the general practitioner. These doctors, in effect, select candidates for the role of mental patient by making decisions regarding referrals.

In the United States the situation is different in that people there may choose to go directly to a psychiatrist. Kadushin's study of patients of psychiatric clinics in New York showed that more than a third of the sample had chosen to turn to a psychiatrist, either in a hospital out-patients department or in clinical practice, as their first contact. Most of the rest of the sample had first consulted a non-psychiatric medical practitioner, while the remainder had resorted to counsellors, clergymen and other advisers. Although there is little research evidence, it is possible that American non-psychiatric doctors share the feelings of the practitioners of Shepherd's study; for example Freidson (1973) is of the opinion that the American first-line doctors also under-diagnose mental illness as they would not wish to alienate their clients by unpopular diagnosis.

Selection by Psychiatrists

When the prospective patient reaches the consulting room of the psychiatrist the latter has to make a decision as to whether the patient suffers from a mental illness or not. In the former case a diagnosis is made, treatment is suggested and the individual is moved towards the role of the mental patient: in the latter case the patient, the general practitioner and the family is told that no mental illness is present, and so the process of becoming defined as mentally ill comes to a halt.

A great deal of interest has been paid by sociologists in recent years to one aspect of psychiatric decision-making, namely to the readiness with which psychiatrists endorse tentative lay definitions of mental illness. Mechanic (1968) has pointed out that in crowded hospitals and clinics, where a patient is typically seen by a very busy psychiatrist, there is not sufficient time to make a complete psychiatric examination. Nor does psychiatry necessarily provide the practitioner with appropriate tools to screen patients quickly and to distinguish the 'sick' from the 'well'; his theoretical psychiatric knowledge may be too abstract and too uncertain for quick judgements. It is safer for the psychiatrist to assume that if the patient is in the consulting room complaining about his symptoms, or if members of the family are there complaining of the patient's changed behaviour and strangeness, or if the general practitioner or law-enforcing agencies referred the patient for psychiatric examination, then something is wrong. The psychiatrist therefore sees his task as being to determine what is wrong rather than whether anything is wrong.

> The criteria he holds are at times indefinite and the physician who practises in large treatment centres often must assume the illness of the patient who appears before him and then proceed to prescribe treatment. Both the abstract nature of the physician's theories and the time limitations imposed upon him by the institutional structure of which he is a part make it impossible for him to make a rapid study of the patient's illness

or even to ascertain if illness, in fact, exists. Instead, it becomes necessary for him to assume the illness of the patient and to apply some label to the alleged if not recognisable symptoms. The consequences are that the basic decision is more or less made by non-professional members of the community. (Mechanic, 1968, p. 197)

Mechanic studied two mental hospitals over a period of three months and found no case where a psychiatrist told a patient that he needed no treatment.

Scheff, the leading exponent of the labelling theory in mental illness, argued even more strongly that psychiatrists, when faced with uncertainties, presume illness. Scheff suggests that there exists a 'medical decision rule' which can be stated thus: 'When in doubt, diagnose illness' (Scheff, 1966, p. 111). This is so because psychiatrists share the general medical orientation that it is far more culpable to dismiss a sick patient than to retain a well one.

Scheff supported his arguments with his research results and some aspects of his work were discussed in Chapter 1. He collected information by studying the ratings psychiatrists made of patients who were newly admitted to mental hospitals, by interviews with psychiatrists and by observing psychiatric examinations for court proceedings (Scheff, 1966). His results were that considerable uncertainties existed in the psychiatric screening of patients and that there was a strong assumption of illness prior to the examinations of patients, which were perfunctory. Specifically, Scheff found that psychiatrists recommended for treatment every one of 196 consecutive cases seen by them; that the average length of psychiatric examinations was just over ten minutes; and that the content of the examinations (i.e. questions asked and conclusions drawn from the patients' answers) showed uncertainties and carelessness.

The research results and arguments of Scheff and Mechanic have been challenged, however. On the basis of data from several secondary sources Gove (1970) argued that psychiatrists screen out a large proportion of persons who come to them as prospective patients. Recently Bean (1979) studied the work of psychiatrists in England who operated a scheme to deal with emergency domiciliary visits, requests for such visits having been made by general practitioners, police and social workers. Bean found that far from admitting every prospective patient to a psychiatric hospital, the number of non-admissions was high; only about one patient in three was admitted. The psychiatrists in this study presumed mental illness, especially as the requests came from professional sources, and had often made some preliminary arrangements for admission to a psychiatric hospital. It is all the more significant then that they often changed their minds when interviewing the patient; it seems that presumption of mental illness did not influence the interviews and the final decisions of the psychiatrists. Bean noted that uncertainties certainly existed; 'It would have been unrealistic to expect no uncertainty, for the nature of the task demanded that a decision be made quickly and often under strained circumstances' (Bean, 1979, p. 126), but he concluded that uncertainties did not dominate proceedings. Bean also found that some psychiatrists at least, spent much longer on the examination than the 10 minutes mentioned by Scheff.

The study by Bean is small scale, but nevertheless most welcome in a field where more arguments and suppositions are put forward than empirical findings.

Selection by the Social Group

It was shown in the previous chapter that there exists among lay people a marked reluctance to define someone as mentally ill and that frequently the condition is accommodated until some crisis precipitates the seeking of professional help. At what point, then, does the layman finally concede the mental illness definition?

Researchers during the 1950s and early 1960s argued that the turning point is admission to a mental hospital. For example, as the Cummings observed in America, 'Mental illness, it seems, is a condition which afflicts people who must go to a mental institution, but up until they go almost anything they do is fairly normal' (Cumming and Cumming, 1957, p. 102). Similarly, in England, according to the study of Enid Mills, (1962) 'Admission to hospital, rather than the behaviour itself, determines that a person is mentally disturbed' (p. 46). Admission is a definite event upon which someone, however regarded until then, becomes defined as mentally ill and assumes the role of the mental patient; but more recent research has shown that those not admitted to hospital may also assume the mental patient role. For some, the turning point comes when the general practitioner refers them to a psychiatrist and psychiatric treatment begins; for others, it comes when normal activities and roles are abandoned.

As stated, stigmatised illness can be thought of as a continuum: from the hardly stigmatised to the very stigmatised. Similarly, the various stages of assuming the role of the mental patient can be thought of as increasingly stigmatising, from consulting the general practitioner through to admission to a mental hospital. This was shown in an interesting research by Derek Phillips (1968) who was particularly concerned with the stigma and rejection which may follow the action of seeking help with mental disorder from one source or another. Phillips studied help-seeking from four help-sources often consulted by people with mental disturbance, namely the clergyman, the physician, the psychiatrist and the mental hospital. In his research, interviews were conducted with 300 women in a New England town whom he categorised according to whether they themselves were acquainted with a relative, a friend, or with no one who sought help for problems of psychiatric disturbance. Each of the women was presented with a series of cards bearing descriptions of various kinds of behaviour (taken from case abstracts) in conjunction with information as to the help sources being utilised by the individual described. The respondents were then asked about the closeness of the relationships that they themselves would be willing to tolerate with the individuals in the case abstracts, the research being designed to relate the replies separately to the type of behaviour and to the help-sources consulted (see also next chapter). With regard to help-sources the results for all three categories showed that the highest degree of rejection was accorded to those consulting the mental hospital and for two of the three categories those consulting the psychiatrist were next in order of rejection.

TABLE 3.2 Rejection Scores[a] for Mentally Ill Cases by
Help-Source and Acquaintance with Help-Seekers

Help-source utilized	Relative ($N = 37$)	Acquaintance Friend ($N = 37$)	No one ($N = 190$)
No help-source	2.81	1.64	1.16
Clergyman	2.20	1.65	1.86
Physician	1.51	1.91	2.46
Psychiatrist	2.45	2.88	2.90
Mental Hospital	3.04	3.14	3.51

[a] Rejection scores are represented by the mean number of items rejected on the Social Distance Scale.
Source: D. L. Phillips (1968), p. 223.

One point shown by these results is that a person with a problem behaviour is more stigmatised by strangers if he seeks help of any sort than if he does not. The reason for this may be that the help-seeker becomes defined as someone who has a problem, and thus compares unfavourably with those who have not and that, moreover, he is defined as someone who is unable to handle the problem himself. The ability to 'manage one's own problems by oneself' and to 'stand on one's own feet' is much valued (especially in American society) and the help-seeker demonstrates his inability in this respect. If an individual must seek help, then from whom makes a great deal of difference: Phillips' data show that it is far more socially acceptable to turn to a clergyman or to a physician than to a psychiatrist. It seems therefore that those general practitioners who feel that referral to psychiatric services would bring about stigmatisation are quite right in that assumption. Contact with a psychiatrist or with a mental hospital selects the individual for the role of the mental patient.

There was an interesting exception to these findings: respondents with a help-seeking relative rejected persons represented in the abstracts more if they did not seek help than if they sought it from a physician, clergyman or psychiatrist. Possibly these respondents were more able to recognise the mental disturbance depicted in the abstracts and had had personal experience of problems created by relatives who had not sought help for mental disturbance. Even for these respondents, however, rejection scores were highest in the case of persons seeking help from a mental hospital.

Phillips' respondents were women living in a small New England town, but there is evidence to show that their findings represent widely held views (Mills, 1962; Shepherd *et al.*, 1966; Hollingshead and Redlich, 1958). There is a small section of contemporary society however which has that 'psychiatric sophistication' discussed earlier: in certain circles to see a psychiatrist or a psychoanalyst (especially on a fee-paying basis) has a different connotation from the one shown by Phillips' respondents: it is not stigmatising but makes a person more 'sophisticated', 'insightful' and 'interesting' (Kadushin, 1969).

Entering a mental hospital is the most decisive of the events which lead to the assumption of the mental patient role. It is also a socially structured event. Many disturbed individuals live in the community without recourse to hospital admission, and their families accommodate their symptoms, whether or not out-patient treatment is undertaken. Accommodation of the mentally ill at home can be taken to great lengths; for example, Yarrow's study revealed that the mental hospital is regarded as a last resort by wives of patients (Yarrow *et al.*, 1955a). Research elsewhere has likewise indicated that many families make tremendous efforts to keep their members out of hospital. An example from the study of Enid Mills in London:

> Mrs. Gathercole . . . is fully absorbed in the family because all the attention of her female relatives is centred upon her. They tend her like a small child and defend her from the outside world. She goes alone to her local doctor and almost every day she walks alone in the park. . . . She does as she is told and is washed, fed and dressed by her relatives. They arrange their entire life around her needs. They are all elderly and retired. (Mills, 1962, p. 82)

Accommodation of the mentally ill at home can collapse

however and hospital admission follows for a variety of reasons.

In a study of schizophrenic patients in England, Brown and his colleagues categorised the events which led to admission to a psychiatric hospital (Brown et al., 1966). First they placed the category of 'danger to self or others', (category A) including violence, threats, suicidal attempts and destructive behaviour. For example, 'Mrs. A. A. had been tearful and depressed for nearly a year. More recently she had been threatening her husband and children and had accused him of infidelity . . . she began to wander at night and threatened suicide.' 'Mr. A.B. attacked his wife when she came in late one evening. He struck her and threatened her with a knife.' 'Mr. A. D. lived with his sister and parents. He was found by the police wandering in a neighbouring town after trouble at his home . . . his parents said that he had been breaking up the furniture in the house' (Brown et al., 1966, p. 46).

The second category (B) included 'other grossly abnormal behaviour', such as bizarre conduct, shouting, marked noise or restlessness, wandering from home. 'Mrs. A. E. lived with her husband and daughter . . . she had taken to walking about the house with nothing on, and on the day of admission walked down the road to see her general practitioner with only a nightdress on.' 'Mr. A. G. a single man . . . his mother said that for two weeks he was like a cat on hot bricks and became wild in manner . . . he couldn't sleep and walked into his mother's room at night' (Brown et al., 1966, p. 47).

Finally, the third category (C) included other, unclassifiable behaviour such as being grossly dirty, etc.

Most admissions in this study were consequences of events of the A and B type.

> Of the 339 patients, 36 per cent were placed into category A, and 35 per cent into category B, that is 71 per cent were either a danger to themselves or others, or acted in a manner that was markedly disturbed. The behaviour that preceded admission was not, in the majority of patients, merely a matter of exhibiting psychotic symptoms. By the time of admission the patient's behaviour had become so deranged that admission was sought largely to deal with troublesome, frightening or embarrassing behaviour rather than with the symptoms of

schizophrenia that are described in psychiatric textbooks. (Brown *et al.*, 1966, p. 48)

Admissions following events such as those described in the preceding paragraph are examples of selection for the mental-patient role, by the social group. The action which finally leads to hospitalisation can be taken by the patient's family (when the disturbed behaviour cannot be contained in the home any longer); by the neighbours, workmates and others in the social group (when unacceptable behaviour causes distress, threats or nuisance); or by law-enforcing agencies on their own initiative (when unacceptable behaviour occurs in public places).

It is important to bear in mind that disturbed behaviour of the type that in some cases leads to complaints and actions by the social group does not produce like social reaction in other cases. Brown noted that 'The crises which did not lead to admission were not notably different, at least as described in the case-notes, from those which did', and that it was 'Difficult to see why some crises should have been followed by an admission and others not' (Brown *et al.*, 1966, p. 50). More research is needed to establish why this is so.

A suggestion from someone that psychiatric treatment is necessary, especially if treatment involves hospital admission, is often received with dismay and refusal. It is a common feature of stigmatised roles that they are accorded to unwilling members of society, who assume the role reluctantly. Often, it is a question of 'acceptance' rather than 'assumption' of the role. The young, blonde, music-loving undergraduate does not choose to play the social role of the 'blind girl'; neither does the boy affected by polio assume the role of the 'cripple' from choice. The question is rather in what manner do they accept their situation?

The position of the prospective mental patient is different in that benefits as well as costs are attached to the role: perceived benefits have to be balanced against perceived costs.

A general point to be noted is that stigmatised individuals tend to hold the same beliefs about social identity and stigma as the rest of society (Goffman, 1963). Especially is this the case where the stigma is not an inborn attribute but is acquired later in life by adults who, until then, had held the beliefs of their group about the stigmatised. Thus, many of the mentally ill themselves share the traditional negative stereotypes of mental illness. The individual's response to the suggestion that he should now become a mental patient is much coloured by his image of what this means.

Accounts of patients entering psychiatric hospitals show that many deny the necessity for so doing prior to admission, and assert that very little is wrong with them.

Nevertheless, the great majority of the patient population enter the psychiatric hospitals on a 'voluntary' basis, that is, they are not compulsorily detained. They usually sign a document indicating their agreement to undergo treatment. A difference has to be made, however, between entering a mental hospital as a 'voluntary' patient in the legal sense, and entering it as a genuinely willing patient. One may be willing to undergo treatment in a mental hospital even though committed by a court of law; another may be unwilling to go into a mental hospital, but enters nevertheless, on a 'voluntary' basis, as a result of strong social pressures. In this sense a willing patient is one who wishes to enter the hospital because of the benefits it offers.

When members of the immediate social group decide that mental hospital treatment is necessary for an unwilling person they may persuade, press, or in extreme cases, trick or threaten that person into agreement. Examples of social pressure being exerted abound in the literature:

> One patient had been separated from his wife for about eighteen months. He had been in arrears in his payments to her for the support of their children, and she had sought legal assistance. Their respective attorneys suggested reconciliation as a way of settling his obligations. The wife – who was an aide in the hospital – readily consented, providing the patient would agree to come to the hospital 'for him to find out what was wrong with him'. The patient had been abusive and quite suspicious of her since his discharge from the service in the last ten years. He agreed to come into the hospital 'to prove she was wrong'. His wife arranged the admission. (Spitzer, p. 254)

Wives may threaten to leave their husbands, bosses to dismiss them or relatives to evict them unless in-patient treatment is agreed to.

Some patients are tricked into entering and signing a document, as Mills shows: 'Mrs. Kerstein explained . . . he didn't know what he was doing and wouldn't sign the form, but I said I'd get him to sign it and I did – I told him it was something else,' and from another respondent 'He thought it was his pension form' (p. 19). Other patients may enter the hospital because they mistakenly think it a different sort of institution; 'Nine of them had been receiving treatment for physical illness and were advised by their doctors to enter a mental hospital – though the words "mental hospital" were rarely, if ever, mentioned. Mr. Atterbury for instance . . . was led to believe that he was going to a convalescent home in the country for a rest and a chance for his nerves to recover' (p. 18). Once in the hospital, the patient may be too apathetic, frightened or submissive to insist on leaving, and in any case the same pressures that brought about entering would operate against immediate departure.

Once the individual is firmly defined by his social group as mentally ill, he is likely to be pressed to accept the mental patient role; at this stage the patient's acceptance of the role is rewarded and denial is met with sanctions by the group. This tends to be the case with other stigmatised roles as well, those who accept the position in which they have been placed by their social group and behave in the ways that the stigmatised are expected to behave are more tolerated than those who constantly deny the right of the group to consign them to stigmatised roles.

The cases of unwilling patients entering mental hospitals have to be seen in perspective, however, by bearing in mind the enormous efforts made by some families to keep a mentally disturbed member out of hospital. The persuasions, threats or tricks described often come after a very long period of normalisation and caring-for at home. Moreover, although some patients resent tricks and deception by their families to get them to hospital, others may prefer such tactics. In an essay by a schizophrenic man about his experiences, the narrator recounts how his wife, having listened to his confidences about his worries and feelings, then immediately telephoned the doctor, following which he was taken to hospital.

The part of the above story I found hardest to write was the interaction with my wife just before my third hospitalisation. Why did I have to write it? Because it is something that should never, never have happened. I certainly don't mean by this that there are never times when people like me need to be taken away from their homes, if only as a protection for their home and family. It is how it is done that is all-important. If only there could have been some subterfuge which I could have found convincing: for example, if the doctor had apparently called to see my wife and then, as if by accident, had found that I needed help (while my wife pretended that I need not go to hospital). Surely there must have been some way to have managed it better? (Wing, 1975, p. 43)

Finally, there are patients who enter the psychiatric hospital willingly: they ask for treatment there because they believe that it will be beneficial to them. For a person who comes to see himself as mentally disturbed, admission to hospital may bring much relief: he does not have to make efforts to maintain normal social roles and to appear to the world as if he had no problems. Relief can also be experienced by someone whose behaviour was regarded as socially unacceptable and sanctioned as such; the acceptance by the social group that the behaviour was due to mental illness, as testified by hospital admission, can be a welcome development.

CHAPTER 4

The Social Role of the Ex-Mental Patient

In recent years much attention has been paid by social scientists to the position of ex-mental patients in society; their ability to play ordinary social roles, their acceptance by the community, their feelings of being stigmatised, their employment prospects and many other aspects of their lives have been studied. Before discussing the various aspects of the ex-patients' position, some preliminary questions must be raised. Why talk of ex-mental patients at all? Who are they?

Many of the studies referred to have assumed, without spelling it out, that the concept 'ex-mental patient' is meaningful and that individuals so designated form a social category. This is largely correct but some explanation is needed. After all, individuals who have had a specific illness, even one necessitating a hospital stay, are not customarily thought of as ex-patients once the illness episode is over. Thus, people do not talk of ex-tonsillitis patients or ex-pneumonia patients (who share the experience of illness and of having been in hospital) although they may remember that this man or that had a heart attack or a stroke. But these latter will be met with sympathy and understanding whereas mental illness is so negatively evaluated by the public that it devalues the sufferer's position and social identity (this was discussed in the previous chapter); moreover public opinion tends to attribute mental illness to faults or weaknesses of character. In that respect, the evaluation of mental illness has much in common with certain other stigmatised states for which responsibility is imputed, such as being in prison or being an alcoholic. These states are so damaging to the social position of the person that once acquired they become bound up with identity, and constitute part of the social information relevant to that person, who will henceforth be referred to as the ex-alcoholic, the ex-prisoner or the ex-mental patient.

Another reason for the existence of the ex-mental-patient category is that public opinion attributes poor prognosis and lasting effects to mental illness. As also discussed in the previous chapter, according to the view of the lay public it is difficult, if not impossible, to cure mental illness, and so, having had it, an individual is thought of as liable to have it again. In this, to the public, it resembles certain physical conditions: for example, if someone has had a heart attack people feel that he is liable to have another. Whether this lay view of the outcome and treatability of mental illness is grounded in clinical reality or not is of little relevance here (in any case the clinical picture would vary according to the type of illness); what is important is that this lay view gives a social reality to the ex-mental-patient category and that there exist certain social consequences of belonging to this category.

Who is an ex-mental patient? It has been shown previously that not everyone with psychiatric symptoms assumes the role of mental patient; a distinction has been made between the 'primary' development of having symptoms and the 'secondary' development of assuming an organised social role, as mentally ill, which is known to others in the social group. Thus, an ex-mental patient is someone who was, in the past, placed in the role of a mental patient. Most often, admission to a mental hospital signifies the assumption of the role and discharge from the hospital marks the beginning of being an ex-patient. Someone may become an ex-patient without hospitalisation, however, if it is known to the social group that mental disturbance was experienced and treatment received from a psychiatrist.

From a sociological perspective, there are several important issues concerning the social category of ex-mental patients, such as whether they perform ordinary social roles or whether being an ex-patient carries with it a special, dominant role. What is the social standing of ex-patients, relative to that of others in society? Is belonging to this category temporary or permanent?

There has been much controversy about the lasting effects of having been a mental patient on a person's social position. Social scientists who adhere to the school of thought known as the labelling theory (or societal reaction perspective) have argued, in general, that once a stigmatised deviant role is assigned to an individual social responses (or societal reaction) will stabilise the role, i.e. will ensure that he continues to play it (Scheff, 1966). In this perspective, the public labelling of someone as criminal, alcoholic, mentally ill, etc., is seen as having most important social consequences. It is argued that once labelled in such a way, the original actions which gave rise to the labelling (e.g. stealing, drinking, violence) matter less to the social group than the attached label; that social responses (for example rejection, hostility, fear) are evoked by the label itself independently of the bearer's observed behaviour. It is also argued that the individual is likely to accept the ascribed label because the system of social expectations, sanctions and rewards will ensure that he does. Once the ascribed role is accepted, he will develop the self-image of the stigmatised deviant and so all-embracing will his role become that he will no longer have the chance to play normal social roles.

Applying this perspective to the mentally ill, it is argued that being admitted as a patient to a mental hospital constitutes public labelling and that after discharge the person becomes an ex-patient, a role which is dominant and irreversible. The initial or continued disturbed behaviour is of lesser social importance than the fact of having been in a mental hospital.

The view of the labelling theorists has not passed uncriticised. Others think that although adverse social responses may meet the newly discharged patient, these are not so permanent nor so important as the labelling theorists would have it (Gove, 1970; Kirk, 1974). It is argued that many ex-patients return to normal social roles, that stigma may exist for a period of time after hospitalisation but does not necessarily become permanent and that where the stigmatised ex-patient role continues this is due to continued disturbed behaviour or to relapses, rather than to the act of labelling.

There is not a great deal of empirical evidence relating to the effects and permanence of stigma in the lives of discharged psychiatric patients. This is mainly due to the lack of follow-up studies: the long term effects of a hospital stay on social position could be best seen by studying patients ten and twenty years after their discharge, but such studies are expensive, time consuming and difficult. Available empirical evidence is more of a short-term nature, relating to between one and five years after hospital stay: more evidence exists about those who continue under medical supervision and treatment than about those who do not.

The research evidence concerning the position of the discharged mental patient in society can be reviewed under three headings: public attitudes towards discharged patients; these patients' own interpretation of their social situation; and the extent to which they re-assume ordinary social roles.

THE CLIMATE OF PUBLIC OPINION

Attitudes towards Ex-Mental Patients

The evidence relating to the public opinion of mental illness, discussed in the previous chapter, has already indicated the generally negative evaluation of the discharged mental patient by lay people. The view that mental illness is not amenable to treatment and that it can be brought on by character defects shows the stigma attached to the experience of mental illness. Studies specially designed to elicit information about people's attitudes to ex-patients found that distrust, social distance and unfavourable sentiments were widely expressed. Several studies used some form of attitude or social distance scale to investigate public opinions and attitudes, a good example being the study carried out by Phillips (1966) whose investigations were also mentioned in the previous chapter. His respondents (married women in New England) were given five cards, four of them describing the behaviour of disturbed individuals (a paranoid schizophrenic, a simple schizophrenic, an anxious-depressed person and a phobic individual with compulsive features) and the fifth, the conduct of a normal individual. These case abstracts were presented in combination with information purporting to show whether each person described had or had not been in a mental hospital. The respondents were then asked a series of questions about their willingness to associate with the described individuals. The questions were:

1. Would you discourage your children from marrying someone like this?
2. If you had a room to rent in your home, would you be willing to rent it to someone like this?
3. Would you be willing to work on a job with someone like this?
4. Would you be willing to have someone like this join a favourite club or organisation of yours?
5. Would you object to having a person like this as a neighbour?

Table 4.1 shows the respondents' replies to these five questions concerning the individuals described by the case histories when they were not said to have been in a mental hospital, and Table 4.2 shows the replies concerning individuals similarly described, but with the added information that they had been in a mental hospital. Table 4.1 indicates that respondents almost totally accepted the portrayed normal person and rejected in various degrees the disturbed individuals, suggesting that the public certainly recognise disturbed behaviour (whether they call it 'mental' or weak, vicious, bad, etc. is not relevant to this point) and respond to it by social sanctioning, i.e. rejection. From this it seems that the social importance of continuing disturbed behaviour should not be underestimated: it is not the attached label alone which has adverse consequences, the behaviour itself is sanctioned.

Table 4.2 shows that the various categories of disturbed behaviour were more severely sanctioned by respondents when they were told that those portrayed had been in a mental hospital, indicating that this added factor increases the

TABLE 4.1 Percentage Willing to Associate with Five Hypothetical Cases[a]

	Cases				
Association	Paranoid schizophrenic	Simple schizophrenic	Depressed-neurotic	Phobic-compulsive	Normal individual
Allow children to marry	1.7	31.7	10.0	60.0	98.3
Rent room in home	3.3	76.7	63.3	88.3	100.0
Work on job	11.7	91.7	91.7	98.3	100.0
Have in club	43.3	93.3	93.3	100.0	100.0
Have as neighbour	70.0	96.7	96.7	100.0	100.0

[a] N for each cell in the table is 60.

Source: Phillips (1966).

TABLE 4.2 Percentage Willing to Associate with Five Hypothetical Cases who are Ex-Mental Patients[a]

Association	Cases				
	Paranoid schizophrenic	Simple schizophrenic	Depressed-neurotic	Phobic-compulsive	Normal individual
Allow children to marry	0.0	0.0	1.7	1.7	16.7
Rent a room in home	1.7	1.7	6.7	16.7	40.0
Work on job	8.3	8.3	28.3	73.3	86.7
Have in club	11.7	43.3	50.0	88.3	95.0
Have as neighbour	43.3	78.3	83.3	93.3	96.7

[a] N for each cell in the table is 60.

Source: Phillips (1966).

degree of rejection likely to be experienced by those already liable to sanction for their objectionable behaviour. The stigmatising effect of the hospital is clearly shown by the attitudes of the respondents to the person described as normal; while recognised and accepted when not said to have been in a mental hospital, Table 4.2 shows that once previous mental hospital treatment is known normal persons are to a large extent rejected: less than 17 per cent of the respondents would allow their children to marry such a person, and only 40 per cent would rent a room in their home to someone in this category.

Several other studies showed that unfavourable attitudes are commonly exhibited towards persons who have had a mental illness, that they are variously regarded as socially incompetent, unpredictable and undesirable (Whateley, 1968; Cumming and Cumming, 1968; Freeman and Simmons, 1968). Some researchers, impressed by the investigations of Phillips, carried out comparable studies: while Phillips chose married women as respondents, the others chose psychiatric nurses (Schroder and Ehrlich, 1968) and college students (Bord, 1971; Kirk, 1974) and studied attitudes to case abstracts similar to those used by Phillips. The finding of these studies was that objectionable behaviour was a more important determinant of rejection than was indicated by Phillips' results. For example, Kirk, who was particularly interested to test the labelling theory, said: 'This study has found that the influence of labelling relative to the actual behaviour, is negligible.'

Of course, young college students of the type used in Kirk's study are likely to be more knowledgeable and sophisticated about mental illness and its indications than a sample of housewives as used by Phillips, who may place more reliance on labels provided by professionals.

The question of whether it is the unacceptable behaviour or the label of previous hospitalisation that is the more important determinant of social response is a significant one. If the former, then the stigma is reversible; the ex-patient can demonstrate his now unobjectionable behaviour and shed the stigma. But if mental hospitalisation itself is stigmatising, irrespective of subsequent behaviour, then the stigma is irreversible. Research evidence indicates a complex situation in this respect: both the disturbed behaviour and the known fact of having been a mental patient evoke negative attitudes from the public. As Kirk observed, the information about previous hospitalisation is likely to be particularly damaging in the absence of other information being available about one person to another (such as that person's known, observable behaviour) and therefore strangers are likely to be judged on such damaging information.

Unfavourable attitudes are not expressed with equal force by everyone. Factors which were shown to influence people's opinions and knowledge of mental illness, especially age and education (see Chapter 3), are also connected with attitudes to discharged patients. The younger and the better educated tend to express the more favourable, accepting attitudes. Thus, Whatley (1968) found that in a stratified sample of 2,000 people, among whom unfavourable attitudes were commonly exhibited, age emerged as the most substantial source of variation. This was closely followed by education, while factors such as sex, religion and rural–urban residence showed no correlation with unfavourable attitudes. Phillips (1966), whose sample of married women was more homogenous, also found that the better educated respondents expressed less reluctance to associate with individuals exhibiting signs of disturbed behaviour.

People express more willingness to associate with discharged mental patients in some situations than in others. Phillips' respondents (see Table 4.2) showed more reluctance to associate with ex-patients in situations of great intimacy or closeness than in relatively impersonal situations. Thus, rejection is greatest when respondents are asked whether they would encourage their children to marry ex-patients or whether they would have them living in their homes and slightest when it is a question of having them as neighbours. Whatley (1968) explains his similar findings in terms of self-involvement. He found that 81 per cent of the respondents disagreed with the statement: 'It is best not to associate with ex-mental patients.' But to this, rather general, observation, which has no direct reference to self, a respondent may merely express disapproval of the practice of shunning ex-patients; no demands are made on him in terms of his safety, job, family, etc. Whatley argues that it is 'safe' to give a response which is favourable to ex-patients because nothing of personal value is committed by so doing. When he asked respondents about situations such as living near a person who had been a mental patient, the proportion of responses which were favourable to ex-patients dropped to 68 per cent; here the respondent's involvement is potentially greater, some primary group interaction with the ex-patient is implied by the question. When questions were put to respondents about employing an ex-mental patient or approving a daughter's marriage to one, the percentage of favourable responses dropped to 57 and 36 respectively. In these situations the respondent's self-involvement is great, he is asked to commit himself, his livelihood or his family to an association which is intimate and may be threatening.

Social acceptability is an important aspect of the position and prestige of an individual in society; those who are not regarded as desirable, acceptable companions by their fellows have thereby an inferior position compared to those who are so regarded. Thus, studies demonstrating that interaction with ex-mental patients is avoided by the public, in effect show that the social position of these ex-patients is inferior to that of persons who have not suffered from mental illness.

Public Behaviour towards Ex-Mental Patients

Studies of the type described above aim to investigate the attitudes of the public; they are not designed to study people's actual behaviour towards discharged mental patients. Verbal statements of attitudes do not necessarily correlate with actions; on the contrary, empirical observations tend to show a lack of association between words and deeds (Rabkin, 1974). Sometimes, the discrepancy between verbal statements of intentions and what happens in practice, is very striking, and brings to mind an early classic investigation. In the 1930s in America, a researcher, La Pierre (1934), drove around the country with a Chinese couple, visiting hotels and restaurants. They called on some 250 establishments and found only one which refused to accommodate them. A few months later the researcher sent each of the visited hotels and restaurants a questionnaire, in which he asked whether they would accept Chinese guests in their establishments. The answers were consistently negative – a most interesting demonstration of discrepancy between behaviour and professed attitudes.

Such discrepancy manifests itself consistently in observations of the attitudes and behaviour of the public towards ex-mental patients. While verbal statements are commonly negative and rejecting, indicating lack of willingness to associate, behaviour is often sympathetic and helpful. In many different situations, where on the basis of attitude studies, rejection would be predicted, in fact acceptance of ex-mental patients is often found. This is not because the findings of the attitude studies were wrong, but because they refer to different dimensions of social life. A person may well hold definite views on how ex-patients should be treated, for example, that they should not be accepted for certain jobs, but when faced with the actual situation he may behave in a way which seems, at first, inconsistent with his views.

Several factors are likely to have an impact on actions. For instance, there are what may be called situational factors. An employer receiving an application from an ex-mental patient would be influenced, besides his attitudes towards such people in general, by the number of other applicants, their relative skills, whether there is an urgent need to fill the job, and what the other employees might feel about working with the applicant. There may also be competing attitudes and values present: the employer may feel that ex-patients should be rejected, but not wish to appear harsh, illiberal or inhumane in the eyes of others, preferring to preserve his self-image as a kindly, helpful person.

There is also another consideration: it is easier to express attitudes of rejection and negative sentiments about a category of persons, in reply to interview questions, than to reject a particular person standing in front of one. Moreover, interview questions refer either to an 'ex-mental patient' which would evoke the cultural stereotype, or to a person described as behaving objectionably; but when a job applicant stands politely before the employer and behaves in a perfectly acceptable manner, not in any way resembling the stereotyped image of the 'mental patient', the response may be very different from the expressed attitude. The employer may then decide that the applicant before him is not really 'mental'.

The size of the problem also matters: people are often willing to interact with one individual, even if his behaviour is not entirely socially acceptable (displaying, for example, signs of anxiety, agitation or apathy) when they would reject interaction with many. It is often the case that local residents oppose the establishment of a hostel or a workshop for ex-mental patients in their area when they would be willing to accept one such individual to live and work among them. Larger numbers carry the implication of enhanced threat and objections multiply.

Thus, behaviour towards discharged patients is determined by a multiplicity of interacting variables, besides professed attitudes. However, public opinion is a legitimate and important area of study, apart from the degree of its relationship to actual behaviour, because it constitutes a climate of opinion, an atmosphere of acceptance or rejection which the discharged patient encounters in his everyday life.

Helpfulness and kindness shown towards discharged patients by people in certain situations is illustrated by several research studies. One investigation concerned with schizophrenic patients five years after their admission to hospital in England (this study, by Brown et al., (1966), will be discussed in more detail later) found that employers were often helpful and understanding. It was found that many employers were willing to wait and take back ex-employees after a stay in a psychiatric hospital, and that some went to considerable trouble to help and support ex-patients.

> For example, a man who had been a baker's roundsman for twenty years at the key admission was taken back later and moved to lighter work in the bakery because he was getting depressed and agitated about being alone all day. Another man who had been a skilled factory worker for seven years at the key admission was subsequently given a small room where he could work on his own. Another man who had worked for one firm for seven years before the key admission was taken back after two years in hospital, and stayed on, alternating

between being a fitter's mate and floor sweeper, depending on how well he was. (Brown *et al.*, 1966, p. 78)

It must be borne in mind, however, that tendering assistance to discharged patients does not signify an absence of stigma. If ex-patients are regarded as unfortunates, weak, vulnerable and in need of help, this view considerably lowers their social standing and prestige and is deeply stigmatising; it is not inconsistent with helpfulness and kindness however. Indeed, research findings that people help and assist ex-patients imply the latter's relatively low social prestige. Only those who are accepted as equals, capable of providing as well as receiving help, can be said to have shed the stigma.

THE MANAGEMENT OF STIGMA

Ex-mental patients are much aware of public attitudes towards them. As Goffman pointed out, those who acquire a stigma later in life had shared the social values of their group before that event, and would be aware of the social group's evaluation of their particular stigmatised condition (Goffman, 1963). Moreover, there is social pressure on people to define their own attributes and characteristics in the same way as these are defined by their fellows, as anything else would undermine the certainty of shared values. For example, if a bachelor or a spinster shows too openly that he or she is comfortable and happy in the unmarried state, this can seem like a challenge to the value of marriage prevailing in the social group; if a man with a deformity or disfigurement asserts that this is no great hardship and has positive aspects, he challenges the value of health and physical fitness. The others in the social group usually respond to such assertions with disbelief; anything else would mean an uncomfortable need to revise their values. In a society where mental illness is viewed unfavourably and the ex-mental patient is regarded as an undesirable associate, the individuals so regarded are likely to be aware of and share, at least to a certain extent, the group values which place them in an inferior position.

Evidence that feelings of stigma exist among ex-mental patients can be found in research reports and in the personal accounts of those with experience of mental illness. The Cummings say, in a study concerned with discharged patients, 'We found two basic evidences of stigmatization: the first an outright expression of shame or inferiority because of the hospitalisation, and the second an expectation of discrimination or inferior treatment from others' (Cummings, 1968, p. 412). The authors interviewed patients discharged from mental hospitals and their feelings of stigma showed up in remarks like: 'I didn't want anyone to know that I was at a mental hospital and call me crazy'; and, 'I don't want everybody knowing I was there – you know what they might think.' Other studies also showed that ex-patients, especially when they are newly discharged, expect to meet negative public attitudes (Yarrow et al., 1955b).

Personal accounts of ex-patients also reveal the feelings of stigma. The following illustration comes from a man who had been in a mental hospital with schizophrenia:

> After graduating, I found I was unable to get a job. The University Appointments Board sent my name to dozens of employers, and I answered umpteen advertisements for university graduates. This was at a time when it was practically unheard of for students from my particular college not to get snapped up, even before graduation. Eventually, after months I got one interview. The man who interviewed me said he had a very good report about me from the Appointments Board. There was just one thing he wanted to ask me: 'It says you should have got a good first but because of an unfortunate breakdown and subsequent long illness you were only able to get a third. Would you mind telling me exactly what happened?' Needless to say, I did not get the job. (Wing, 1975, p. 32)

Ex-mental patients may respond in a number of different ways to their expectations and feelings of stigma; in Goffman's words, there are many ways of 'stigma management'. One response is the redefinition of the situation. When a patient returns from a mental hospital to find that he is now one of a category of persons regarded as socially incompetent, unpredictable and undesirable, he may try to change this situation. To change attitudes towards ex-mental patients in general may seem impossible; indeed, he may have shared these attitudes himself in the past. But he can attempt to change the classification of himself as an ex-patient. One way of doing this is to assert that the hospitalisation was a mistake, he never was 'mental', he should have gone to a different type of hospital, it was only a nervous breakdown or a physical illness. This redefinition of the situation aims to show that the person was not, in the past, socially incompetent, unpredictable, etc., and therefore he is not any of those things now: the stigma should be reversed. Attempts to redefine the situation are helped by the public stereotype of the mentally ill person as someone bizarre, recognisable and dangerous: confronting someone who, although an ex-patient, does not appear to be like the stereotype and had not appeared so in the past, may encourage belief that his assertion of a mistake may well be true.

This method of stigma management aims to restore the ex-patient to the world of competent, acceptable, predictable people. There is no concealment of the fact that an illness has occurred, only an attempt to disguise its nature and minimise its social consequences.

Another method of stigma management is 'passing'. This term refers to the method whereby the stigmatised attribute or characteristic is concealed so that others will not become aware of it. Not all stigmatised persons can attempt to 'pass', some attributes such as physical deformity, disfigurement or blindness, are so apparent that this response is not possible, nor may it be for a mentally disturbed individual whose odd and unacceptable behaviour is generally observable; however, an ex-mental patient may attempt to conceal the fact of hospitalisation. Passing is a favoured method of stigma management by those for whom it is available; the social rewards of being considered an acceptable, unstigmatised person, make it very attractive. Concealment of past mental illness from acquaintances made later, and from children in the family is often attempted (Yarrow et al., 1955b); it is the rule rather than the exception to hide past mental illness from prospective employers. The university graduate with a history of schizophrenia, whose lack of success in obtaining a job was quoted earlier, said: 'From then on I applied for jobs on the strength of my GCE and school references. What had I been doing since then? Helping my father with his gardening business. (My father did not have a business)' (Wing, 1975, p. 33). Thus, passing may involve deliberate mis-statements of the truth; but often silence on the subject is enough, as new acquaintances or interviewing employers seldom make deliberate inquiries about the mental history of the person before them.

Goffman describes persons whose stigma is neither known to their associates nor immediately evident, as the 'discreditable'; in contrast to the 'discredited', whose stigma is known or evident. Ex-mental patients attempting to 'pass' belong to the former category, and Goffman explains the problem facing them:

> While the mental patient is in the hospital, and when he is with adult members of his own family, he is faced with being treated tactfully as if he were sane when there is known to be some doubt, even though he may not have any; or he is treated as insane, when he knows this is not just. But for the ex-mental patient the problem can be quite different; it is not that he must face prejudice against himself, but rather that he must face unwitting acceptance of himself by individuals who are prejudiced against persons of the kind he can be revealed to be. Wherever he goes his behaviour will falsely confirm for the others that they are in the company of what in effect they demand but may discover they haven't obtained, namely, a mentally untainted person like themselves. By intention or in effect the ex-mental patient conceals information about his real social identity, receiving and accepting treatment based on false suppositions concerning himself. (Goffman, 1963, p. 42)

Continued concealment of past mental illness often means a constant dread that the discrediting information will be discovered. To avoid long-term fears of this sort, ex-patients sometimes use passing as a temporary measure; for example, they may attempt to obtain employment by concealing past mental illness while planning to admit it later. The hope is that once a person is accepted as a good worker and colleague the disclosure will not be so damaging.

Redefinition of the situation and passing are not the only responses available for ex-mental patients. An alternative is to tell the social group about the experience of mental illness, to talk openly, to hide nothing. Some ex-patients decide to explain the nature of their problems and how they overcame them; others, to demonstrate that they are changed, transformed persons (Cumming and Cumming, 1968).

PERFORMANCE OF SOCIAL ROLES

Adult men and women are accepted as full members of their society where they perform major social roles as employees, husbands or wives, parents, etc., and meet social expectations. As said before, if someone does not meet social expectations in the performance of his roles and the reason for this failure is thought to be inability rather than unwillingness to do so, then he is defined as 'unfortunate', 'sick', 'weak', 'wanting', etc. and assigned an inferior status. Thus, the extent to which an ex-patient performs social roles, especially work and family roles, is a very important determinant of his social position.

In the case of physical illness those leaving the sick role are assumed to be returning to their pre-illness social roles. Complete recovery carries with it the expectation of a complete resumption of normal activities and even in the case of heart attacks, disablement and other conditions which may have long-lasting or permanent consequences, the social group expects at least a partial return to former roles. The family will be waiting, the employer willing to re-employ (perhaps in a less demanding capacity) friends and neighbours ready as before to pursue normal social intercourse, and so on.

However, a complete or even partial return to previous roles may not be possible, or in some cases even desirable, for the discharged mental patient. The spouse may have decided on separation, the parent with whom the patient had formerly lived may have died; indeed some such event may have precipitated hospitalisation in the first place. The job may have been filled, a circumstance which may occur in any case of prolonged absence but rendered much more serious for the former mental patient who has the additional burden of negative public attitudes to contend with. Also, it is likely that his relatives or doctor may advise against a return to the pre-illness work or family situation, if that were regarded as having had an adverse effect on him.

The social roles performed by the patient prior to hospital admission are not necessarily 'pre-illness' roles in the same sense that a physically ill person may be said to have performed his normal roles before developing pneumonia or having a road accident. Mental illness often has no clear starting point which can be identified retrospectively and the roles performed prior to hospital admission may have been affected by the illness for some considerable time. Thus the patient for whom the onset of the illness was relatively sudden may be favourably placed to pick up the threads of his former existence whereas one who had been going downhill for a long time prior to hospitalisation may have no stable situation to return to.

Employment

One of the most important measures of the position of an ex-mental patient in society is his or her work record. Social expectations in Western societies are clear and consistent: an adult man is expected to work, and failure to do so seriously affects social standing. For people in general a long period of unemployment brings financial problems together with loss of prestige and self-esteem, but for ex-mental patients, in addition, it brings a reaffirmation of the ex-patient status. Social standing and prestige in Western societies are largely determined by occupational status; if this is non-existent then an alternative determinant, in this case the ex-mental patient status, will gain importance. Conversely, if a former mental patient manages to function in a work role, his occupational status eventually may replace his status of ex-patient.

Social expectations are less clear regarding the work of women; even so, employment records of working women can usefully be examined and the housework done by housewives also provides an important measure of normal role performance.

Work record is a useful practical measure in that it is relatively easy to examine, easier, for example, than it is to determine role relationships within the family, and for that reason it is favoured by researchers.

An important British study by Brown and his colleagues

examined the experiences of 339 schizophrenic patients during a five year period following their admission to mental hospitals in 1956 (Brown et al., 1966). They obtained information from interviews with the patients and with other informants (usually a close relative living with the patient) and from many different kinds of records (e.g. hospital, employment, welfare records). The majority of the patients left hospital within six months, and many much sooner (a quarter were discharged within seven weeks). When the authors analysed the employment records of male patients the striking result was that at the end of the five years 55 per cent of the men were out of work. The result was very different however when first admissions were examined separately: only one-third of the men admitted for the first time were unemployed at the end of five years against two-thirds of those with multiple admissions.

Of those whose admission had been for the first time two-thirds had had an employment held open for them and most had returned to it after discharge. It seems that many employers were willing to wait and take back employees after a stay in a psychiatric hospital and that many discharged patients were willing to return to the same work setting, colleagues, and workmates. Type of work apparently did not affect the chance of returning to the job; professional and clerical workers had the same chance of returning to their jobs as had skilled and unskilled manual workers.

Although much helpfulness on the part of employers was reported in this research, it seems clear that the occupational status of many ex-patients seriously declined compared to their peak employment status. More than half of the men who worked in professional, clerical or skilled manual jobs at their peak·employment, were working at considerably lower level after the five year period following their admission.

For the female sample, both paid employment and housework were investigated. Paid employment has not the same meaning attached to it as a measure of social standing for women as for men; many married women have no paid employment and even for unmarried women, housework and looking after parents or relatives, is socially acceptable. Ability to carry out household duties, especially for married women, can be very important: self-esteem and the esteem of others may depend on it, and several people are affected by it. In their research Brown and his colleagues rated the performance of household duties by housewives: they collected information about five types of household activity – cooking, shopping, washing and ironing, cleaning and tidying, and looking after children – and rated the competence of women ex-patients at these activities.

They found that two-thirds of the women whose admission to hospital had been for the first time were either in employment or were performing competently as housewives at the end of the five year study period, a finding very similar to the work record of men in the sample. It has to be borne in mind, however, that household work can be carried out in privacy, less public criticism and fewer comparative standards exist and for these reasons it may be easier to function competently in household tasks than in open employment.

Employment record, however useful a measure, cannot be taken as the sole indicator of an ex-patient's functioning in social roles. There are some whose behaviour continues to be disturbed and socially unacceptable yet who are able to work, and others whose behaviour is entirely acceptable and free of disturbance who are, nevertheless, unemployed. In the study of Brown *et al.* each patient's behaviour at the end of the follow-up period was rated as not disturbed (or minimally so), moderately disturbed or severely disturbed. Very few of those rated severely disturbed were at work, which is not surprising; but almost half of the moderately disturbed patients were employed while a third of those with no (or minimal) disturbance were not in employment. There are many possible reasons for this situation; some employers go out of their way to help former patients in spite of some disturbed behaviour, while others are not so sympathetic or are less able to accommodate these patients. The particular skills of some men may be more difficult to utilise; the overall unemployment situation of the country or region, at the time of discharge can vary, and all these factors would affect employment.

Thus, while it can be argued that unemployed male ex-patients do not meet social expectations as adult members of society but continue in their dependent ex-patient roles, the converse cannot always be said: those who are employed, although not dependent, may not invariably shed the stigmatised role of the ex-mental patient.

The Influence of Family Settings

Functioning in normal social roles is much influenced by the type of social setting the patient returns to on discharge from the hospital. A patient may go back to the parental home or to the marital home, may go to live with relatives or friends or may, from choice or necessity, find himself living alone; the type of home as well as the relationships within it have a bearing on the patient's subsequent normal functioning.

Most patients who lived with their families before hospital admission return to them when discharged; the majority go back to either parental or marital households. It is an intriguing finding of researchers that ex-patients who live with their spouses are more likely to function in normal social roles than those who live with their parents.

The follow-up study of schizophrenic patients by Brown and his colleagues revealed that married men, living with their wives, had the best employment record: they were far more likely to be found in employment at the end of the five year study period than were men living with their parents (or indeed those who lived with other relatives, friends or alone). Married women living with their husbands also functioned well at work: only a small proportion of them was rated severely incompetent at housework.

Similar results were found by other studies. Freeman and Simmons (1968), for example, investigated the post-hospital experiences of male patients in the Boston area, and demonstrated that married men living with their wives were much more likely to perform social roles well than those men who returned to parental homes on discharge. High performance of social roles in this research included employment, reports by relatives as to social participation and absence of disturbed, unacceptable behaviour.

Another study, by Angrist and her colleagues, showed similar results with women ex-patients; high performance in normal social roles was found to be strongly associated with marital status and family setting (Angrist *et al.*, 1968). In their sample of 287 former patients in Ohio, 'high performers', i.e. those functioning well in social roles, were found to be living in conjugal families with their husbands rather than with parents, adult children, siblings, other relatives, or alone. Under all living arrangements other than conjugal settings, former patients performed at a lower level.

Not only is there an association between types of family setting and normal functioning, but also between family setting and readmission to mental hospital. Ex-patients who live with their spouses are not only likely to function better but are also more likely to return to the mental hospital if they do not, than ex-patients who live with their parents. An explanation could be that marital partners have higher expectations of their spouses' normal functioning than have parents of their adult children. In parental homes the ex-patient's family status is that of a son or daughter of the house; although an adult, the family position of such ex-patients may revert to that of the child who, traditionally, is in a dependent position and of whom social expectations of usefulness and exemplary behaviour are relatively low; therefore parents are more ready to accept that their son or daughter is at home, unemployed, dependent in a childlike fashion, than are marital partners ready to accept such behaviour from their spouses, from whom they expect 'adult' behaviour. The higher expectations of the marital setting would encourage and press former patients to function normally.

Not only may spouses and parents have different expectations but the fulfilment of social obligations may be of more practical importance in one setting than in another. The feasibility of keeping a socially non-functioning ex-patient, occupying a modified sick role for a long period, is greater in parental than in marital homes where the need to assume adult social roles is more pressing. An ex-patient, back with her husband, who fails adequately to look after her young children is more likely to return to the mental hospital than is another ex-patient in difficulties living with her parents. Angrist found that female ex-patients, living in conjugal homes where another woman was available to take over the duties, functioned less well than those in a similar situation with no such assitance on hand. Similarly, childless women living in conjugal homes performed less well than those with children under the age of sixteen. This pattern illustrates the importance, for high social performance, of the expectations of others and the need to fulfil tasks and obligations.

Another explanation of the different performance of ex-patients in diverse family settings may be that married patients tend to be less severely ill at admission and in better shape at discharge than those who are single, divorced, or separated. Angrist examined this possibility for women but found no evidence for it; neither the extent of the former patients' psychiatric illness at admission nor its extent at discharge, as rated by therapists, were related to marital status or to the type of household in which they lived. However, more research is needed concerning this point.

Homes of friends and relations may resemble either the parental or the marital home in respect of social expectations of the ex-patient. An aunt or a sister may take the position of the mother, expect little, accept the unemployed status of the ex-patient in the home; while another sibling may expect more and encourage the patient much as a spouse would.

Living alone constitutes another, and quite different, environment. Brown's study showed that men living alone were much less likely to be in employment than those living with marital partners, which indicates a lower level of functioning for such men, at least in work roles (Brown *et al.*, 1966). These ex-patients are not under pressure to meet social expectations as there is no one in the home to provide encouragement. Freeman and Simmons (1968) showed that men living in non-familial settings and performing social roles at a low level, are more likely to return to the mental hospital than those from marital homes.

The Influence of Family Relationships

Not only the type of family unit the patient returns to but also the emotional climate and the relationships prevailing in the home influence the functioning of the patient in normal roles. One intriguing and influential line of investigation has been pursued by a team of British researchers associated with the

Social Psychiatry Unit of the Medical Research Council. Their particular interest was to assess the influence on discharged psychiatric patients of family life, especially the emotional relationships obtaining between ex-patients and the closest of the relatives with whom they lived (parent, spouse, or other) (Brown et al., 1962; Brown et al., 1972; Vaughn and Leff, 1976).

A standardised method was developed by this team to measure the quality of emotional relationships; they interviewed the close relatives and used an index of the 'expressed emotion' (or EE) shown by them towards the patient and the illness. This index has three components: critical comments made by the relative when talking about the patient, hostility expressed by the relative, and what the investigators called 'emotional over-involvement'. The rating of the relatives' criticism was based on the number of critical comments made by them during the interviews; hostility was rated according to statements of resentment, dislike and rejection, tone of voice and to gestures indicating disapproval; emotional involvement was rated according to the degree of concern, anxiety and protectiveness shown towards the patient. This index was then used to categorise homes as high EE or low EE; the former indicating that the close relative is critical, hostile or markedly over-involved, the latter that the relative was none of these things. The influence of the patients' returning to each type of home on subsequent functioning was then explored.

The investigators found that much the greater proportion of patients who relapsed and again developed symptoms of mental disturbance were living in high EE homes. They measured relapse nine months after discharge and said that the relative's expressed emotion was the best single predictor of whether a patient would relapse or not, during that time. Thus, according to these studies, there exists a very significant association between the emotional involvement of the closest relative and the functioning of the ex-patient.

The extent of face-to-face contact with a critical, hostile or domineering close relative is of great importance to the discharged patient: the more such face-to-face contact, the less likely a return to normal functioning. In high EE homes, reduced contact with relatives, for example, by the patient attending a day-centre or work-place during most of the day, or even by sleeping during the day and being active at night, can serve to protect the patient's well-being.

More research is needed (and is being undertaken in different countries) to show whether the association between the emotional involvement of the close relative and the functioning of the ex-patient is a causal one; that is whether the patient's returning to a certain kind of emotional climate in itself reduces his chances of normal functioning. The researchers themselves think it very possible that there is a causal relationship; and certainly it would not be surprising to find that in a sympathetic and understanding family setting the patient is able to function well.

The index of expressed emotion has received some adverse comments, as well as praise, from social scientists. In a highly critical letter, Harris has argued that the index is no more than the interviewers' common-sense judgements about the emotions, hostile–critical or otherwise, of the relatives they have interviewed (Harris, 1978). Harris argued that these judgements, on the whole, are more likely to be right than wrong, because the 'researchers are ordinary, competent members of society who can, as a matter of fact, recognise, say, a criticism when they hear it' (p. 8). The point Harris makes is rather that the judgements are not invariably right and even if they are there is no need to pretend that they constitute a complex measuring instrument rather than the use of common sense.

This comment rather underestimates the EE index however; in several respects it is more than a common-sense judgement which may be right or wrong (Rutter and Brown, 1966). It measures the extent of the relative's hostility and criticism and gives an indication of the degree of intensity that these reactions have to reach before they are associated with relapse. Moreover, there is one element in the EE index which is not an indication of dissatisfaction with the ex-patient: the marked emotional over-involvement. This, according to the studies, was associated with relapse irrespective of criticism and hostility. It seems that the fact of a relative (most often the mother) being to a marked extent emotionally over-involved with the ex-patient, increases the prospects of a relapse.

CHAPTER 5

The Family of the Mentally Ill

In contemporary Western societies most people live in family groups. A 'family' may be defined in many different ways: for example, narrowly, to include parents and their non-adult children only (elementary or nuclear family), or more broadly to include grandparents, uncles, aunts and cousins (extended family). For the present discussion the most useful description of a family group is the one often used for census purposes: relatives living in the same household, sharing common table and living room. Thus, an adult may live with spouse and children or with parents, siblings or other relatives; in all these cases the family group constitutes the immediate social environment. It is indeed a 'social' environment because relationships within the family group, the division of work among its members and the routines of daily life are much dependent on cultural and social factors: on the culturally transmitted notions that people have about how they ought to behave in such relationships and settings.

The importance of the family setting for the mentally ill has frequently been mentioned in preceding chapters: the close relatives' recognition of the patient's mental disturbance, their influence on the patient's admission to hospital and on the ex-patient's adjustments to post-hospital life and many other issues have been examined. This chapter will focus attention on the family group itself rather than on the mentally ill member of it. The family will be looked at as a meaningful social entity and the ways in which mental disturbance affects its social position, life-style, internal relationships and links with the outside world will be scrutinised.

Illness, whether physical or psychiatric, can seriously affect the family group: if someone assumes the sick role, he discontinues normal social activities and various tasks have to be reallocated and carried out by others; in addition, the care of the sick person has to be undertaken. It has been argued in recent years that family groups in contemporary Western societies are, in many respects, ill-equipped to cope with sickness in the home. The modern family is quite small: frequently only two adults, the husband and wife, are present, and if one becomes sick, the other perforce has to undertake all the manifold duties of the household. With a high proportion of women in employment there is often no one in the family group who routinely spends all day within the home, and is thus available to care for the sick person. A great deal of geographical mobility, typical in contemporary industrial societies, takes people away from the vicinity of close realtives who could otherwise undertake some of the tasks involved.

To cope with short-term sickness may be difficult enough for the modern family, but accommodating the long-term sick and the handicapped poses problems of a far greater magnitude. With improved living standards and the advance of medical knowledge, increasing numbers of chronic sick and handicapped persons, most of whom live with their families, are enabled to survive to a far greater age than such people of earlier generations. In the case of mental illness, the growing popularity of 'community care' and apprehension of the possible harm done to patients by long periods in hospital have meant that increasing numbers of mentally disturbed people continue to live with their families rather than in institutions. Much of the psychiatric treatment provided is now on an out-patient basis and most hospital admissions are for short periods.

The family group of the mentally ill individual is thus likely to live with that person during the first phase of the illness, prior to contact with professional help; during the illness if treatment is on an out-patient basis, and, in some cases, more or less permanently where the impairment is long-lasting. In these circumstances it is important to examine the effect of living with a mentally ill person on other members of the family group.

THE BURDEN OF MENTAL ILLNESS

Many aspects of daily life are profoundly affected by living with a mentally ill relative; information about the dislocation of normal routines has been collected by several researchers who interviewed relatives and observed the lives of the families of identified psychiatric patients.

It is common observation that families often accommodate mental illness by adjusting the daily routines of the household to it. If the mentally ill person cannot be left alone in the house (for example because of the apprehension that he might harm himself or because he is afraid to be alone) then the family may rearrange their lives so that someone is always at home. Mealtimes may become unreliable, established routines of washing, cleaning, shopping and so on may have to be varied and even sleeping arrangements adapted to the new situation if the disturbed person is liable to interrupt the sleep of others.

The accounts of relatives contain many illustrations of practical daily problems, such as a woman who was described by her husband as very forgetful – she would start to fill the oil stove and then go on to something else, so that the stove overflowed; or a young man who was said to be willing to mow the lawn or wash up if asked but who tended to stop halfway through the job and wander away so that supervising him took more effort than doing the job oneself (Creer and Wing, 1974).

The demands made on members of the family in terms of extra duties, less leisure and disrupted routines, can be very considerable and the effect on their regular employments, damaging. Sometimes, relatives feel that they have to take less demanding jobs than they would otherwise have chosen, or take early retirement or part-time work to compensate for the extra drain on their time and energy at home. If this happens then the family income can become much reduced at a time when the unemployment or partial employment of the mentally disturbed person reduces the income of the family group in any case.

One attempt to assess the extent to which the presence of a mentally ill person affects the household routines and the employment and leisure activities of the rest of the family was made by Grad and Sainsbury (1968) who compared two areas in the South of England which provided two different types of psychiatric service. One, Chichester, provided a community care service in which a much lower proportion of psychiatric patients was admitted to mental hospitals than in the other area, Salisbury, which at that time provided a more hospital-orientated service. Researchers visited the homes of a sample of psychiatric patients and interviewed close relatives soon after the patient was referred to a psychiatrist and again two years later.

By rating the effect of the patient on the work, leisure, income and health of the families and on relations with neighbours they concluded that in both areas around 20 per cent of families were suffering a severe burden at the time of the patient's first referral and a further 45–50 per cent were suffering some burden. During the two years these proportions changed little in Chichester but fell dramatically in Salisbury a finding which could be taken to indicate that at least in respect of the problem areas studied, removal of the patient to hospital considerably alleviated the burden on the family and, conversely, that the continued presence of the patient in the home constituted an ongoing burden.

Although the disruption of the household and the reduction of income constitute considerable difficulties, relatives do not usually regard these practical matters as their main problems (Mills, 1962; Creer and Wing, 1974). The problems most emphasised by them have to do with the emotional climate of the family, the relationships within it and the health of adults and children.

Emotional Climate

The strains, stresses and conflicts caused by living with a mentally disturbed person frequently constitute the most severe problems for families. Some of the stresses are directly attributable to the symptoms; for example, the excessive silence of the disturbed person, frequently met with, can cause a great deal of stress in the family. A constant stream of talk, confused and muddled, can also be exhausting for relatives to listen to. A sister said of a patient who kept up a continuous fretting conversation: 'Sometimes when she stands behind me

TABLE 5.1 Percentage of Families Affected at Referral, During and at the End of Two Years

Effect on:	At referral Chichester	At referral Salisbury	At any time during Chichester	At any time during Salisbury	In the last 3 months Chichester	In the last 3 months Salisbury
Household routine	25	36	32	27	13	6
Social and leisure life	32	32	38	28	22	14
Income	27	25	35	30	20	10
Mental health	53	77	No rating		38	19
Physical health	17	8	14	7	6	4
Children	36	37	40	30	40	32

Source: Grad and Sainsbury (1968).

while I'm working and goes on like that I begin to feel so ill I say to her, "Iris, go upstairs and shut the door, if you don't go away from me I shall scream".' (Mills, 1962, p. 84).

Excessive silence can be equally trying. Some patients are withdrawn, apathetic and silent, hardly speaking to members of the family for days on end, nor appearing to hear when spoken to. As one father told a researcher: 'You can't get a word out of Vincent now – sometimes he won't speak all evening and sometimes not much in a week' (Mills, 1962, p. 85); and a relative in another study complaining about a young man who went home from hospital each weekend said: '... quite often doesn't speak a word the whole weekend, then, when it's time to go back you ask him "have you enjoyed your weekend?" and he just says "No".' (Creer and Wing, 1974, p. 10).

Unpredictability of the patient is another source of stress in the home. As discussed previously, unpredictable behaviour undermines social expectations and gives rise to sensations of uncertainty and insecurity. For relatives living with this situation the basic certainties of daily life are undermined: waking up each morning with the feeling that anything may happen during the day, is distressing and stressful. No wonder relatives often talk about 'living on the edge of a volcano' or of being 'constantly on a knife-edge' (Creer and Wing, 1974, p. 30). It is likely that this fear of what might happen is particularly severe in cases where relatives remember past incidents of the patient doing something unexpected and disastrous.

> One father, for example, recounted how he had once been taking his son somewhere in the car. There had been no sign that anything was amiss, nor had anything happened to upset the patient that day. But when the father turned around to reverse, the patient suddenly punched him hard, breaking his nose. This kind of incident need only have happened once for relatives to have it permanently at the back of their minds, making them always slightly uneasy and watchful of the patient's reactions. The unpredictable always tends to be frightening and because the patients often seem to respond to internal rather than external stimuli, this could give the relatives a panicky feeling of having no control at all over the situation. (Creer and Wing, 1974, p. 31)

Symptoms such as excessive talk or silence and unpredictability, are not the only causes of a stressful emotional climate. The relatives' own feelings about the patient and his illness contribute to the strains experienced by the family, and these feelings often include guilt, anxiety and anger.

Guilt feeling, that is the notion that one is to be blamed for the mental illness of a close relative, is usual and very distressing. It is well described by Elizabeth Bott in an essay about the contemporary Western family's responses to crisis situations such as the mental illness of a family member:

> Whatever explanation of the illness they adopt, the conclusions are disheartening. If the husband is ill, the wife may ask herself, consciously or unconsciously, what she has done to produce it or make it worse. If she adopts the hereditary hypothesis, she will worry about her children: 'Are they tainted?' The children ask themselves the same questions, 'Am I such a bad child that I have driven him mad?' 'Is it going to happen to me? Will it happen to my children?' If a child is ill the parent may ask 'What have we done?' (Bott, 1971, p. 25)

Guilt feeling for the misfortune of a close relative is a characteristic emotional response to all types of illness; for example, in a study of families in which a child contracted polio, Davis described how parents felt responsible and guilty for the child's illness (Davis, 1963). This study was carried out in the mid-1950s in America (before the full-scale introduction of the anti-polio vaccine) at a time when there was nothing parents could have done to prevent their children from contracting the disease; but parents nevertheless felt guilty. A father in the study said:

> I think it's just an inner-self letdown that you as a parent have not guided your family and your household the way that you would have guided it had you known this was coming. Let's put it this way. Suppose instead of living here, I was living in the state of Washington. Why didn't I decide to go to the state of Washington?... What made me come here? I don't know.... But I did, I did come here. Here's where Gerry got sick. (Davis, 1963, p. 37)

The guilt response to illness is connected with important cultural assumptions in the value systems of Western societies.

Parsons (1958) pointed out that there is a general value commitment in these societies to man's mastery of the environment, to the notion that man is able to modify and conquer his environment instead of just having to adjust to it. This general orientation leads to the unwritten, seldom enunciated, but nevertheless strongly-held cultural assumption that misfortune rarely hits those who take proper precautionary measures. Empirical research on illness behaviour has shown this orientation to be especially marked in the middle classes who are therefore particularly prone to the view that serious illness and other crisis situations are somehow due to negligence or to wrong actions.

The emotional climate of the family with a mentally ill member is also characterised by much anxiety over the correct way of dealing with the patient and by the enhanced problems of family life. Mental illness is surrounded by uncertainties for the layman; because it is a stigmatised condition and because in the past the mentally ill were locked up and put away there are no socially agreed, acceptable ways of dealing with the mentally ill who live within the family group. No available models of behaviour exist that people can make use of. Usually, in health matters, a great deal of advice-seeking and advice-giving goes on among lay people, but advice about dealing with a mentally ill relative is rarely sought or given. The stigma of mental illness makes it a much less comfortable subject for lay discussion than physical illness and, in any case, the lay-group has no feelings of competence to deal with problems associated with it. Neighbours, parents or in-laws will volunteer advice about physically sick children or husbands, as they have had personal experience with similar problems or heard discussions about them; but the same people are likely to be uncertain and silent on the subject of mental disturbance. Not only is social group-experience lacking but very little professional advice is forthcoming. Relatives often complain that even when a patient is receiving psychiatric treatment, or on his return from a psychiatric hospital, they receive no advice and are left 'to sink or survive', to find out for themselves how to deal with the patient and the unfamiliar problems of family life (Creer and Wing, 1974; Wing, 1977). Relatives are uncertain whether they are looking after the patient in the best way, not sure what they should tell young children about the mental illness and how much contact between patient and child they should encourage, and are confused over many other things. It is only by trial and error that relatives find solutions and, meanwhile, the lack of socially and medically approved norms of behaviour applicable to the situation in which they find themselves causes much anxiety.

Relationships within the Family

In a stressful, emotional climate, relationships between family members are likely to become strained. In any case, illness in one member of a family affects relationships not only between the sick person and the others but also between the healthy members of the family. Internal relationships and roles have to be adjusted to accommodate the illness. For example, if a father falls ill and becomes dependent on the care of his wife, he displaces their children to some extent, as the mother can devote less time and attention to them. If the illness is long-term, the mother may have to assume the role of breadwinner and supporter of the family and in consequence of her changed family status, her relationships with both husband and children are likely to change. In general, with a family group, a change in someone's major social role, such as the assumption of the role of the patient, brings about changes in the role-relationships of others. Such changes mean that the previous balance of family relationships becomes disturbed and a new, changed balance has to be achieved for the continued functioning of the family unit.

So far, little systematic research has been undertaken into changes in relationships among relatives of psychiatric patients following the onset of the illness. Yarrow and her colleagues, in their study of women whose husbands were admitted to a mental hospital, gave some interesting preliminary information. They examined the relationships of the wives with their own parents, with their husbands' parents and with their children (Yarrow *et al.*, 1955b). The researchers found that relationships between wives and their husbands' parents were frequently characterised by accusations, criticisms and hostility. If the mental illness of the husband was attributed by the wife to character weaknesses or defects (as it often was) the wife was inclined to blame her husband's parents for these shortcomings; she would allege that the parents spoiled him, made a baby out of him, that the parent–child relationship in the husband's childhood was to blame. The husband's parents, in turn, were inclined to accuse the wife of lack of understanding and of keeping the patient in hospital. Even where prior relationships had been good, interaction between wives and in-laws deteriorated. Yarrow points out that parents and wife are the relatives closest to a sick husband and thus the ones most readily available for the ascription of responsibility and blame.

Usually, once a husband had entered a mental hospital, the focus of the problem shifted from what to do about him, to coping with the children and managing the finances in his absence. The wives then often looked to their own parents for help and several assumed, at least partially, the dependent daughter role. These relationships were not trouble free either; old parental opposition to the daughter's marriage was revived, parents' expressed reservations about the choice of husband re-stated and bitterness over their unrealised hopes for a successful marriage made evident. Wives attributed strained relationships with their parents to such recriminations.

Where possible the wives in Yarrow's study turned most readily to their adult, or adolescent, sons and daughters for support in facing up to the problems of their father's illness: they shared the anxieties and the responsibilities. Almost all wives with young children tried to conceal from them the mental disturbance of their fathers, avoiding the subject as much as possible giving various false explanations to the children to account for their father's absence. These concealments left the mothers anxious lest the children found out the truth, and added to the problems created by the illness.

Thus, according to Yarrow's study, family relationships were characterised by conflicts and anxieties, findings confirmed by other researchers. In parental homes, the illness of a son or daughter is often followed by stress brought on as a consequence of differential treatment being accorded to the patient by a parent: siblings and the other parent tend to resent the increased attention and care that the patient receives. Family relationships in contemporary society are governed by strong social norms with which differential treatment conflicts. In the realm of childrearing and sibling relations, egalitarianism is the governing principle, the notion being that, allowing for certain age/sex differentiations, all children receive equal care, love and attention from their parents and have equal standing *vis-à-vis* each other. A short-term physical illness, understood to be such, may not seriously affect this arrangement, as the sick child receives more attention only temporarily. However, long-term conditions can disrupt the previous balance of family relationships (Davis, 1963). When a mentally ill son or daughter receives extra attention from a parent (usually from the mother) over a long period of time, this conflicts with the expectations of other siblings and of the other parent. For example, a mother in Mills's study said of her daughter: 'She'll come in and I'll perhaps put her dinner down and she'll say "I don't want that", and I get her something else – my boy Johnny gets mad and yells at her and the other girl gets cross too. I tell them to leave her alone because she's ill' (Mills, 1962, p. 67). Another mother in the same study said that she put her schizophrenic son before her daughter's wish to bring home a boyfriend (p. 67). In another study Creer and Wing (1974) found that parents struggled with divided loyalties: they wished to do their best for the mentally ill child, but were much aware of distress and possible injury to their other children. This study also revealed strains between parents; the mother and the father would blame each other for handling the patient wrongly.

The Health of the Family

Mental illness in the home can affect not only the quality of family life but also the health of family members. A stressful emotional climate, anxieties and practical burdens, can have harmful effects on the physical and mental health of both adults and children. Concerning adults, the study of Grad and

Sainsbury has shown that the mental health of a very high proportion of relatives suffers from living with a mentally disturbed patient. Table 5.1 shows that at the beginning of that study, between half and three-quarters of the close relatives' mental health was affected, and that at the end of the two year follow-up period this proportion was still considerable in spite of the patient having had treatment. The relatives themselves attributed their own emotional disturbance to worry and concern about the patient and to the problems created by his presence. Other studies also show that relatives think their own health and well-being are affected; in the study of Creer and Wing (1974) nearly half of the relatives thought their health was 'severely' or 'very severely' affected by having a mentally ill member of the family living at home, and only 15 per cent of them said that they experienced no such effects. Several illustrations of the health problems reported by wives of schizophrenics are given by Brown *et al.* (1966): for example: 'At times she felt trembly and could not eat and sleep; wanted to run a mile. Obtained sleeping tablets from her general practitioner.' 'Her nerves had been "all shattered". She had bad headaches and pains in her stomach attributed by her general practitioner to "nerves".' 'Said that she worried a lot and had bad headaches. Got wound up and bubbled up inside; had lost weight and did not want to eat. Her doctor attributed this to anxiety and considered sending her into hospital' (p. 127).

Children as well as adults can experience adverse effects on their health and this possibility has been studied extensively. An important consideration is that if children's mental and physical health are affected, with possible long-term consequences, then the social costs of having mentally ill people in the home may be very high. In an interesting research, Rutter and his colleagues (1976) investigated a sample of families from which one parent had been referred to a psychiatrist; children in these families were compared with school classroom controls and were followed up for four years. The researchers found nearly twice as many examples of persisting emotional or behaviour problems in the children of psychiatric patients than in their classroom controls. Children especially affected were those in families with continuing marital discord, or where the parent's disorder was associated with hostility or irritability towards the child. In fact, several researchers confirm that it is the deteriorated parent–child relationship and the parent's negative feelings towards the child that are likely to affect its mental health, rather than any particular type of mental illness or the degree of severity thereof in the parent (Rutter and Madge, 1976). Grad and Sainsbury (1968) have also shown that considerable adverse affects on children are caused by having a mentally ill adult in the home (Table 5.1). In their study, between 30 and 40 per cent of the children had become disturbed in some way; relatives mentioned many signs of adverse affects on the children's health and well-being, such as becoming unhappy, worried, unduly naughty and backward at school.

In their survey of psychiatric patients in general practice, Shepherd and his colleagues (1966) studied a small sample of families in order to see how the patients' children were affected as regards both physical and mental health. A group of thirty-two married women were selected for this study, all between the ages of 25 and 45, and diagnosed by their general practitioners as suffering from chronic neurotic conditions. A control group of women of similar ages, who were examined and found not to be neurotic, was also selected. The researchers found that the children of neurotic mothers had higher consultation rates than did the children of those in the control group, the difference being especially marked in respect to girls. Similarly, in the reports of the parents, it was the children of the neurotic women who had the higher incidence of illness and who exhibited the more neurotic traits. Possibly, in the reporting of parents, the neurotic women were the more alert to, and worried by, their children's ill-health and the more likely to attach importance to their aberrant behaviour. However, doctors also (according to a child health survey questionnaire administered by the researchers) diagnosed disturbance in more children of the neurotic than of the non-neurotic mothers. Here, too, the difference was consistently more marked in the case of girls:

The presence in the home of a disturbed relative and the ensuing stressful emotional climate and disrupted household routines are likely adversely to affect children. In addition, the

TABLE 5.2   Indices of Morbidity and Emotional Disturbance in the Children of Neurotic Married Women and Their Controls

Indices of morbidity and emotional disturbance	Sex	Children of neurotic group	Children of control group
Mean number of consultations	Boys	4.4	3.8
	Girls	4.6	2.5
Mean number of days unwell	Boys	72	49
	Girls	81	51
Percentage diagnosed as neurotic	Boys	21.7	10.3
	Girls	34.4	7.4
Percentage reported by parents to have shown neurotic traits	Boys	17.4	17.2
	Girls	40.6	18.5
Number of children	Boys	23	29
	Girls	32	27

Source: Shepherd *et al.* (1966).

extra work involved in looking after a mentally ill patient suggests that a child may be given adult responsibilities too early: when tasks have to be reallocated as a consequence of illness, there may be no one available but the other children to undertake them. It can also be argued that stable parenting behaviour is disrupted when one parent becomes mentally ill and that children are likely to be brought up erratically by such parents. All these factors affect the health and development of children and add to the social costs of mental illness.

THE SOCIAL POSITION OF THE FAMILY

According to Goffman, it is the nature of stigma to spread from the stigmatised individual to his close associates.

> Thus, the loyal spouse of the mental patient, the daughter of the ex-con., the parent of the cripple, the friend of the blind, the family of the hangman, are all obliged to share some of the discredit of the stigmatized person to whom they are related.

One response to this fate is to embrace it, and to live within the world of one's stigmatized connection. It should be added that persons who acquire a degree of stigma in this way can themselves have connections who acquire a little of the disease twice removed. (Goffman, 1963, p. 30)

The family of someone defined as mentally ill is likely to find itself occupying a social position inferior to that which it previously enjoyed. The wife of a mental patient is likely to be regarded by her social group as an unfortunate, deserving perhaps of help and kindness, but essentially different from ordinary, normal wives. In some such cases responsibility may be attributed to the wife (people may say that she should never have married that husband or that she should have handled him differently, etc.), while in others she may be deemed blameless; but whether responsibility is imputed or not, the position of the wife is that of someone who has been singled out by misfortune. In this, close relatives of the mentally ill are in a situation similar to that of near relations of other stigmatised individuals, such as the physically disabled and the criminal.

Families with a mentally or physically disabled member tend to have a feeling of being 'different' from other families, of being alienated from a universe of 'normal' experiences (Davis, 1962). The family's previous conception of itself, as a 'normal' family changes: 'normal' families do not have such misfortunes. The relatives tend to have the expectation that others will stigmatise them even before the social group comes to know about the condition. These expectations are based on previous social experience: the relatives feel that people in like situations are treated in this way. In the study of Yarrow and her colleagues (1955b) wives of mental patients had expected social discrimination when their husbands entered hospital: they expected to be avoided by their old friends, they were afraid that their children would be excluded from play groups or taunted by other children. Uppermost, and distressing, is likely to be the feeling that others may avoid one, a common fear also in families of the physically disabled: relatives frequently complain that their friends and acquaintances changed towards them, that they lost their previous social circle (Miles, 1979).

Indeed, many families, having in their midst a mentally ill member, experience an over-all reduction in social contacts. There are several reasons why this should be so. In most situations of crisis, where a family faces such misfortunes as physical illness, death or accident, there are social expectations as to how the social group should behave towards that family. There are socially prescribed forms of offering help and expressing sympathy: visits to hospital, the sending of flowers, messages of condolence, offers of financial or domestic assistance, etc. However, when the misfortune has attached to it a stigma, as with imprisonment for a crime or commitment to a mental hospital, people lack the appropriate response. There are no socially accepted forms of behaving towards the family in such cases; people lack certainty and become puzzled or confused. As discussed previously, stigma undermines social expectations and predictability; when a family member acquires a stigmatising condition, such as mental illness, people become uncertain as to what this implies for the rest of the family, unsure of what it means for their relationships with the other family members, and confused as to what their own attitudes should be. It is tempting, in situations which involve uncertainties and embarrassments, to take the easy way out and avoid the issue altogether.

According to Yarrow's study (1955b) people became confused on learning of a friend's admission to a mental hospital: the wives they studied received very few visits, written messages or gifts from friends, only vague promises of 'wanting to visit' which never materialised, during the period of their husbands' hospital stay.

There are other reasons for the discontinuance of relationships; where the social life of a married couple is based on contacts with other married couples, the elimination through illness of one spouse tends to leave the other in the situation of 'odd one out' when it comes to visiting, holidays and outings. The spouse of the patient may be unwilling to meet the couples who formed the previous social circle and unacceptable to them. Acquaintanceship based on the workplace tends not to survive prolonged absence from work.

The family's social contacts can also become reduced if a mentally ill person with unacceptable or embarrassing habits lives in the home. Friends are not then invited to the house, while if the patient cannot be left alone, the chance of meeting friends outside it is lessened. There are many illustrations of the impact of a patient's behaviour and habits on the social contacts of relatives; in one study, a nineteen-year-old girl who shared a flat with her schizophrenic mother described her parent as 'smelling awful', her clothes as 'ruined' and the whole house as becoming so unpleasant that she did not like to invite her friends round. She rarely went away at weekends, although she would have liked to, because her mother would then be alone (Creer and Wing, 1974, p. 28). Relatives frequently complain that even if they invite people to the house few will come a second time; that school children cannot ask their friends home and that invitations to visit others also stop after a time. Social relations are thus surrounded by embarrassment and become reduced.

In spite of these many sources of difficulty in social relations, not every family with a mentally ill relative experiences major disruption of its social life. The nature and the duration of mental illness account for some variations: it is the long-lasting conditions and those with symptoms causing social embarrassment that tend to be the more disruptive. However, what also matters is the family's attitudes to the outside world and the extent to which the family members wish to maintain their social relationships.

There are three main approaches open to the relatives of the mentally ill; they can attempt to 'pass' (i.e. conceal the sick person's condition), they can 'normalise' their relationships (i.e. continue normal interaction) or they can 'disassociate' (i.e. withdraw from social contacts). Following Goffman's terminology, these different ways of conducting social relationships can be called 'interaction stratagems'. Of course, it is not suggested that people, on learning of mental illness in a relative, make conscious choices, in the sense of having duly deliberated the possible stratagems; rather is it postulated that they interact with their social group in one way or another according to the situation in which they find themselves and according to their attitudes, value orientations and personalities. Such forms of interaction are not peculiar to mental illness and several researchers have explored the various interaction stratagems pursued by other sick and disabled people and their relatives (Goffman, 1963; Davis, 1962; Miles, 1979).

'Passing' as a response to mental illness was discussed previously in the context of discharged mental patients attempting to conceal their past illness and hospital stay. Members of the family also may feasibly adopt this tactic and conceal from their friends and acquaintances the mental illness of one of their number. Passing, as an interaction stratagem, is linked to the assumption of stigma: people conceal that which is shameful or discrediting. Concealment is likely to succeed more with new acquaintances and those who are physically or socially distant than with close friends, but even in such cases it is not always easy. For example, the long absence of a spouse has to be accounted for; many wives of patients in Yarrow's study told their friends and neighbours that their husbands were in hospital for physical complaints or that they were in the country taking a rest, etc. 'To keep the neighbours from knowing the husband's hospital (having reported that he was in a hospital because of suspicion of cancer) Mrs. G. must rush to her apartment house to get the mail before her neighbours pick it up for her as they used to do. . . . Before she can allow visitors in her apartment, she must pick up any material identifying the hospital. . .' (Yarrow, 1955b). Relatives say that new acquaintances can also become a problem: '. . . sooner or later the conversation was bound to turn to "And do you have any children?" "Oh, yes, and what does your son do?" Mention mental illness and an awful hush descends on the whole room' (Creer and Wing, 1974, p. 36).

Disassociation is a stratagem involving the avoidance of social contacts with former friends, neighbours and colleagues. The choice of this stratagem is linked to considerable fear and anticipation of stigma; the relatives prefer to isolate themselves from normal social relations rather than risk adverse responses. A person disassociating may go to great lengths to avoid others, to the extent of changing his address, or place of work. Some typical remarks illustrate this stratagem: 'Of course, I have cut out seeing all but a couple of our friends'; '. . . I've cut off all our other friends. I didn't tell them that I was giving up the apartment and I had the phone disconnected without telling anyone so they don't know how to get in touch with me'; 'I haven't gotten too friendly with anyone at the office because I don't want people to know where my husband is. I figure that if I got too friendly with them, they would start asking questions' (Yarrow, 1955b, p. 36).

One of the main problems with both passing and disassociation as interaction stratagems is that the relatives adopting them can become isolated and lonely. If interactions are deliberately limited, or are based on concealment and lies, then those relatives are likely to be left with little or no companionship. Moreover, the expectation of stigma is never put to the test, as in such circumstances they are not able to assess the validity of their assumptions about adverse social responses.

The third stratagem is 'normalisation' which means attempting to minimise the problem of mental illness and entering into or continuing normal relationships with the social group. The choice of this stratagem is linked to an assumption that stigma is absent or slight and should be ignored. Relatives pursuing the normalisation stratagem tell others about mental illness in the family and are willing to discuss its nature and impact.

The choice of interaction stratagem is not always clear cut: people may oscillate between one and another or try to combine them.

There is a set of people available in whom relatives may confide without fear of adverse response, who will understand and discuss the mental illness, namely, those in a similar situation to themselves. Association with such others reduces loneliness and isolation. For example, the wife of a mental patient in Yarrow's study explained how she and her husband had met, and liked a great deal, a couple who lived in the same apartment house; that husband had needed to see a psychiatrist, and their mutual understanding of the problem constituted the basis of a friendship (Yarrow, 1955b).

There is a lack of systematic research into the proportion of people choosing one stratagem or another and into the sociopsychological correlates of responses. In the study of Yarrow and her colleagues, a third of the wives communicated minimally with others around them and were predominantly motivated to conceal their husbands' illness; another third extensively discussed the husbands' condition with others, while the rest of the wives were distributed between these extremes. In another study, close relatives of patients discharged from a mental hospital and living in the Boston area were interviewed (Freeman and Simmons, 1968). The researchers found that a quarter of the relatives showed great sensitivity to the reactions of the community and chose a stratagem of concealment of mental illness and of withdrawal from the community. From this study comes the finding that the type of relationship to the patient (i.e. whether spouse, sibling, parent) has a bearing on the feelings of stigma experienced by the relative. Wives of mental patients were most likely to feel stigmatised and to choose to withdraw from community associations. Possibly this was so because the wives felt their status to be greatly dependent on the evaluation of their husbands' status by members of the social group. It is somewhat less easy to explain why the other group of relatives with a strong stigma feeling and the wish to conceal and withdraw, should be the sisters of female (but not of male) patients. The researchers suggest that sisters may be very anxious lest they are classified by their community as similar to the other sister (i.e. the patient) as such negative evaluation may deter prospective marriage partners.

The Boston research also investigated the correlates of stigma-feelings. The strongest association was found between a feeling of stigma on the part of a relative and that person's report on the post-hospital behaviour of the patient: those who reported that the ex-patient still had problems and was difficult to manage at home also felt most stigma, suggesting that relatives fear that the community will stigmatise them because of the discharged patient's current unacceptable behaviour rather than that individual's past history of mental hospitalisation.

THE ATTITUDES OF RELATIVES

So far in this chapter the impact of mental illness on the daily life, internal relationships and social position of the family has been discussed. It seems apparent that families experience much disruption, distress and conflict as a result of mental illness. The question to consider then, is why families tolerate this situation, as so many undoubtedly do, and what alternatives are available to them.

Accepting the Patient

Perhaps a general point should first be made: a great deal of sickness, of many types, is accommodated in the community without people fully realising the extent, or spelling out the effects of it. A common observation of researchers and health-professionals is that people under-report the existence of illness and the problems it causes (Brown *et al.*, 1966; Creer and Wing, 1974; Davis, 1963). Symptoms which develop gradually tend to be disregarded or not taken seriously (see Chapter 2) because people get used to them and adjust their lives to accommodate them. Likewise with problems caused by a mentally ill relative in the home: families tend to adjust their daily lives, and, above all, their level of expectations so that after a period of time earlier hopes and goals are abandoned and even forgotten. When interviewers ask questions about the problems of mental illness in the home, relatives are inclined to minimise them. According to Brown and his colleagues:

> A number of relatives denied that they had problems when, by common-sense standards, they must have had many. Although extreme examples were rare, our impression throughout the work has been that there is a tendency for relatives to understate the amount of trouble and distress.... Some relatives, for example, apparently coped by lowering their expectations of the patient and of family life.... It was rare for any complaint to be made, even in cases where it was clear from the hospital and local authority records that extreme difficulty had been experienced. (Brown *et al.*, 1966, p. 99)

Indeed, this is why, in many of the studies quoted earlier, researchers preferred to assess the impact of mental illness independently of the complaints made by relatives.

Of course, human beings have a remarkable ability to adjust to adverse circumstances: wars, famines, painful diseases and political oppression can be tolerated. People manage to get through many distressing situations, living from day to day. A perception of situations as unalterable, or an apathetic acceptance of the *status quo*, may account for the willingness of many to adjust. It may be, then, that for some families the problems caused by mental illness become part of everyday life, and are accepted as 'just one of those things' albeit distressing. Illustrations of the extent to which relatives can be unaware of the full weight of their burden and of the adjustments they make, are given in many studies. For example, a young girl who lived alone with a schizophrenic mother said: 'I never knew I was depressed until I was able to get away for a fortnight and I went abroad on holiday with a friend. It was only after I'd been away a few days that I suddenly realized how lighthearted I felt. It was such a contrast to how I normally feel' (Creer and Wing, 1974, p. 67).

Acceptance of a situation, perceived as unmodifiable, explains the toleration of the mentally ill exhibited by some families; others however have different reasons. There are those who care for a mentally ill family member at home because they feel it their duty to do so. It is important to bear in mind that powerful social norms govern many aspects of people's behaviour towards members of their family: in contemporary Western society the obligation of parents to care for their children is very strong, and so is the expectation that the family provides help in sickness, trouble and need. Some people may be very conscious of the adverse effects that a patient's presence has on their lives, but are willing to carry on out of a sense of family obligation. Many examples of such feelings can be found in studies of the relatives of mentally ill patients.

The behaviour of relatives can be better understood however, if not only the costs but the possible benefits of caring for a mentally ill person are considered. Illness is evaluated negatively in society and it is easy to overlook the possibility of any benefit accruing from it, but there is much research evidence to show that to some people, in some situations, illness in oneself or in another seems desirable (Miles, 1978). After all, the sick role has privileges as well as obligations: the sick person may enjoy abandoning social responsibilities and obligations if these seem too heavy and unwelcome. Likewise, the illness of a relative may have positive aspects: an overbearing, unpleasant person can be temporarily removed from the family group or be changed as a result of the illness.

An interesting illustration of the positive aspect of mental illness in a relative was given in the study of Rogler and Hollingshead (1965), who investigated the effects of schizophrenia in Puerto Rican families. The authors described the traditional marital roles of Puerto Rican husbands and wives as typically non-egalitarian: it was generally accepted that husbands were the dominant partners in marriage and that they showed their independence and 'masculinity' by spending time and money on drink, women and gambling. The socially accepted position of wives was subordinate, they showed resignation and acceptance. When a husband became mentally ill and exhibited symptoms of withdrawal, associated with schizophrenia, the wife's subordinate position in the household improved. She could take outside work, nurse the husband and be the supporter of the family. The husband's previous demands, marital infidelities and gambling ceased and wives reacted positively to their changed situation in spite of the odd behaviour exhibited by their men.

Having a mentally ill patient in the home may also have benefits in that it can satisfy some emotional need in a relative. The presence of a dependent, no matter how disturbed or demanding, can be a source of satisfaction, giving meaning and usefulness to the life of someone who feels the lack of these qualities. The presence of another human being, even if withdrawn or depressed, can help to reduce loneliness as in situations where the patient lives with an elderly, retired parent or sibling. An elderly widow may be glad not only to have some companionship but also to have someone do the shopping occasionally or be on the premises to call a doctor if the need arises. For such lonely and isolated relatives, the patient's habits would not constitute a big problem; not being able to leave the patient alone or being prevented from seeing friends for example, would not worry them. Studies concerned with relatives' problems make the point that patients are not invariably a liability to them (Mills, 1962; Creer and Wing,

1974) though there is certainly more evidence of the burden on the family than of any benefits deriving from the patient's presence. But concentration on the clearly negative aspects of having the patient in the home can make the behaviour of relatives seem incomprehensible.

Thus, the motives for caring for disturbed relatives in the home are various and complex. Some accommodate mental illness because they gain something from doing so, some out of feelings of duty; these and others are often able to adjust their lives and expectations until the burden of living with mental illness becomes an acceptable part of existence.

It is difficult to estimate what proportion of relatives of any particular type of patient are likely to show acceptance or rejection, and it is also difficult to say whether certain types of family are likely to be more accepting than others. From various studies it seems that the majority of families accept, or at least tolerate, patients at home. Creer and Wing judged the relatives' general attitudes from the way they spoke about the patients during interviews. About a quarter of the relatives were unfavourable in their attitudes and nearly three-quarters of them were tolerant or accepting. Similarly, Brown and his colleagues found that almost three-quarters of the relatives of schizophrenics living at home at the time of the interviews conveyed that they welcomed the patient's presence and only a small proportion (12 per cent) said that they would rather the patient were permanently in hospital or elsewhere. However, studies based on interviews with relatives who live with patients may give a biased picture: those who have rejected, and consequently do not live with, such a patient, are not included in these studies. Thus, Brown estimates that patients who left the area during the study period (and whose relatives were not interviewed) had left after periods of difficulty and tension at home. Rejection and unfavourable attitudes therefore may be more common than the studies quoted above indicate.

In an earlier study by Wing and his colleagues (1959) it was reported that no family of a male patient refused to take him back when he was discharged from hospital, and that relatives, on the whole, were more likely to be welcoming or accepting than rejecting. The willingness of English families to care for their mentally ill relatives has often been noted (Mills, 1962); and a recent American study found similar attitudes there: the majority of families interviewed after patients were suddenly returned home due to an unexpected hospital strike in New York State expressed pleasure at the turn of the events (Barrett *et al.* 1972).

Whether a family is willing and able to accept the mentally ill relative depends not only on its motivation and internal resources but also on the support it receives from its social network. It has been argued that families living in a close-knit network of kin group and friends, all of whom know each other well and reside in the same neighbourhood, would receive more support than families in loose-knit networks, where friends, kin and neighbours are geographically scattered and not in contact with each other. Members of close-knit networks are more likely to provide informal support, both emotional and in the form of practical help, partly because they are conveniently located to do so and partly, and even more importantly, because they are influenced by a strong informal social control. In a community where people all know each other well, the news about a family's need for assistance quickly spreads; more than that, the news concerning who does and who does not provide help is likewise soon known by everyone. Failure of someone to help, against social expectations, is then followed by the disapproval of the others; in other words, a strong informal social control operates in such communities.

By contrast, in a loose-knit network, where a family's friends, neighbours and kin live in different places, not knowing each other, informal social control is very much weaker. The news about specific needs is not spread quickly, nor does it become known whether any particular kin or friend helped or not.

An example of the strongest form of social support is that of the Hutterite communities in North America. Members of these communities are held together by strong social bonds of shared religion, life style (agricultural work and commonly owned property) and a high rate of inter-marriage. The Hutterites look after their mentally ill people themselves, but the burden is not borne by small family units alone.

The onset of symptoms serves as a signal to the entire community to demonstrate support and love for the patient. Hutterites do not approve of the removal of any member to a 'strange' hospital ... all patients are looked after by the immediate family. They are treated as ill rather than 'crazy'. They are encouraged to participate in the normal life of their family and community, and most are able to do some useful work ... no permanent stigma is attached to patients after recovery. The traumatic social consequences which a mental disorder usually brings to the patient, his family and sometimes his community are kept to a minimum by the patience and tolerance with which most Hutterites regard these conditions. (Eaton and Weil, 1968, p. 189).

A family living in such a community has a far lesser burden than the small urban family living in a loose-knit network.

Rejecting the Patient

Not all families accept the burden of living with a mentally ill relative. A most interesting study, which revealed the rejection of psychiatric patients by their families, was carried out in Greece and its findings were surprising because they showed that even in cohesive, close-knit communities rejection may be the accepted practice (Alivisatos and Lyketsos, 1968). The study was concerned with relatives' attitudes towards hospitalised psychiatric patients in a traditional society, where inter-familiar emotional bonds and moral obligations were strong and would normally hold the members of the families together through a lifetime. The expectation of the researchers was that in such a society families would accept and welcome the patients back from hospital. The result of this study showed a different picture: in the majority of cases (88 per cent of the patients) the responsible relatives said that they wanted the patient to remain in the hospital. They gave several reasons for this: being afraid that the patient's living at home would constitute an unbearable burden, cause family conflicts, disturb the neighbours and cause financial problems. A reduced interest in the patient himself was very evident. The relatives of nearly half the patients expected them to remain in hospital forever and refused to have them home; the others were willing to accept home those patients who were able to take care of themselves, were capable of working and were not aggressive. The researchers concluded that

> although it is generally accepted that tight bonds hold members of the Greek family united through life, the results of this research showed that in many of the families of mental patients their responsible relatives ceased to consider them as family members. They did not feel any obligation for their care, and their interest was limited to rare visits, if any, to the hospital. (Alivisatos and Lyketsos, 1968, p. 366)

An interesting finding of this study was the attitudes of the families' immediate neighbours. In nearly half of the cases (46 per cent) the neighbours were hostile to the mentally ill patients. They exposed and stigmatised both patients and families, and showed themselves afraid of mental illness. For the rest of the cases the neighbours were either indifferent or, in about a third of the cases, supportive towards the afflicted families. It seems, then, that a close-knit, cohesive structure and strong kin bonds do not necessarily guarantee social support for the families of the mentally ill; the particular attitudes of the social group also matter a great deal. It is also possible that the action of removing the patient to hospital severed the family feelings in the case of the Greek families and that without such a removal (as in the case of the Hutterites who kept the patients in the community) the family bond would have continued to hold.

A good indicator of rejection is the rate of separation or divorce among married couples following mental illness in husband or wife. According to Brown's study, the rate of separation and divorce for schizophrenic patients is substantially higher than for the general population: possibly as much as three times higher. While the rate of separation and divorce for the general population in Britain was no higher than 10 per cent for people married between 1930 and 1950, the married patients of comparable age in Brown's sample had a considerably higher rate: 44 per cent of the men and 27 per cent of the women had been separated or divorced by the time of follow-up. Similarly, higher divorce rates for patients have been reported by American researchers (Adler, 1955; Evans *et al.* 1961).

The acceptance or rejection of psychiatric patients by their families is a complex issue. The picture that emerges from most studies is that of families willing to accommodate and to receive back the patient from hospital, but which are hard-pressed by the strains and demands of living with a mentally disturbed person. Entire families shoulder a burden because one of their members is mentally ill. With an increasing shift in hospital policy towards early release of patients and home care, the degree to which the family is able and willing to undertake this burden is a most important consideration.

CHAPTER 6

Men, Women and Mental Illness

Rates of mental illness are higher for women than for men: this is a consistent result of numerous studies. Gove and Tudor (1973) undertook a review of the literature on sex differences in mental illness in Western industrial societies and found that whether judged by statistics on mental hospital admission, psychiatric outpatient care, general practitioner attendance or community surveys, women had the higher rates of mental illness.

In general practice, where the majority of psychiatric cases are treated, about twice as many female as male patients are identified as suffering from psychiatric illness (Shepherd *et al.* 1966). Table 6.1 shows that for all categories except personality disorder there is a female preponderance in consultation rates.

Hospital statistics also consistently show a predominance of women among admissions for depressive and neurotic disorders but not for schizophrenia alone where the rates for both sexes are equal; admissions for personality disorders are higher for men, but this category accounts for only a small proportion of the intake.

In a community study conducted in Britain, where the mental health of people living in an old residential district was compared with that of people living in a new housing estate, it

TABLE 6.1 Patient Consulting Rates per 1,000 at Risk for Psychiatric Morbidity, by Sex and Diagnostic Group

Diagnostic Group	Male	Female	Both sexes
Psychosis	2.7	8.6	5.9
Neuroses	55.7	116.6	88.5
Personality disorder	7.5	4.0	5.5
Psychosomatic conditions	24.5	34.5	29.9
Psycho-social problems	4.6	10.0	7.5

Source: Shepherd et al. (1966).

was the women who consistently had more psychiatric problems (Table 6.2).

This study clearly indicates the higher incidence of psychiatric problems among women. Even with mild nervous disturbance there were 1.8 females for every male, rising to 4.1 for neurosis in New Adam.

TABLE 6.2 Sex Ratio, Female to Male, for Various Indices of Mental Health

Index (From interview statements)	New Adam[a]	Old Bute[a]
Nervous disturbance:		
Severe	3.9	3.9
Moderate	3.5	2.8
Mild	1.8	1.8
Any degree	2.3	2.3
Neurosis	4.1	2.7
Depression	2.6	2.5
Anxiety	2.1	2.7
Fatigue	2.6	2.7
Insomnia	2.5	2.3

[a] 'New Adam' and 'Old Bute' are respectively the new and the old residential areas.

Source: Hare and Shaw (1965).

It also has been shown by Gove (1972) that these differences between men and women apply far more to married than to single people: mental illness is more prevalent among married women than among married men whereas for single people the difference is minimal.

That such sex-related differences should exist is intriguing and several explanations have been put forward. It is possible that biological factors predispose women to these disorders or that social factors make them more vulnerable; it may also be that men and women respond differently to problems or that there are sex-influenced variations in labelling. In this chapter these hypotheses will be considered, a point to bear in mind being that they are not mutually exclusive; on the contrary, it is likely that a combination of factors accounts for the sex differences in mental illness rates.

BIOLOGICAL FACTORS

The possibility exists that sex differences in mental illness rates are due to biological factors. It has been suggested that women have a greater predisposition to neurosis (Rutter, 1970) and to phobic reactions (Marks, 1969). It has been noted that women are especially vulnerable to mental illness during the premenstrual period (Dalton, 1969) and a similar vulnerability during the months following childbirth has been documented. Hysterectomy is also associated with psychiatric illness as was demonstrated by an investigation in which a sample of women who had had this operation were followed up and compared with a control group who had been operated on for another condition (Cholecystectomy). Psychiatric referral was three times as great among the post-hysterectomy group as among the controls.

Although these biological factors point to the greater susceptibility of women to mental disorders they would not seem adequately to account for the bias towards women in mental illness rates nor do they necessarily explain why that bias is far more pronounced among married than among single people. The changing pattern of the sex-distribution of the illness over time also seems to require some other explanation.

THE POSITION OF MEN AND WOMEN IN SOCIETY

The differences in mental illness rates between the sexes may be related to their respective social situations.

The disadvantageous situation of women has received much attention in recent years from social scientists and feminist writers (Oakley, 1972; Chesler, 1972; Laws, 1971). Their work, social contacts, prestige and power have been analysed and found to compare unfavourably with corresponding aspects of the male situation. It has been argued that modern industrial societies impose greater stresses on women and that consequently depression and neurotic disorders are predominantly female disorders. (The relationship between stress and psychiatric disturbances has been noted by many authors and will be discussed in the next chapter.)

In modern Western societies women work at home doing housework, or have employment outside the home, or both. Housework has a number of special features conducive to the development of stress among women. The work entails very long hours and no free days; a woman's overall working week is likely to be far in excess of the average working week in industry. Much of their work is dull, repetitious and uninteresting, and these intrinsic features of domestic work and the conditions under which it is frequently performed act as sources of dissatisfaction. This is now widely accepted and confirmation is found in the work of Oakley (1974) and other authors. Working alone, or with young children as the only company, housewives can become isolated, lonely and cut off from social contacts. Sociological studies often find that an important reason given by women for taking up employment outside the home is their search for companionship and human contacts (Gavron, 1966). Housework has less status than outside employment, and housewives themselves attach less prestige to it. All these factors combine to make domestic work unsatisfactory and to create a stressful environment for many full time housewives.

Work in paid employment also brings stresses peculiar to women workers. Men traditionally occupy the better paid and more prestigious positions. At each level of the occupational hierarchy women are concentrated in the poorer paid, less skilled and auxiliary work (Westergaard and Resler, 1975). The majority of working women either have unskilled jobs in factories and service industries, which are repetitious, carry little intrinsic work satisfaction, and are badly paid, or they work in female-dominated occupations, such as nursing and secretarial work, which have inferior occupational status precisely because of their image as women's work, and because their function is, by definition, auxiliary to the work of men in those fields (e.g. nurses to doctors in hospitals and secretaries to executives in industry). Laws stipulating equal pay for comparable work are of recent origin in Western countries and despite them many women have lower pay, less satisfaction and less work status than their male colleagues. In trained professional and managerial work, women have to become more competitive, to work harder and be better than men, in order to reach comparable positions; the higher those positions the smaller the proportion of women filling them.

Thus, the work situation of women in contemporary Western societies may well cause special stresses leading to neurotic and depressive disorders. The interesting finding that married women have more mental disorder than married men, while there is no corresponding difference among single people (Gove, 1972), can also be explained in terms of relative social positions. The stresses caused by working full time in the home, by lack of companionship, by isolation and by the low prestige attached to housework, all particularly affect married women, especially those with young children. Those who also have jobs outside the home have an additional source of stress in their dual role-obligation: they try to function as employees as well as wives doing domestic work. Information from wives about their husbands' share in housework tends to show that the role of men in this respect is regarded as 'helping' the wife, to whom is accorded the major responsibility for it and child care (Oakley, 1974). Married women in employment have even longer hours and although not isolated and cut off, they experience the stress of two, often conflicting roles: neither outside job, nor domestic work can be given the attention which each commitment would receive without the other.

Although working married women have stresses peculiar to their situation, several studies indicate that it is the housewives who are in the most unrewarding and stressful situation. In an American research concerning the effect of work-status on women's mental health, a group of hospitalised depressed women was studied (Mostow and Newberry, 1975). The sample was matched for age and marital status and it was found that women who had employment outside the home recovered more quickly than the housewives. According to a review of the literature (Nathanson, 1975) working women present fewer symptoms and recover more quickly than non-working women of the same age.

In Britain, a study of mental health in a new housing estate (Hare and Shaw, 1965) revealed especially high rates of neurosis among married women aged between 25 and 45. An important contribution comes from Brown and Harris (1978) whose research will be discussed in more detail in the next chapter. They studied women with psychiatric illness in South London and identified several factors which inclined women to psychiatric disorder, among them the absence of close, intimate relationships, the lack of outside employment and the presence in the home of three or more children under the age of 14.

The importance of employment outside the home for the mental health of women is shown by a research in which stress symptoms of housewives and unemployed men were compared (National Center for Health Statistics, 1970). Here it was found that the two groups had similarly high rates of stress symptoms; isolation from social contacts and a sense of uselessness and frustration may well be common to both of these groups.

Some types of marital relationship may also be more stressful for women than for men: in many marriages the husband is the dominant partner, with more power and greater control of the affairs of the family. Wives without outside employment are in an economically weak situation in so far as they are financially dependent on their husbands. Studies have shown that wives have to do more of the adjusting in marriage (Komarovsky, 1967). As a consequence, their self-esteem and satisfaction are likely to be diminished, increasing their vulnerability to depression and neurosis.

Thus, literature on the position of women gives ample grounds for contending that many women in Western industrial societies find their situations frustrating and unsatisfactory; writers have related this state of affairs to changes in the social structure. For example, Gove (1978) has argued that recent changes in society have worsened the position of women; that women have become more isolated from each other, that their child-bearing and child-rearing roles have been reduced and that uncertainties about alternative roles have grown. British studies have demonstrated that as a consequence of widespread geographical mobility many married women living in new housing developments, often removed from kinship ties, feel lonely (Willmott and Young, 1962).

The attribution of differential mental illness rates to the unfavourable position of women in society and to the peculiar stresses to which they are exposed has a great deal of support from research. Such attribution is not entirely satisfactory, however, because the stresses peculiar to men in modern Western societies have not been similarly investigated; no movement paralleling the feminists has, with equal enthusiasm, studied the position of men. Such a study might well confirm that women's position is more stressful than that of men; but further research is needed before it is possible to state this unequivocally.

An interesting finding which may contradict the differential stress explanation of mental illness rates, relates to the self-reporting of 'happiness' by men and women: studies reveal very little difference between men and women in the degree to which they report that they are happy and satisfied with life. Women profess themselves just as much (or as little) satisfied and happy as do men, yet they have more psychiatric symptoms and are found to have poorer mental health. Feminist writers, concerned about the paradox of 'happy housewives' who nevertheless suffer from depressive and neurotic illnesses, suggest that professed happiness is a form of 'false consciousness'; they argue that women have long been socialised into uncomplaining acceptance of an unsatisfactory feminine role (Bernard, 1972; Chesler, 1971). Accordingly, when asked, women will say that they are happy or satisfied because that is the socially acceptable answer and because they do not admit dissatisfaction even to themselves; while the reality of the situation is manifested in poor mental health.

THE RESPONSES OF MEN AND WOMEN TO ILLNESS

Attempts to account for the higher rates of mental illness in women in terms of biological and social causes are based on the assumption that there exists a genuine sex-related difference in the prevalence of mental illness. However, it could be that the difference is more apparent than real and reflects only the greater tendency of women in general to interest themselves in health matters and consequently to perceive and report their symptoms.

Numerous studies have shown that women read, discuss and know more about health and illness than do men and that they follow medical advice about habits and life-style more readily; women make greater use of medical services and consume more medicines (Mechanic, 1978; Dunnell and Cartwright, 1972; Wadsworth *et al.*, 1971). This greater interest in matters of health and illness may well be related to the biological nature of women: pregnancy, childbirth and menstruation may serve to focus their attention on health-related problems. Moreover, pregnancy, childbirth and child care bring women into contact with doctors and medical services and familiarise them with the approach and thinking of health professionals. Women's traditional role in looking after the health of the family would maintain their interest in such issues. It is, then, very likely, once their interest is aroused and medical contacts have been established, that women continue to be more concerned than men with health matters and consequently more perceptive of symptoms and more inclined to interpret their problems within a health framework.

It has also been suggested that women are the more willing to report their symptoms to doctors because the role of the help-seeker and of the sick is, in many ways, more compatible with the feminine gender role. The sick role is essentially a dependent one: the sick person is in need of help, care and treatment from others. Seeking medical help is to anticipate the sick role and those more willing to assume it would be more willing to report their symptoms. Help-seeking itself places the seeker in a dependent and submissive position as it implies the superior knowledge and skill of the health professional from whom instructions and advice are sought. The traditional expectation that women are dependent and submissive would accord more with the role of help-seeker than would the male role; it can be argued that women are socialised and pressed into accepting the feminine role and thus find it easier to become patients (Chesler, 1972). This argument of role-congruity applies to both physical and mental illness, and would, at least partially, explain why the reporting rate of illness is higher among women than among men.

In a research designed to investigate the effect of the illness-behaviour and attitudes of mothers on the illness-behaviour of their children, Mechanic (1968), found evidence of this sex-role socialisation. In that study, information was obtained from mothers and their children separately; it was found that boys were more likely than girls to feel that they have to behave in a 'stoical' manner and bear pain bravely. Mechanic also reported that male respondents expect their mothers to be less brave and stoical than their fathers. Thus, it can be argued that the culture of Western industrial societies permits women to complain and to think about their health more than it does men, who are expected to be brave and uncomplaining; to 'fuss' about one's health is not considered 'manly'. These cultural expectations, like so many others, are transmitted through socialisation, to the next generation.

Such cultural expectations are also likely to influence the decision to seek help for psychiatric symptoms. Several studies have shown that women are not only more likely to interpret their problems in a psychiatric framework but are also more willing to disclose intimate information about themselves, to talk about the things that distress them, and to discuss especially their anxieties (Phillips and Segal, 1969; Gurin *et al.*, 1960).

In an interesting research Horwitz (1977) demonstrated the differences between men and women in their willingness to discuss their problems with lay and professional people. His study was based on interviews with 120 patients at a community mental health centre in New Haven who were asked to give information concerning the members of their own particular social networks with whom they had discussed the problems which eventually brought them into psychiatric treatment.

As Table 6.3 shows, a consistently higher proportion of women than men patients had talked to their various lay contacts i.e. kin, friends and workmates, perhaps the most striking difference between the sexes being in their use of friends. There was also an interesting sex-linked pattern of communication: in the majority of cases when a patient approached someone (other than a spouse) about problems, a person of the same sex was consulted. Thus, women spoke to sisters, mothers and girl friends, while men, who more rarely spoke to anyone other than their wives, relied on brothers and fathers.

Inability to communicate may result in the problem being 'bottled up' within the sufferer. Even where distress is apparent from behaviour, people coming into contact with the sufferer may be reluctant to initiate discussion about the observable condition. The willingness of women to discuss

TABLE 6.3 Percentage Distribution of Each Sex who Speak to Selected Types of Network Members who Are Available for Interaction

	Men	Women
Spouse	75	84
Parents	40	80
Siblings	40	72
Extended kin	10	31
Friends	27	82
Workmates	19	52

Source: Horwitz (1977).

their problems with members of the lay group results in those problems becoming 'visible' and increases the chance of their being acknowledged and of professional advice being sought. In addition, through talking to relatives and friends women receive more information about the availability of psychiatric services and are thus in a better position than men to utilise them effectively.

Horwitz's study also showed that women are more active than men in seeking professional help from a variety of sources (clergymen, social-welfare agencies, marriage guidance counsellors, etc.) and that they are more willing to define their own problems as psychiatric. In fact, women were twice as likely as men to self-label their problems as psychiatric and to enter psychiatric treatment voluntarily.

Evidence from large surveys conducted in Britain also support the argument that more women than men report symptoms of psychological problems. (Dunnell and Cartwright, 1972; Wadsworth *et al.*, 1971).

It has been suggested that another reason for differential reporting of symptoms is the difference in the social costs of help-seeking for men and women. There are more women than men without paid employment and therefore housewives are better able to attend clinics and surgeries as they are not in danger of losing wages, and are less inconvenienced by restrictive surgery hours or by long waiting. In addition, housewives may go to doctors more often because they take their children and elderly relatives when they need treatment, visits which give them the opportunity to ask advice about themselves. Indeed, some women take children with minor ailments to the doctor as a conscious or unconscious pretext, when they feel unable to seek help directly for their own psychiatric problems (Balint, 1957). However, there are other cases where heavy home commitments, such as having children or old folk to look after, act as a deterrent to women in seeking help for their own problems; Brown and Harris found that many depressed women with young children did not report their problems to doctors.

Thus, all-in-all, women are more likely than men to conceptualise their problems as psychiatric disorder and to take action by reporting symptoms to doctors, and research evidence supports the existence of sex-related differences in reporting. Gove has argued in several papers that there exists a genuinely higher prevalence of mental illness in women than in men, and that the difference is not merely due to variations in reporting (Gove, 1978; Gove and Tudor, 1973; Clancy and Gove, 1974). Gove carried out several studies in the United States, as well as undertaking literature reviews; he is of the opinion that in modern Western industrial nations women suffer more mental illness due to their unfavourable sex and marital roles. Other writers however have said that differences in illness behaviour distort the psychiatric illness rates (Dohrenwend and Dohrenwend, 1969; Mechanic, 1978). The two explanations are not mutually exclusive; women may have higher rates of mental illness than men while their greater readiness to perceive and to report symptoms may still have a distorting effect on the statistics of this illness.

Differences in Responses to Stress

Another, related explanation of differential mental illness rates as between the sexes, has to do with the patterns of their response to stress. It has been argued that such responses divide along culturally-influenced lines, that women develop neurotic and depressive disorders while men become violent, antisocial or alcoholic (Dohrenwend and Dohrenwend, 1976; Mechanic, 1978). Certainly crime, violence and drink-related offences are more often committed by men than women, indeed, the violent man is a cultural stereotype in modern Western societies, as is the neurotic woman. Socialisation would account for men and women responding to stress by culturally expected behaviour.

There is some research evidence to show that as well as adults, children and young people exhibit sex-related differences in problem behaviour. Studies of children indicate that boys are most often referred to Child Guidance Clinics for problems connected with aggression and destruction, while girls are referred for problems connected with excessive fears, worries, lack of self-confidence and feelings of inferiority (Chesler, 1972). As far as young adults are concerned, a study concerning psychological problems among American college students reported similar findings (Mechanic, 1968).

Personality disorder is more prevalent among male than female psychiatric patients (see Table 6.1). It can be argued that if the figures for crime are added to those of mental disorder under a single umbrella of 'deviant behaviour' then the sexes no longer differ in rates of deviance. It is beyond the scope of the present discussion to explore the extent to which crime or violence and depression or neurosis are merely alternative ways of responding to stress (certainly many background and psycho-social correlates of the two types of behaviour are different – see, for example, Rutter and Madge, 1976); but, in general, sex-influenced differences in behaviour exist and are likely to affect responses to problems.

DEFINING MEN AND WOMEN AS MENTALLY ILL

A further explanation of the higher rates of neurotic and depressive disorders in women relates to the social process of defining people as mentally ill. It is argued that both laymen and professionals are more likely to label a woman than a man as mentally ill.

As far as lay people are concerned, it is likely that cultural expectations and stereotyping would incline them to apply this label more easily to women. Traditionally, in Western societies women are regarded as both weak and complaining, and defining them as 'neurotic', 'anxious' or 'depressed' may seem to be peculiarly appropriate. Such definitions can become derogatory labels, used to express disapproval or contempt.

The notion of differential labelling accords with the general arguments of the labelling (or societal reaction) theorists. An important part of their theory is the hypothesis that people in positions of great power and high status in society are less likely to have derogatory or 'deviant' labels applied to them and are more able to reject labelling attempts than those who are relatively powerless (Scheff, 1966). Women in Western societies have lower status and less power than men and consequently are more likely to be labelled as mentally ill.

Horwitz (1977) in his study of the patients of a mental health centre, investigated the process whereby someone's problems are labelled as psychiatric or otherwise by members of the lay social group, prior to the beginning of treatment. He found that women were more likely than men to be labelled by kin group and friends as having psychiatric problems. An interesting finding was that husbands were more likely to be labelled as having psychiatric problems by their wives, than were wives by their husbands. This result may appear, at first sight, to contradict the argument that such labelling is power-related, since the husbands' dominant position in marriage is much emphasised in the literature (Komarovsky, 1967). However, Horwitz found that those individuals who were labelled by their wives as mentally ill were in a less powerful position *vis-à-vis* their wives than is usual in American marriages. For example, men who had lost their jobs before entering treatment had found themselves in a weakened situation, as had husbands whose wives were able to unite with their grown-up children or with their own kin-group (the husband having no available kin living in the area). In such situations wives were able to enforce the definition of their husbands' problems as psychiatric and to insist on treatment. Other than cases where husbands were in a peculiarly weak position, women were much more likely than men to be labelled as mentally ill.

The argument of differential labelling may apply to laymen, but would it also apply to medical practitioners? Is there any reason to think that diagnosis by doctors is influenced by the sex of the patient?

Several authors have put forward the proposition that doctors are more likely to diagnose women than men as 'neurotic' and 'depressed'. For example, Leeson and Gray (1978) remarked that 'From the way the term is used, you might think it is not so much a diagnosis as a moral failing – and we suspect it is often used like that' (p. 159). These authors argue that doctors, in certain situations, apply the label 'neurotic' to women patients who, for some reason, they consider troublesome. There is the situation of the doctor, who has failed to diagnose any physical illness that would account for the patient's complaints, telling the patient that nothing is wrong, saying or implying that she is 'just neurotic'. Then there are women patients who do not seem to the doctor to conform to the female sex stereotypes, for example housewives who complain about being unhappy and isolated in their homes, or who lament the lack of a meaningful career. Some doctors, regarding these women as unnatural and troublesome tell them, explicitly or implicitly, that 'Normal women don't behave like that, you must be neurotic' and that 'You have a lovely home, a good husband and two beautiful children, everything a normal woman could want, and you're not satisfied. You must be neurotic' (Leeson and Gray, 1978, pp. 161–2).

The majority of medical practitioners in Western industrial societies are men and it is often contended that they view their women patients from a distinctly male cultural perspective. Writers from the feminist movement have repeatedly argued that male doctors have a tendency to stereotype and devalue women, and that, more specifically, they diagnose women's problems as psychiatric or psycho-social rather than organic in origin, thereby implying that these problems are of lesser importance (Chesler, 1972; Boston Women's Health Book Collective, 1973). As already discussed, doctors tend to rank psychological problems as being of lesser importance than physical illness; it is possible, therefore, that diagnoses such as neurosis and depression are more easily given and that this tendency, coupled with a predisposition to apply such diagnoses to female patients, misleadingly inflates the rates of psychiatric problems in women.

The attitudes of doctors are shaped by many cultural experiences, such as their childhood socialisation in sex-stereotyping and their occupational socialisation in medical schools. Most medical school teachers, especially high-ranking professors, are men and several writers argue that these medical educators refer to women in a stereotyped and negative way, implying that they are unreliable reporters of symptoms and are beset by such emotionality that their complaints rarely reflect 'real' disease.

The notion of differential labelling by professionals as part of a general picture showing the relatively powerless and unsatisfactory position of women in Western industrial societies is attractive, and intuitively feels 'right', but little hard evidence can be found in favour of it. Horwitz (1977) collected information from interviews and records about labelling by professionals and came to a different conclusion: while a higher proportion of women than men had been labelled as having psychiatric problems, by professionals other than a physician (e.g. by clergymen and marriage guidance counsellors) there was no sex-difference in labelling by physicians. Horwitz's results were confirmed by an American experiment designed to investigate general practitioners' evaluations of symptoms presented by male and female patients. McCranie and his colleagues (1978) used a clinical simulation technique: case descriptions of patients' characteristics, together with their presenting symptoms and the results of preliminary investigations were given to doctors, who were then asked to answer questions about the diagnostic and treatment decisions that they would make in such cases. Two types of complaint were used in this experiment: chronic headache accompanied by generalised weakness and malaise, and chronic abdominal pain accompanied by intermittent diarrhoea. The results of physical examinations which accompanied the case description were within the normal limits. The researchers designed these descriptions to present the general practitioners with a picture open to alternative diagnostic interpretations. The result of this experiment showed that doctors were not more inclined to diagnose symptoms of female patients as indicating psychogenic illness than those of male patients (Table 6.4). For both males and females the doctors favoured predominantly organic explanations. Moreover, the general practitioners exhibited no sexual stereotyping in their judgements of seriousness and prognosis.

It is, of course, possible that in a real face-to-face encounter with a patient, a doctor is influenced by visual and auditory cues such as physical appearance, tone of complaint, expressions used, etc., which are not reproduced in a simulation experiment. Nevertheless, it is difficult to find any hard evidence supporting the argument of sex-stereotyping by physicians.

TABLE 6.4 Psychogenic Versus Organic Diagnoses

	Headache case		Stomach case	
	Psychogenic	Organic	Psychogenic	Organic
Male patients	27%	73%	6%	94%
Female patients	16%	84%	13%	87%

Source: McCranie *et al.*, (1978).

The Influence of Advertisements

Labelling by both laymen and professionals may well be influenced by advertising material. Drug companies powerfully advertise their many new products developed to deal with psychiatric problems. Much of this advertising is aimed at doctors but some is meant for the general public; if sex-stereotyping is communicated by advertisements, labelling processes may well be influenced. Social scientists have recently become interested in the manner in which women are portrayed in advertisements in general, and in advertisements for psychotropic drugs in particular. Aspects of such advertisements that may influence sex stereotyping are the illustrations, which are designed to attract attention, create interest and transmit information. In drug advertising, the illustrations may, by implication, suggest that someone of the sex, age or type portrayed is likely to suffer from the condition which the advertised drug would help. It has been suggested that psychotropic drug advertisements have a sex bias: that they are mostly illustrated with pictures of women patients, implying that women are the ones most likely to be in need of such products.

The style of illustration and wording also matters: researchers have pointed to the existence of sex differences in the content of advertisements. For example, Prather and Fidell (1975) reported that women tended to be portrayed as emotional, irrational and complaining and men as non-emotional, rational and stoical. They also found a tendency to present women's symptoms in a more humorous manner, implying that their health problems are less serious.

However, this stereotyping in advertising may be changing, according to a recent study by Thompson (1979). She analysed drug advertisements depicting either a male or female patient, in two American medical journals (the *Journal of the American Medical Association* and the *New England Journal of Medicine*). Both of these prestigious journals are published weekly and have a wide circulation. Thompson classified the advertisements according to the condition for which the drug was recommended, grouping them as primarily psychogenic, primarily organic and as including both psychogenic and organic elements. As Table 6.5 shows, about two-thirds of the advertisements for drugs dealing with both psychogenic and organic conditions illustrated male figures, emphasising the male patient as the potential user of psychotropic drugs. The sex bias was shown to be the opposite of that found by previous studies.

Thompson carried out a comparison of the sex distribution of patients as portrayed in the advertisements, with the actual sex distribution of those suffering from the condition which the advertised drug was said to ameliorate. She found that even the advertisements for drugs designed to relieve symptoms of depression, anxiety and insomnia, conditions for which more women than men receive treatment, were more likely to contain a picture illustrating a male than a female figure.

The researcher put forward two interesting explanations for

TABLE 6.5 Percentage Sex Distribution of Patients in Advertisements for Drugs by Type of Condition

Type of Condition	Male	Female	Total
Psychogenic	65	35	100% $N = 120$
Organic	66	34	100% $N = 318$
Functional[a]	37.5	62.5	100% $N = 48$
Total	63	37	100% $N = 486$

[a] 'Functional' was the term used for conditions which have both psychogenic and organic roots.

Source: Thompson (1979).

her findings; one is that the American pharmaceutical industry is reacting to pressures from the women's movement to redress previous sexual bias in advertising, the other is that advertisers may believe that female consumption of these drugs is reaching saturation point and that more would be achieved by making the point that male patients too have symptoms needing medication.

Of course, drug advertisements, especially those designed for laymen, are likely to influence not only labelling but the very perception of illness and illness behaviour. Like marketing techniques in other industries, the pharmaceutical industry advertisements tend to create needs which can be filled by the product. People with vague, unorganised problems may see their troubles as 'depression' or 'anxiety' for the first time when they see advertisements for drugs that purport to 'lift' and to 'relieve anxiety'. It can be argued that women are more exposed to drug advertising because of their greater interest in health matters and because they frequent chemist shops and supermarkets more often than men do. Women are thus more likely to buy the advertised medicine, if obtainable without a prescription, and are more likely to present their problems to the doctor in a way influenced by the knowledge that drugs for certain conditions are available.

DIFFERENTIAL USE OF PSYCHOTROPIC DRUGS

So far, the arguments in favour of biological and social explanations of the reported higher incidence of mental illness among women have been considered and also the arguments for the existence of sex-influenced differences in illness behaviour and of differential labelling. One thing remains certain: more women than men become defined as mentally ill and receive treatment for psychiatric problems. It is not easy to separate the various factors which influence the process of becoming defined as mentally ill; a good illustration of the difficulties involved concerns the use of psychotropic drugs.

Several studies have demonstrated that women take more psychotropic drugs than do men, the ratio often suggested being two to one. This drug use is best considered in the perspective of medicine-taking in general in respect of which women are shown to be larger consumers of many different kinds of medicines.

Dunnell and Cartwright (1972) in a national survey of 1,400 people revealed that in Britain women of all age groups consume more medicines than men do and this applies to both prescribed and unprescribed medicines. During a two-week period, prior to interviews, half of the women respondents had taken something prescribed by a doctor compared with less than a third of the men, and three-quarters of the women had taken some self-prescribed medicine compared with three-fifths of the men. Dunnell and Cartwright also asked questions about the use of certain psychotropic drugs; as Table 6.6 shows, more than twice as many women as men had taken a drug of this type during a two-week period.

Investigations conducted into psychotropic drug use in various countries found that women have higher rates of consumption of these drugs than men have; in a community survey in Canada, it was found that the use of tranquilisers and sedatives was 2.2 times more frequent among women (Chaiton, *et al.*, 1976) and a study in Finland has shown that more than two-thirds of the prescriptions for psychotropic drugs went to women (Hemminki, 1974). Recently Cooperstock (1978) studied sex differences in the use of psychotropic drugs in Ontario. Her information was based on

TABLE 6.6 Proportion of Men and Women Reporting 'Sleeplessness' and 'Nerves, Depression and Irritability' and Taking Sedatives, Sleeping Tablets or Tranquilisers

	Men	Women
Proportion reporting sleeplessness	12%	20%
Proportion reporting nerves, depression or irritability	14%	27%
Proportion who had taken sedatives, sleeping tablets or tranquilisers	6%	13%

Source: Dunnell and Cartwright (1972).

computerised records of prescriptions dispensed during 1970–71 and 1973–74 by a prescription insurance agency. According to her findings, a consistently higher proportion of women than men received prescriptions for these drugs; also women were likely to receive larger numbers of prescriptions during a year and were more likely to go on using drugs continuously.

The use of these drugs is the outcome of many steps in a social process. The individuals who eventually become users of them have to experience problems which they interpret as psychiatric; they have to decide to seek medical help; the doctors, in turn, have to diagnose the problems as psychiatric and having done so must prescribe the drug that the patients have then actually to take. The preceding discussion has shown that at every step of this process, women are arguably more likely than men to find themselves continuing along the path that eventually results in their being defined as mentally ill. It is argued that women have more problems in consequence of their more stressful social situations and work roles; that they are more likely to conceptualise their problems as psychiatric and more likely to seek medical aid, and that it is more likely that doctors will define them as having psychiatric problems and prescribe appropriate drugs for them.

The explanation of the higher rates of mental illness in women as compared to men is multidimensional, all the different factors discussed are likely to contribute to it.

CHAPTER 7

Social Class and Mental Illness

Numerous studies have revealed that there exists a strong association between social class and psychiatric disorder; that the highest rates of the latter are to be found in the lowest social groups. According to a review of the literature by Dohrenwend (1975) twenty-eight out of the thirty-three studies that reported data on mental illness by social class came to this same conclusion.

As early as 1855, in a report on insanity in Massachusetts, Jarvis stated that the 'pauper class' contributed sixty-four times as many cases of insanity, in ratio to its numbers, as the other classes (Jarvis, 1855). One of the earliest systematic studies in this century, by Faris and Dunham (1939), showed that in Chicago the areas having the highest mental hospital admission rates were those with the greatest numbers of people in the lowest socio-economic strata – deteriorated and slum areas with many transient and rootless people from the lowest social classes. Since that time this basic finding of the association between low social class and high mental illness rates, has remained remarkably persistent.

The correlation between social class and sickness rates is not confined to mental disturbance but is a feature of health and illness statistics generally. It has often been demonstrated that it is the people at the lowest end of the social scale who suffer most sickness and for whom the risk of early death is greatest.

It is easier to demonstrate the existence of an inverse

relationship between mental illness and social class than it is to explain it: whether causal relationships exist and, if so, their precise nature are as yet unsolved questions.

Perhaps the most internationally famous study designed to collect empirical data about these questions was carried out by Hollingshead and Redlich (1958), the former a sociologist and the latter a psychiatrist, in New Haven, Connecticutt. The location was chosen because of its proximity to Yale University where the two investigators held professorial appointments.

The investigators based their study on a psychiatric census: they included everyone who was in treatment with a psychiatrist, whether as outpatient or hospital inpatient, between 31 May and 1 December 1950, and who was resident of New Haven when entering treatment. The census did not include unidentified and untreated cases, nor was there any attempt to gather information as to the extent of untreated mental illness in the community. Even within this framework the investigators encountered grave difficulties in locating the persons to be enumerated. The main problems were that not all patients received treatment in the locality, (especially the well-to-do who were likely to go to psychiatrists and clinics elsewhere) and that not all psychiatrists and clinics (especially the private ones) were willing at first to disclose their records. By diligent investigation and public relations work and a great deal of travelling and talking to interested parties the researchers eventually received the co-operation of nearly all of the private and public hospitals, clinics and psychiatrists whom they contacted. They were also able to include the inhabitants of the area who received treatment outside it, mostly in adjacent areas but some at famous treatment centres elsewhere in the United States and in Canada. Psychiatric and sociological information was gathered about everyone enumerated in the census: demographic particulars, family, work, and social history, details of diagnosis and treatment were collected. Additionally, detailed case studies of fifty of the patients were carried out.

In order to make comparisons between patients and the general population, a 5 per cent sample of the households in the area was also enumerated, and individuals in these households were interviewed. The two samples were then categorised according to an index of social position, constructed on the basis of education, occupation and area of residence. A five point scale was used (Class I to Class V) and the subpopulations were described in terms of life style, ethnic origin, religion, income and social standing.

Table 7.1 shows that there was a distinct inverse relationship between social class and mental illness: class V contributed many more patients than its proportion of the population warranted; all the other classes contributed fewer. The Table also shows the concentration of the mentally ill in classes IV and V, which accounted for just over 78 per cent of the patients.

Thus, a major finding of this study is that the lowest social class had a much greater rate of identified psychiatric disorder than the other classes. These researchers also found that the association between identified mental illness and social class held whether measured in terms of prevalence, i.e. the number of cases in treatment at the time, or incidence, i.e. new cases coming into treatment.

At the start of the research the authors postulated that a relationship exists between types of mental illness and the patients' position in the class structure, and this, too, was confirmed. The census showed that the association between social

TABLE 7.1 Class Status and the Distribution of Patients and Nonpatients in the Population

Class	Population (%) Patients	Nonpatients
I	1.0	3.0
II	7.0	8.4
III	13.7	20.4
IV	40.1	49.8
V	38.2	18.4
	$n = 1,891$	236,940

Source: Hollingshead and Redlich (1958), p. 199.

class and mental illness was strongest when psychoses, principally schizophrenia, were considered alone.

Another significant finding was that the kind of treatment a patient receives varies with his social class position. The most time-consuming and expensive treatments were given almost exclusively to patients in social classes I and II while class V patients were most likely to be accorded custodial care only.

A follow-up study by Myers and Bean (1968), carried out with the same New Haven patient population a decade later, confirmed these results. Again, it was shown that social class position carried with it an implication as to the clinical course of the disorder. The lower class patients tended to stay in hospital continuously or if released were more likely subsequently to be readmitted than were the higher class patients.

The early studies of social class and mental illness evoked a great deal of interest and were followed by many more during the 1950s, 1960s and 1970s. With increasingly sophisticated methods, investigators tried to ascertain the reasons for the relationship between high rates of mental illness and low social class and several explanations were put forward. These can be categorised under three headings:

1. the 'downward drift' explanation: people who develop mental illness drift down into the lowest social class;
2. the 'environmental stress' explanation: working class environment produces stresses which become causal factors in mental illness;
3. the 'differential labelling and differential treatment' explanation: working class patients are more likely to be labelled mentally ill and less likely to leave the role of mental patient than those from the middle class.

'DOWNWARD DRIFT'

According to the hypothesis of downward drift, people who become mentally ill are unable to hold responsible, important and well-paid jobs and have to undertake work which is less demanding and less skilled. As the illness develops and increasingly damages the person, these individuals have to find occupations which are increasingly simple, less and less demanding and less and less well paid. They 'drift' down the occupational scale. They are also forced to move into poorer housing and to cheaper neighbourhoods where such housing can be found. In other words, a downward social mobility takes place, as a consequence of mental illness.

This explanation says nothing of what causes the individual's mental illness in the first place: whether it was due to genetic, organic or interpersonal factors or whether it was mainly a result of labelling, the argument is that once a person becomes mentally ill, or is so regarded, the downward drift is set into motion. Such a person, who had started life in a middle class family and drifted down the social scale, has experienced downward mobility, whatever the cause of his affliction.

In fact, such a middle class individual would experience downward mobility whether his social standing was compared to that of his parents (intergenerational mobility) or to his own beginnings (intragenerational mobility). Somewhat different may be the position of those who are born into working class families and become mentally ill; it has been suggested that in a society with much intergenerational upward mobility, it is quite possible that healthy members of the working class move upward, leaving behind a 'residue' of less healthy ones. Thus, for those born into the lower social strata, not so much a downward drift, but an experience of being left behind may occur.

In certain ways the drift explanation may be peculiarly applicable to schizophrenia. Individuals with this disorder may withdraw from social contacts and seek isolation, living in lodging houses situated in poor sections of urban areas, in comparative isolation and undergoing long periods of unemployment. Moreover, neighbours living in poor urban areas may be more used to, or more indifferent to, types of behaviour which would seem unacceptable in middle class neighbourhoods.

It is a common clinical observation of psychiatrists that mentally ill patients, especially those with schizophrenic disorders, tend to hold jobs which are considerably below their educational and intellectual level and that they are frequently unemployed. Several researchers investigated the drift hypothesis empirically, trying to find evidence for or against it, and the findings up to date are somewhat contradictory.

Perhaps the strongest evidence in favour of the hypothesis came from a study by Goldberg and Morrison (1963). They obtained data on 509 male schizophrenic patients, aged twenty-five to thirty-four, all first admissions to mental hospitals in England and Wales. Similar to the findings of other studies, a disproportionately high percentage of these patients were in class V (primarily unskilled labourers). The researchers then collected information about the occupation of the patients' fathers, at the time of the patients' birth, and compared it with census data on employed men at the same period. It was found that the social class distribution of the patients' fathers was essentially the same as that of the general population and was not concentrated in class V. Thus, the conclusion was that the schizophrenic sons had drifted down the social scale.

Goldberg and Morrison also carried out a complementary study of male schizophrenics living in outer London; they again found a decline in the occupational status of the patients compared with that of their fathers. The sons' occupational drift had occurred within their own educational and work careers. Interestingly, the most marked drift took place in the case of patients who had been in the highest and lowest social classes. Examples of the former category were patients of good education, who had failed in their attempts to gain university degrees or to build successful business careers and, unable to hold their places, had drifted down the social scale. Patients who were born into families of unskilled workers and who worked in unskilled occupations themselves, also fared badly: it seems that they dropped out of the labour market entirely and became permanently unemployed. It was the patients in middle range employment, having some degree of repetitive skill, who were best able to keep their jobs and least likely to drift down. Goldberg and Morrison attributed the lower social status of the schizophrenic sons as compared to that of their fathers, to the illness itself.

Earlier, Hollingshead and Redlich in their New Haven study also tested the drift hypothesis, but unlike Goldberg and Morrison they found no evidence for it. Hollingshead and

Redlich adopted several approaches to evaluate the hypothesis. They collected information about the geographical mobility of patients and found that most of those who lived in poor parts of the city had always lived there, just as the class I and II patients had always lived in better residential areas and still did at the time of the study. There was no evidence, either, of drift into the poor parts of the city from other parts of the country. The investigators also looked into the possibility of an occupational drift: they compared the patients' class position at the time of the study with the class position of their families during their childhood and adolescence (family of orientation). It appeared that over 90 per cent of the patients were in the same class as their families and Hollingshead and Redlich concluded that neither geographical nor occupational mobility accounted for the concentration of mental illness in the lower social classes.

It is interesting to speculate on the reasons why two studies, both careful, painstaking and meticulously carried out, came up with such contradictory findings. Goldberg and Morrison suggest that a reason may be the different definition of social class used in the two studies: in the New Haven research the residential area of the patients' homes constituted part of the social class index. However, many schizophrenic patients live with their parents in their higher class homes, a factor that would mask the discrepancy between the class of parents and sons in other respects. Other studies, too, are contradictory. For example, the Midtown Manhattan Study (Srole *et al.*, 1962) compared patients' social class (based on occupation, education, income and rent) at the time of the study with the social class of their fathers (based on occupation and education) when the patients were children. They found that 55 per cent of the patients were non-mobile, and of the rest, equal proportions were upwardly and downwardly mobile. Kohn (1979) argues that no evidence for the drift hypothesis can be found, while others, like Dunham (1965) argue that evidence in support is available. There is also a finding that not so much a downward drift but rather a lagging behind (the 'residue' explanation) occurs (Turner and Wagenfeld, 1967).

Thus, the drift explanation has become a matter of sharp controversy, with British workers being inclined to accept the hypothesis for schizophrenic patients, though not for others, while American writers are not agreed even on that. It has to be pointed out that a major difficulty with the quoted studies is that they employed different measures of social class (or socio-economic status) and much of the controversy may be a simple consequence of that.

There is, of course, much evidence to support the drift theory in one sense: once a person becomes a mental patient, i.e., is assigned a social role which is stigmatised and which carries low social status, he moves down the social scale to a position of little prestige and rewards. The social position of the mental patient was discussed previously and the disadvantaged situation of such patients was discussed. The controversy surrounding the drift hypothesis is not about loss of status consequent on the assumption of a stigmatised role, but questions rather whether the concentration of the mentally ill in lower social classes can be satisfactorily explained by downward drift, following the damage done by the onset of mental illness. It must be borne in mind that the drift explanation does not preclude the possibility of other explanations, on the contrary, it is likely that several processes combine to produce the association between mental illness and social class.

ENVIRONMENTAL STRESS

According to the environmental stress explanation, there exists a causal relationship between the environment of lower social class life and mental illness. This explanation (also called 'social causation hypothesis') postulates that certain environmental factors of poor, mainly urban, working class life are excessively stressful and so conducive to psychiatric disorders.

Central to this hypothesis are the notions of stress and stressful life events and the part these play in the causation of mental illness. Mental illness is often seen as the outcome of a combination of causal factors. Schwabb and Schwabb (1978) say that 'For hundreds of years, concepts of mental illness have stipulated that it is the result of remote and immediate causes or, in more modern terms, of predisposing and precipitating factors. The immediate or precipitating causes consist of events and conditions that we now label 'stressful'.

Stress and Stressful Life Events

According to the Shorter Oxford English Dictionary, the word 'stress' is probably a shortened form of 'distress', meaning hardship, straits, adversity, affliction or a force of pressure exercised on a person. In the social sciences, the definition and investigation of stress pose many problems (Dohrenwend and Dohrenwend, 1974). In a narrow sense, the term has been used to refer to externally induced events which can be assumed to be painful or discomforting to most people who experience them. In this sense, a variety of social, personal and physical events can produce stress situations: natural disasters, such as earthquakes or floods; war and battle conditions; illness, injury, pain; crises of life such as bereavement, loss of employment and many others.

This usage of the term raises several questions. There are situations which are not 'externally induced' but which can also be stressful; for example those involving isolation, loneliness and frustration. Also, to include only those events which are distressing or painful to 'most people' begs the question of how many these 'most' have to be: 80 per cent, 90 per cent perhaps? If only experiences that can be assumed to be painful for nearly everyone are included in the concept of stress, then the term may embrace very few situations; only the death of a much loved relative, a life-threatening illness, prolonged hunger and other extremities would be included.

Moreover, given situations and events are distressing to different people in different degrees: the loss of home through a natural disaster is likely to be far more distressing to people whose lives centred around it, whose treasured possessions, full of memories, were in the home and who planned to live there for the rest of their lives, than a similar event would be to people who were not very fond of their house or who regarded it only as a temporary domicile. Thus, ideally, stress events should be studied in relation to the personal meaning they have for particular individuals. This is a formidable research task however; large scale investigations of stress situations become extremely complex if every respondent's personal interpretation of possible stress events has to be separately studied. Most researchers, in the past, settled for some operational definition of stress for the purposes of their particular studies.

Broadening the concept to include any event which is subjectively experienced by someone as painful is also unhelpful. It has been asserted that to be alive is to be under stress, an extreme statement which may have some truth in it, but which hardly helps to define and to operationalise the concept of stress.

In recent years researchers have become much interested in the cumulative effects of discrete, widely-spaced, stressful events on the psycho-social functioning of individuals. Early work in this field was carried out by Meyer, who, without using the term stress, described events which disrupt the lives of individuals and argued that illness was associated with such 'life-events' and that mental illness in particular was a reaction to them (Schwabb and Schwabb, 1978). Meyer described as life events such occurrences as birth and death in the family, moves, success or failure at school or at work, etc. Subsequent researchers have argued a great deal about the sort of occurrences which should be considered as stressful life events.

Much of the research on this subject is concerned only with distressing or discomforting happenings in people's lives (Parkes, 1972; Mechanic, 1962) but some investigators have contended that research should not be restricted in this way, maintaining that it is often impossible to categorise life events as wholly pleasant or unpleasant. Thus, according to Mechanic

> Most events have elements that are both comforting and discomforting. For example, most people will define such changes as getting married, being promoted on the job and moving into a new and more attractive home, as positive, favourable events. But consideration of each of these events reveals considerable challenges which may be discomforting if they tax the individual's abilities and resources. Marriage poses new problems of adjustment and accommodation of

living with another person. A promotion may raise doubts in the person's mind as to his ability to meet the new demands, and they may require, as well, considerable adjustments in routines and work patterns. Moving to a new home may lead to a break away from secure social networks, and require the need to make new friends. Moreover, the process of moving may be arduous and harassing. In short, we must recognise that positive social events may contain components that are significantly discomforting and present the person with challenges that may be trying and which threaten possible failure. (Mechanic, 1968, p. 298)

The central theme of contemporary research on life events is that these constitute a change in an individual's life, necessitating readjustments. This is a very important issue. People's lives are built around routines, and changes which disrupt those routines also disturb people's sense of security. Even when events are viewed in a positive light (*vide* Mechanic) they require the rethinking of values, commitments and choices, a process which may well disrupt the previously unthinking acceptance of routines.

Moreover, not only the event itself, but the anticipation of it may also be disruptive. For a woman anticipating desertion by her husband or the marriage of her daughter (which she feels would leave her lonely or useless) the threat of such an event would constitute a disruptive change.

Researchers not only have the difficulty of deciding what events (or the anticipation of them) to include, they also have considerable methodological problems. One concerns the weight to be attached to particular events. Desertion by a husband or a daughter's marriage may both be disruptive changes, but the meaning and importance attached to them is likely to vary from one person to another; the one event is more disruptive than the other, but how much more? Twice as much perhaps? It is also likely that cultural subgroups, as well as individuals, will attach varying degrees of importance to similar events, according to their values. Difficulties of this sort make the assigning of a weight, or numerical value, to an event very problematic. Nevertheless, attempts have been made to evaluate the significance of various events, and scales of life events and of readjustment have been constructed by investigators (Holmes and Rahe, 1967; Paykel, 1974; Brown *et al.*, 1973).

Another methodological difficulty arises from the retrospective nature of most studies: people are usually questioned about events in their lives long after their occurrence and the researcher is faced with the problem of selective recall and bias by the respondents.

In relating the notion of stress and life events to mental illness, it has been argued that these precipitate or contribute to its onset. There is much evidence in favour of this argument. Investigators have found repeatedly, although not invariably, that a high number of stressful events often precede the onset of psychiatric disorder and appear to have causal importance.

Thus, Brown and Birley studied schizophrenics in London and found support for the hypothesis that life events are of causal significance in the onset of schizophrenia (Brown and Birley, 1968; Birley and Brown, 1970). These researchers made efforts to avoid what they called the 'contamination' of data in retrospective investigations; when studying psychiatric patients it is necessary to guard against not only the usual problems of recall and bias but also the specific post-onset reinterpretations of events. In the light of the subsequent illness people reconsider the meaning of past life events and their own reactions to them and what they are likely to report is the end product of such re-interpretations. More than that, they are likely to exaggerate the stress of past events in an attempt to explain the illness. To overcome this problem, Brown and Birley elicited lists of events in their respondents' lives according to a predetermined schedule, without using the respondents' accounts of what they had thought of the occurrences and how they had reacted to them. The results of this study showed that the patient group had nearly double the number of events per person, compared to a control group drawn from the general population, during the thirteen week period studied.

In what sense can it be said that life events may 'cause' mental illness? Brown argues that

> Two positions can be taken about the causal role of events: one

emphasises the importance of predispositional factors and plays down the influence of events. At most, events are seen as triggering something that would have occurred before long for other reasons. We refer to this as a triggering effect. An event for the most part simply brings onset forward by a short period of time and perhaps makes it more abrupt. The opposing position is that onset is either substantially advanced in time by the event or brought about by it altogether. The event is in other words of fundamental aetiological significance. We refer to this as a formative effect. Of course, triggering and formative effects are opposite ends of a continuum rather than entirely different processes. (Brown and Harris, 1978, p. 122)

Regarding the study with schizophrenic patients, Brown's conclusion is that 'events for the most part trigger florid schizophrenic symptoms in those already likely to break down for other reasons ... events may at times have a formative effect. Some susceptible individuals might never have broken down with schizophrenia without the event in question' (Brown and Harris, 1978, p. 126).

The London Study of Depression

If it is accepted that stress and stressful life events play an important part in precipitating mental illness, then the concentration of the illness in the lower social classes may be explained by the existence of an undue incidence of stress and life events in the working class environment. Two questions arise then: are there more stresses in the lives of people at the lower end of the social scale, and what types of difficulty in that environment are likely to precipitate the onset of mental illness? An important British research on depression provided a great deal of relevant information on these issues (Brown *et al.*, 1975; Brown and Harris, 1978).

Brown and his colleagues based their research on women respondents, living in an Inner London Borough (Camberwell). Two samples were obtained: one consisted of 114 patients with a diagnosis of depression who were undergoing in- or out-patient treatment. The other, the comparison group, consisted of a random sample of 458 women. In both groups the respondents were aged between 18 and 65. The comparison sample was investigated for possible untreated psychiatric disorders, and it was found that 17 per cent of its members were psychiatrically disturbed and a further 19 per cent were considered 'Borderline': the remaining 64 per cent were 'normal'. The women suffering from depression reported clusters of symptoms, such as sleep disturbance, loss of weight, lack of energy, heightened anxiety, etc.

The respondents were categorised in respect of social class, the measure of social class used being based on a ranking of occupations in terms of criteria such as standard of living, education, etc. (Goldthorpe and Hope, 1974). The social class of each woman respondent was classified according to the occupation of her husband or father if she was living with either, otherwise according to her own occupation. The resulting categories were then used to establish two groups: the middle class and the working class group.

The researchers collected a great deal of interview material on life events. As in the previous work by Brown and his colleagues on schizophrenics, in this study too, life events were established according to an arranged list of items and irrespective of how the respondents reported themselves to have felt about the events. But here the researchers also wanted to gather information about the meaning attached to life events by the respondents; they asked the women what the occurrences meant to them, and about their responses thereto. The study period was the nine months prior to the interview for non-patients, and the same length of time before the onset of the illness for patients. Life events were rated in terms of severity according to the threat they implied.

The basic results of the research showed that an association between life events and depression existed: events categorised as 'severe' were almost four times more common among patients than among normal women during the period studied. In addition to life events, information was collected about ongoing 'difficulties' in the respondents' lives and these were also found to be closely associated with depression: major difficulties were three times more common among the patients than among the normal women.

A case history cited by Brown and Harris will serve to illustrate an 'event'.

> Mrs. Ferguson, a married woman of 51 with two adult children living at home, was one of the seventy-three women admitted as an in-patient. Her husband told her one day 'out of the blue' that he was having an affair. Before this she said she had no reason to think her marriage was not 'fine'. She said she had suspected nothing. Almost at once she said she felt depressed. She began to cry a great deal and did so every day. She felt life was not worth living and she thought carefully about various methods of committing suicide. She began to feel guilty and in some way responsible for the failure of her marriage. She sweated a good deal and generally felt tense. These symptoms came on within a week or so of the event and for the next five to six months she gradually got worse. (Brown and Harris, 1978, p. 111)

Here, clearly, was an 'event'. In contrast, examples of ongoing difficulties included: a son's drug-taking, living in a damp flat, receiving unpleasant letters from a parent about living with a man, being forced to move from a house to furnished rooms because of non-payment of rent, and a son who was caught several times stealing from local shops. Both events and difficulties were more numerous in the patient group.

Much information was collected about the relationship between social class and depression. The survey showed large class differences: depression was much more common among working class than among middle class women. To determine the meaning of this association, however, was a complex matter.

On analysing the samples according to age, marital status and number of children, an interesting finding emerged: there was no class difference in the risk of developing depression among women without children. Among those with children at home, working class women were much more likely to suffer from a psychiatric disorder, the proportion being about one in five compared with about one in twenty in the comparable middle class group.

When the researchers examined the class distribution of events and difficulties they again found that there was a class difference only among women with children; women without children at home showed no class difference in the number of their problems. An interesting part of the research is concerned with the particular problems which are more common in the lives of working class women, and is of special relevance to the argument that lower social class life is very stressful. It appears that it is in the realm of 'household events' that the class difference is really manifested. The researchers listed some life events for working class women: being given a month's notice to quit her job in a laundry; husband losing his job; husband sent to prison; son in trouble with the police; notice to quit flat; threatened with eviction by landlord; court appearance for not paying rent; forced to have an unwanted abortion because of housing conditions. Household events for middle class women were of a rather different nature: finding her husband had got involved with a women at work; husband staying away for a week; a son having to go to a special school because he was backward; husband discovering her affair; builders working on their house leaving owing them money (pp. 162–3). The life events experienced by working class women were more numerous, more severe and of a type clearly related to their economic and social situation. The research finding concerning the 'difficulties' of the women was the same: the most unpleasant difficulties were experienced more commonly among working class women, and, more importantly, their difficulties lasted longer, because they were less easy to resolve. Interestingly, here it is not only household difficulties which show class differences but also another category: health difficulties.

One of the surprises of this research was that although there existed such a distinct class difference in the number and severity of the life events and difficulties experienced by the women, this alone did not explain the class difference in depression. When comparable groups of working class and middle class women, who had children and who had experienced similar numbers of events and difficulties of equal severity, were examined separately, the working class women were still four times more likely to develop depression than were their middle class counterparts. To explain this greater vulnerability some other factor, related to social class, had to be at work.

Brown and Harris indicated four factors which make women vulnerable to depression. The first concerned the general question of social support, and in particular the notion that it is important for a women to have a close, intimate relationship with someone in whom she can confide, especially about things which trouble her. The researchers found that women who had such an intimate tie (usually with husband or boyfriend, but possibly with a woman friend or sister) were less vulnerable to depression than those without such a tie. The other vulnerability factors were: loss of a mother before the age of 11, having three or more children under 14 living in the house and lack of employment outside the home.

It can be argued that several of these factors are class-related. Researchers on marriage and family life have documented the loneliness of many working class wives; for example, in a study of American working class marriage, Komarovsky (1967) described the lack of communication and intimacy between many husbands and wives. Wives in this study frequently reported that they did not discuss with their husbands their dissatisfactions and troubles, but kept their worries to themselves. Working class couples are more likely to have segregated marital roles, i.e. to have separate duties and responsibilities as well as separate leisure activities and social relationships (Bott, 1957). This is especially so during the years of child rearing; the woman's world is then centred around the care of young children and household tasks, in which the husband, in a segregated marriage, does not participate. It is likely, then, that the isolation of the housewife and her lack of social contacts (also discussed in the previous chapter) are particularly severe for working class wives.

These same wives are also most likely to experience the second vulnerability factor indicated by Brown and Harris, i.e. having three or four children under fourteen in the home. There are more children, often coming close together, in working class families, which accentuates the difficult position in which working class married women find themselves. Loss of one's mother before the age of eleven, the third factor, is also class-related. It is in the working class, where the risk of early death is greater, that children are more commonly left without a mother in their early years.

Brown and Harris themselves found that these three vulnerability factors were more common among working class women, although they found no evidence of class difference in respect of the fourth factor; employment outside the home.

A further interesting finding was that as far as close ties are concerned the situation of both working and middle class women improves with age. As they get older and the children grow up, relationships with their husbands become closer. Women are also more likely to develop social ties outside the home once they cease being too preoccupied with young children. A class difference was found in these matters also: the level of intimate relationships was higher at all life stages among middle class women than among working class women.

To summarise: the study of Brown and his colleagues has shown that working class women have a higher risk of depression, due to the greater number of severe life events and major difficulties experienced by them, problems concerning finance, housing, husband and children being especially important. These women are additionally vulnerable because of the likelihood of their having experienced certain vulnerability factors, that, although not capable of producing depression of themselves, were found to increase the risk when life events and difficulties were present.

Stress and Social Class

Several investigators found an association between the number of stressful life events experienced by psychiatric patients and their social class background. These studies are not entirely comparable to the London research on depression (or, indeed, to each other) because the diagnostic categories and the definition of events varied a great deal. However defined though, stressful life events occur more frequently in the environment of people at the lower end of the social scale.

An important longitudinal study was carried out by Myers and his colleagues in New Haven (Myers *et al.*, 1974; Myers *et al.*, 1975). They interviewed a community sample of 720 randomly selected adults about events, both desirable and undesirable, which brought about changes in their lives. They found that the greater the number of events experienced by an individual during the year prior to the study, the greater the likelihood of his developing psychiatric illness. Moreover, an increase in the number of events was associated with a worsening of symptoms while a decrease was related to an improvement. This finding was true for all social classes and there was no significant class difference in the number of events respondents experienced. However, the ratio of undesirable to desirable events was also related to symptoms and this was quite different for the various social classes. Upper class subjects had just as many events as those in the lower social classes, but a significantly larger proportion of their life events were pleasant and desirable. From a follow-up study by Myers and his colleagues it seems that respondents who experienced numerous events and still did not develop psychiatric symptoms were more common among the upper classes; conversely, those who developed psychiatric disorder despite experiencing relatively few events were more likely to be in the lower classes. The investigators reported that catastrophic events, outside the control of the individual, were especially important for the development of psychiatric illness.

Of particular interest in Brown and Harris's research was their finding that the severe life events which precipitated depression were of the type closely linked to economic problems. Brown and Harris called these 'household events' because they were centred around the home and the family. It is noteworthy that the preponderance of these events was connected with insecurity of housing, insecurity of employment and the involvement of husband or child with law-enforcement agencies. This suggests the possibility that it is the insecurities of working class environment which act as special stress agents.

Insecurity has traditionally been a part of working class life and an element of insecurity and unpredictability is still an inherent component of this environment today (Westergaard and Resler, 1976). A good illustration of this is the case of unemployment, which has been shown to be related to psychiatric hospitalisation (Brenner, 1973). In a review of the literature, Liem and Liem (1978) show that unemployment is a most important source of stress: it is closely connected to loss of self-esteem and deterioration of personal relationships. Loss of work and income give rise to self-blame and to estrangements from friends and relatives, thus combining financial and psychological pressures. These stresses apply to the unemployed of all classes; but the risk of unemployment is greater for manual workers than for white collar employees and the consequences can be considerably harsher. At the lowest end of the occupational scale, unskilled workers have much higher rates of unemployment than skilled manual or non-manual workers. (Rutter and Madge, 1976).

Insecurity in working class life goes much beyond unemployment: uncertainties about housing and income are also more common in this environment. In Britain, Westergaard and Resler argue that insecurity and unpredictability are partly connected to the composition of the manual worker's wage packet: one-third of the income comes from overtime earnings, premiums for shift-work, and unsocial hours, etc., which are unpredictable. Penalty if the worker is sick, exclusion from employer-run security schemes, are part of the picture.

> Above all, the contrast remains striking between the 'life cycles' of ordinary workers and those of managers, executives, professionals and some sections of the salariat below these levels. ... This contrast between the flat life cycle of workers, descending into or near poverty in old age, and the incremental and promotional curve which the bourgeois life cycle typically follows – underlines the insecurity of working class life. (Westergaard and Resler, 1976, p. 95)

It seems then that life events concerning employment and housing are part of the stress of working class life. This also appears to be the case with the problem of husbands or sons being involved with law-enforcement agencies, a circumstance often mentioned by women respondents in the London study of depression. Crime and delinquency among young people (where it is most frequent) is a predominantly working class event, more usual among youngsters who are sons of manual workers than in those from middle class homes (Rutter and Madge, 1976).

Thus, certain features of working class life are likely to be excessively stressful. However, as Brown and others have demonstrated, the concentration of psychiatric problems in this environment is not entirely explained by reference to the presence of stress: at any given level of stress, people in the low social classes are more likely to develop psychiatric illness than those of higher social position. Brown and Harris explained this by pointing out that special vulnerability factors are at work. It can also be argued that the explanation lies in the differences in the type of events experienced and in how effectively people can deal with stress (Dohrenwend and Dohrenwend, 1969). Working class people are in a weak position in this respect because the stress-producing situations they face are less alterable by individual action than those most often encountered by middle class individuals. Stress in the working class environment most often arises from structural economic factors over which individuals have little control, and moreover, they have fewer resources, in money and power, to mitigate the consequences of stressful events.

It has also been suggested that working class life may limit people's internal resources to cope with problems. For example, Kohn (1979), writing about the concentration of schizophrenia at the lower end of the social scale argues that individuals in that class have a characteristic conception of the external world: a fearful and fatalistic belief that one is at the mercy of forces beyond one's control and even understanding. This orientation, according to Kohn, is too limited and too rigid for dealing effectively with stressful situations and reduces the ability of such people to cope. This argument comes very close to the view that a distinct lower working class 'culture' exists (a 'culture' of poverty and deprivation) which conditions people to be apathetic and unable to cope with problems of life. This view however is not supported by evidence (besides being derogatory and dismissive of the very real problems); on the contrary recent research points to its untenability. If there is inability to cope in the environment of lower social class life, this is far more likely to be the consequence and not the source of existing problems.

Geographical Differences

Adverse features of working class life can vary according to type of environment. Several studies have found geographical differences in the rates of mental disorder: in general, rates are higher in densely populated urban areas of low social status and lower in long-established rural communities. The pioneering study in Chicago in the 1930s, by Faris and Dunham (1939), showed that the majority of psychiatric patients admitted to a state mental hospital had come from the inner city. This area was described as poor, overcrowded and disadvantaged, providing a harsh social environment. The implications of this study awakened the interest of many researchers in the possible influence of poor urban environment on mental illness and raised the question of whether there are certain characteristics of poor inner city environments that, by themselves, may cause or precipitate mental illness and that are not present in the rural environment.

It has been argued that social cohesiveness, a sense of belonging to a community, is characteristic of the type of environment associated with mental well-being: in well established communities, there is a lesser incidence of mental disorder than in areas which lack such cohesiveness. This was argued by the Leightons in their famous *Stirling County* studies (A. H. Leighton, 1959; D. C. Leighton *et al.*, 1963). These studies were conducted in a predominantly rural county in Nova Scotia, and the fundamental hypothesis of the investigators was that a community's integration or disintegration is related to the mental health of its population. The studies were based on more than 1,300 interviews with a randomly selected sample of respondents. The authors found that psychiatric illness was more frequent at the lower end of the social scale and that it was more common in depressed, disintegrated slum areas than it was in integrated, socially cohesive areas.

The Stirling County studies were conducted in different types of rural areas; subsequent researchers compared rural and urban environments. In Britain, Rutter and his colleagues examined the rates of psychiatric disorder in inner London and the Isle of Wight, the latter being an area of villages and small towns (Rutter *et al.*, 1975a,b). Their study was based on interviews conducted with representative samples of the general population in the two areas, using the same measurement methods in both. They showed that psychiatric disorder was twice as common in inner London as on the Isle of Wight. Moreover, this difference between the rates of disorder applied generally to long-time residents of the respective areas just as much as to the others, so that a 'drift' to London by the mentally ill could be eliminated. Respondents in the study who lived in London experienced more problems of poor housing and overcrowding than those living in the Isle of Wight, but this difference was not enough to explain the higher mental illness rates in London. The authors suggested that there exists some additional disadvantage of living in inner city areas, which creates stress. London has a considerably higher population turnover and a higher proportion of immigrants than the Isle of Wight, factors that would affect the social cohesiveness of the area. Short-term residence in a neighbourhood and the consequent lack of integration into it may well create stresses precipitating psychiatric problems.

Perhaps the most important question which arises concerns the relationship between social class and geographical area: do inner city stresses operate across the social scale or do they affect any particular social classes more than others? In order to answer this question, Brown and his colleagues compared their data on psychiatric disorder among women living in London with similar data obtained in North Uist, a rural area in the north of Scotland (Brown *et al.*, 1977). North Uist is an island (about sixty miles from the Scottish mainland) and the majority of the women respondents in the study were born and bred there. There is a traditional culture which is slow to change, perhaps because of the relative isolation of the community. The majority of the people live in crofting and fishing households and the community is well integrated.

The researchers used the same methods of measurement in London and North Uist thus ensuring the comparability of their data. They found, as expected, that psychiatric disorder was higher in London than in the island. A most interesting part of their findings was that, in contrast to London where social class was related to psychiatric illness, in North Uist there was no difference between the rates of disturbance for working class and middle class women. A similar connection between class and area was mentioned by Rutter, who found no significant association between social class and rates of mental illness on the Isle of Wight, while in London the association was considerable (Rutter *et al.*, 1975a,b). It seems therefore that working class women are more vulnerable than middle class women to mental illness in the inner city areas but that this is not so in rural communities. Moreover, there was no marked difference in mental illness rates between middle class women living in cities and rural areas: whether in inner London, the Isle of Wight, or in North Uist the risk of mental illness for middle class women was similar.

Thus, these studies indicate that it is the association between social class and mental illness in the cities that has to be explained. It is quite possible that there is a certain kind of stress which is felt particularly by working class women living in cities; housing problems, unemployment, trouble with police and general insecurity, all of which typically affect the working class, are urban problems. These troubles are exacerbated by the lack of social cohesiveness in these areas, thus becoming the 'inner city stresses' of working class people.

It is also argued that urbanisation may increase the rate of mental illness because of the social changes associated with it. For women, urban life has meant the loss of traditional functions and importance: in earlier times their responsibility for household work, such as cooking, marketing and sewing made their contribution to the family far more important than similar work can be in a contemporary urban environment, where ready made articles and 'convenience' foods are available. In rural areas, like North Uist, women face fewer such changes and have retained in greater measure the security of traditional roles. For men also, role changes and disruptions of long-established patterns are associated with industrialisation and urban living. This argument is suggested by Hagnell, whose studies in a predominantly agricultural district of Sweden showed that for both men and women who moved to a large city the risk of developing mental illness was greater than for those who stayed in rural areas (Hagnell, 1966).

Interestingly, in his surveys in Sweden, Hagnell found no social class difference in mental illness rates similar to those demonstrated by North American and British investigators. Even in towns, the risk of becoming mentally ill was distributed much more evenly across the social classes, if anything the lower risk being found in the lower occupational groups. It is possible, as Hagnell suggests, that a more egalitarian system produced these results: people in the lower occupational groups in the study area saw themselves, and were seen by others, as middle class. It is also possible that the worst of the working class problems associated with mental illness, such as insecurity and deprivation in housing, employment, etc., had been eliminated in Sweden (Leighton *et al.*, 1971).

DIFFERENTIAL LABELLING AND DIFFERENTIAL TREATMENT

This explanation of the relationship between rates of mental illness and social class is concerned with the social processes by which people become defined as mentally ill and with the treatment accorded to them after they are so defined. It is argued that people from the lower end of the social scale are the most likely to become defined as mentally ill and encounter most difficulties in returning to normal social roles. It is suggested that the apparent concentration of mental illness among people of the working class is greater than the real prevalence of it would warrant.

There are several different components of this explanation which often become intertwined. Regarding the process of becoming a mental patient, it can be argued that given psychiatric problems of equal severity, people from poor, deprived homes are more likely than those in better circumstances to be admitted to a mental hospital. Medical and welfare authorities, when deciding whether to recommend admission, take into consideration the circumstances of the individual; bad housing, lack of money and absence of available family to care for the patient render more likely the decision to admit to hospital. Patients whose psychiatric problems come to light through the police and the courts are also more likely to be sent to hospital if they are of low social class background: legal authorities would feel that such individuals are not likely to enter treatment and to pursue it unless as hospital in-patients. In some cases, diagnosis and referral to treatment may seem to a psychiatrist as the more desirable and liberal alternative to a prison sentence.

From a different perspective, labelling theorists say that the psychiatric label, like other stigmatising labels, is most likely to be applied to those who are powerless to resist it. In this framework, psychiatric treatment is a punitive way of dealing with those who offend and it is argued that authorities are more likely to victimise and to stigmatise the weak. Similarly, lay people in authority, e.g., employers, are seen as exhibiting a discriminatory readiness to perceive signs of mental illness in working class behaviour. Thus, according to this explanation, the concentration of mental illness in the lower social classes is a consequence of the greater chance of such people becoming defined as mentally ill.

Hollingshead and Redlich (1958) in their New Haven study found considerable evidence of a tendency by authorities to perceive and appraise behaviour according to the social class background of individuals. They cited the case histories of two adolescent girls of similar behaviour. A class I girl came to the attention of the police when, after 'one of her frequent drinking and sexual escapades', she became involved in a traffic accident while drunk. Her family arranged for bail and returned her to school where it was discovered that she was pregnant. A doctor was called in with a view to abortion, but he refused and recommended psychiatric treatment. The girl started psychotherapy; eventually her baby was placed for adoption, and she continued in treatment with a highly regarded psychoanalyst.

By contrast, a class V girl came to the notice of the police when she had been observed to have intercourse with several sailors from a naval base. She was arrested and sent away to be 'reformed'. In the institution she created such disturbance that a psychiatrist was called in, but he later reported that the girl's 'inability to communicate' with him on most subjects and her 'crudeness' made her unsuitable for psychotherapy (Hollingshead and Redlich, 1968, pp. 175–6).

This illustration shows not only that the class I girl was dealt with differently (i.e., her family arranged for bail and for a private psychiatrist) from the class V girl, but also that psychiatric treatment itself can vary according to the patient's social class. This was in fact a major finding of Hollingshead and Redlich; they showed that prolonged psychotherapy (including psychoanalysis) was given almost exclusively to class I and II patients. This type of therapy is very expensive and time-consuming, much more so than treatment by drugs or electric shock, which was given to patients in the lower social classes. Moreover, psychotherapy requires a certain amount of verbal skill on the patient's part which is more likely to be found in the well educated. Psychiatrists tend to choose higher class, well educated people for this treatment, assuming that lower class people would lack the aptitude to participate. This assumption may well be correct for a different, though allied, reason: Hollingshead and Redlich argued that cultural differences in value orientation between psychiatrists and lower social class patients presented a serious obstacle to psychotherapy as psychiatrists were unable to understand and to communicate with these patients.

In some sophisticated urban circles of America, psychotherapy has become associated with high social status, and with mild rather than severe disturbance; with verbal skills and pleasant hours spent on the couch of the analyst (Kadushin, 1969). Not surprisingly, this treatment carries far less stigma (if any) than a stay in a mental hospital and drug treatment. Those who are able to afford it will understandably obtain the more pleasant and less stigmatising treatment and thus will not appear in the records of mental hospitals and mental health clinics.

In Britain, where medical services are freely available, it has often been demonstrated that middle class people are able to make better use of them because they are more informed, have more contacts and demand better services (Cartwright and O'Brien, 1976). In addition, private treatment is available for those who are able to pay the fees or who belong to private insurance schemes. Thus it can be argued that upper and middle class people with more resources, are better able to avoid treatment in mental hospitals and clinics.

Differences in social and economic resources (education, money, knowledge of the system, etc.) play another part in differential treatment and labelling: more resources promote prompt and effective action to obtain psychiatric help. Higher social class patients are likely to enter into treatment early, when the disorder is not yet very severe, at a stage when the illness may be treated without the individual becoming defined as a mental patient. By contrast, those with fewer resources, lacking knowledge of the world of psychiatry, may not obtain professional help until the symptoms are severely disruptive. Hollingshead and Redlich found that people in classes I and II were considerably more aware of psychological problems than those in classes IV and V. 'The lower status patient will attribute his troubles to unhappiness, tough luck, laziness, meanness or physical illness rather than factors of psychogenic origin. The worst thing that can happen to a class V person is to be labelled 'bugs', 'crazy', or 'nuts'. Such judgement is often equal to being sentenced for life to the 'bughouse' (Hollingshead and Redlich, 1958, p. 175).

Thus, there are several reasons why the association between lower social class people and rates of treated mental illness may be over-emphasised by differential definitions and treatment, and the fact that many higher social class people with psychiatric problems may receive help but still not appear in official statistics. Similarly, differential patient-management would play a part at the stage of discharge from treatment. Psychiatric personnel are much more willing to discharge a patient to a comfortable home where life is not harsh than to a poor, deprived home; indeed, this is why reports on home circumstances are taken into consideration. It has been suggested that lower social class patients stay in hospital longer and have a greater chance of becoming institutionalised (Fied, 1975). Decisions concerning discharge may also be influenced by the hospital staff's expectations regarding the patient's medicine-taking behaviour. Often, patients can be returned to their homes on condition that medication continues: the patient has to follow instructions concerning prescribed medicines. Psychiatrists might expect the better educated, higher class patient to have more understanding of medication and of the importance that doctors attach to it; they would also expect the relatives of such patients to be more reliable in ensuring that their instructions were observed. Therefore, the middle class patient would have a greater chance of being discharged from hospital quickly. Studies have demonstrated that working class patients tend to stay in hospital longer than higher class patients with the same condition (Fied, 1975), and this too influences differential definitions of people as mental patients.

CHAPTER 8

The Expansion of Psychiatric Problems

In the first chapter of this book the difficulty of answering the question: 'Who is mentally ill?' was discussed and in subsequent chapters social definitions of, and responses to, mental disturbance were examined. During these discussions the comment has been made more than once that norms of behaviour and thinking are not static but change constantly. Sociologists are especially interested in changing patterns and one trend in particular has lately been attracting attention, namely that increasingly more personal and social problems are being interpreted within a psychiatric framework. In other words, the boundaries of psychiatry are being stretched, by laymen and professionals alike.

THE EXPANSION OF MINOR PSYCHIATRIC SYMPTOMS

It has been argued that the threshold at which the problems and discomforts of daily life become unacceptable is, as it were, being progressively lowered. In modern industrial societies people's expectations regarding standards of living have been and are rising. In Western countries people have come to accept comfortable housing, an abundance of consumer goods, a variety of food and clothing produced for the mass market, shorter working hours, longer annual holidays (often spent abroad), clean working conditions and so on, as no more than the ordinary entitlement of the average citizen. A range of welfare and social provisions such as pensions, unemployment and sickness benefits and a longer full-time education are also aimed at making life more problem free for each successive generation. In other spheres increased knowledge of medicine, pharmacology and medical technology have combined to solve many health-related problems; changes in the legal system, such as easier divorce and legal aid, also have the intention of making life easier. These and other developments have all added to a general feeling that troubles can be overcome and that more advances, more inventions, more wealth, would lead to a situation where fewer and fewer difficulties would have to be borne. The argument is not so much of a life genuinely becoming free of problems (after all, plenty of problems remain, especially for some sections of the population) but rather of a general expectation that problems are capable of solution, if not at present, then in the future. What Parsons called a commitment to an indefinite progress in Western societies, has become general (Parsons, 1951).

Adding to this commitment, a proliferation of various professional 'helpers' – health workers, social workers, counsellors, advice bureaux – has developed, all with the aim of easing problems; and the availability of these professionals has added to the feeling that all difficulties should be amenable to solution by some means or other. Many of these helpers emphasise that people should be able to spend their lives happy and satisfied, that it is the 'quality of life' that matters; teachers tell their pupils, nurses tell young mothers and career advisors say to job-seekers that the 'important thing is that you should enjoy what you do'.

In this climate of expectation of a problem-free, happy, satisfied life, understandably the feeling creeps in that if one is not entirely happy, if one feels depressed, anxious or tense, then something is wrong, that such feelings are not natural or normal and something should be done about them.

Of course it can be argued that heightening expectations of a good life constitutes a desirable trend: people should be freed from the harsh conditions experienced by many during the early and middle years of the industrial era; there should be more to human existence than endless worry over lack of food and shelter. It is something to be glad of that people can turn their minds to the quality of life rather than having to concern themselves about sheer survival. The trouble is that expectations of a completely problem-free life cannot be fulfilled, there are some problems which have no solutions and have to be borne; moreover, higher standards and rising expectations and demands bring new problems in their train. Leisure can lead to boredom, mobility to loss of community and the prolongation of life to loneliness in old age.

One result of higher expectations is that people turn to their doctors with a range of minor physical and psychological symptoms which previously seemed to be acceptable parts of daily life. General practitioners in Britain complain that patients frequently consult them unnecessarily, with trivial problems (Cartwright, 1967). Not only frequently unimportant physical symptoms but also a variety of minor psychiatric symptoms such as sleeplessness, feelings of depression, worry, irritability, anxiety, etc., are reported.

Nor is it the expectation of a problem-free life alone that

Figure 8.1

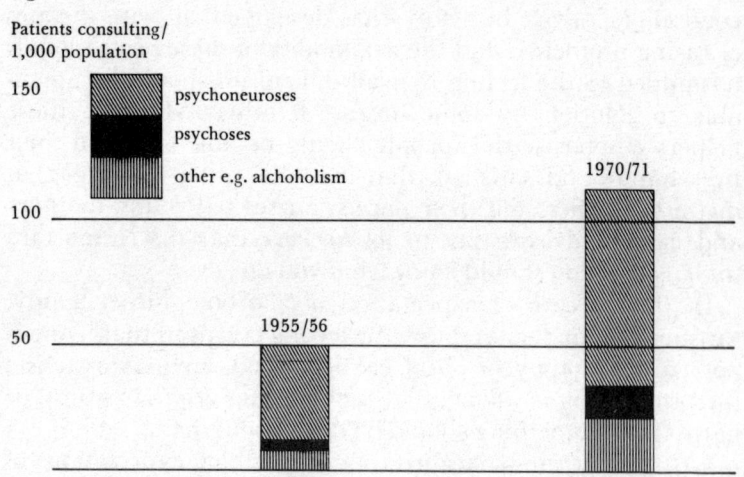

Patients consulting/
1,000 population

- psychoneuroses
- psychoses
- other e.g. alchoholism

1955/56
1970/71

Source: Office of Health Economics, 1975.

fosters this trend, but also the knowledge that remedies are available. It is widely known, among lay people, that drugs are available to help one to sleep, to relieve tension and worry, and to lift depression; magazine articles, advertisements, television and radio programmes all transmit information about these medicines, and consequently it seems worth while to complain to the doctor about symptoms that these remedies might alleviate.

While, undoubtedly, consultations for minor psychiatric problems have increased, it is not easy to find reliable historical evidence as to the extent of this increase. The difficulty is that past records of family doctors are often inaccessible and unsophisticated, diagnostic terms used by the doctors have changed and in any case, there exist considerable variations of diagnoses, especially where ill-defined conditions of psychological origin are concerned. So a meaningful study of consultation patterns over a long period of time is not really possible. However, indications of recent changes (during the last two decades) and of present patterns can be found.

Perhaps the most dramatic picture of changes over time is that given by the two National Morbidity Surveys carried out in England and Wales (the first in 1955–56 and the second in 1970–71); these showed that the number of patients consulting their general practitioners for mental disturbance more than doubled during the fifteen-year period between the two surveys.

The consultations illustrated in Figure 8.1 include those for both minor and major disorders and there are reasons for the increase in both. For example, the modern tendency for shorter stays in psychiatric hospitals and the maintenance, in the community, of patients suffering from disorders of a greater degree of severity than hitherto has meant that many more psychiatric patients are in the charge of general practitioners. However, consultations for minor conditions increased more than those for severe conditions; within the psychoneurosis category the diagnosis of 'neurotic depression' was given twenty times more frequently and the category of 'other e.g. alcoholism' had also increased substantially by the time the second survey was conducted. Michael Shepherd and his colleagues in their study of psychiatric illness in general practice in the London area found that 10 per cent of the patients consulting general practitioners were diagnosed as suffering from a 'neurotic' disorder (Shepherd *et al.*, 1966).

The increase in consultations goes hand-in-hand with an increase in the consumption of psychotropic (i.e. mind-affecting) drugs. The vast majority of general practice consultations, for whatever complaint, end with patients receiving prescriptions (Cartwright, 1967). It is not surprising then that so many patients complaining of minor psychiatric problems leave the consulting room with a prescription, usually for a sedative, tranquiliser or anti-depressant. There has been growing concern in recent years regarding the large quantities of psychotropic drugs being consumed. In their survey concerned with medicine takers and prescribers, Dunnell and Cartwright (1972) asked some 1,400 people in Britain about their consumption of medicines and found that a tenth of their sample had taken a sedative (which term included tranquilisers and sleeping pills) during the two-week period prior to the interview, and a further 1 per cent had taken an anti-depressant. The main reason people gave for taking sedatives was sleeplessness; about half of the drugs were taken for this reason and another 30 per cent for 'nerves', 'depression' or 'to calm me down'. Thus, the majority of those taking psychotropic drugs were doing so for minor, ill-defined complaints. In this survey only 16 per cent of psychotropic drugs were being taken for specific psychiatric conditions or for diseases of the central nervous system.

Dunnell and Cartwright found that sedatives and antidepressants had been taken by more people in the survey population than any other category of drug that is obtainable only on prescription from a medical practitioner (94 per cent of the psychotropic drugs in the survey were prescribed); moreover, many of these drugs were taken regularly by respondents, two-thirds had been taken every day during the fortnight prior to the interview. Also, the majority of these drugs were taken over long periods, many for more than a year.

Studies conducted in other Western countries showed similar results; a survey in Western Europe revealed that the proportion of people using a tranquiliser or sedative was 17 per cent in Belgium and France (Balter, 1974) and it has been calculated that in Denmark every person is prescribed a dose of tranquiliser every second or third day (Laurence and Black, 1978).

As the majority of psychotropic drugs are obtainable on prescription only, there has been much concern over the alleged tendency of general practitioners to 'over-prescribe' these medicines. In Britain, one in five of all National Health Service prescriptions are for tranquilisers, sedatives or anti-depressants. Perhaps the most graphic description of the size of the problem is that in England and Wales in one year (1970) 47 million prescriptions were issued for these three types of drugs, that is, one for every man, woman and child (Parish, 1971). During the 1960s and 1970s the number of prescriptions issued for psychotropic medicines in Britain shot up and in the United States, Australia and Canada the trend was similar (Office of Health Economics, 1975; Cooperstock, 1978).

Why do general practitioners issue such large numbers of prescriptions? It can be argued that they, like their patients, adhere to the expectation that life should be more and more problem-free; that they, too, are influenced by the availability of the preparations. Also, doctors are committed, by their training and professional orientation, to actively helping the patient who seeks their assistance. When faced with a patient complaining of mild psychiatric problems (caused perhaps by some temporary domestic upset or work difficulty) the doctor may well prefer prescribing a medicine to sending the patient away unaided. Writing a prescription may also be a relatively easy way for a hard-pressed doctor to terminate the consultation and to satisfy the patient's demands, as has been suggested by researchers (Stimson and Webb, 1975).

It seems, also, that in the British National Health Service repeat prescriptions for psychotropic drugs are frequently issued by general practitioners. This means that a patient can obtain a repeat of the prescription by writing for it, or by applying to the doctor's receptionist, without seeing the doctor. Large numbers of repeat prescriptions save the doctor's time. Dunnell and Cartwright found that tranquilisers, sedatives and anti-depressants were often obtained by patients in this way: more than a third of these medicines had been obtained on prescriptions repeated ten times or more; other researchers, e.g. Balint and his colleagues (1970) had similar findings. The doctors in these studies tended to under-estimate the number of repeat prescriptions they were issuing, and appeared surprised and embarrassed when they realised the extent thereof. Balint suggested that a large number of repeat prescriptions indicated a failure of communication between doctor and patient.

Some commentators have argued that very active advertising by pharmaceutical companies has pressed family doctors into prescribing large quantities of psychotropic medicines and has fostered inappropriate prescribing habits (Parish *et al.*, 1973; Stimson, 1975). General practitioners seem to be unsophisticated in diagnosing psychiatric problems and lack the knowledge and experience which would enable them to make the best use of psychotropic drugs – this was a finding of Shepherd and his colleagues (1966).

There are several reasons why the large consumption of psychotropic drugs, taken for minor conditions, causes concern. An obvious consideration is the hazard of drug-dependency and chronic intoxication; another is that the side effects of these medicines are not sufficiently known to the prescribing doctors and even less to the patients. Dunnell and Cartwright found that people taking drugs were remarkably badly informed about the possible side effects, few respondents could recall having been told about not driving a car or taking alcohol, etc.

Some important general criticisms have been made of the trend of increasing consultations and prescriptions for minor psychiatric symptoms. A strong case against the 'medicalising' or 'psychiatrising' of problems was made by Ivan Illich (1975), whose books have achieved popularity and found a wide readership. Illich points out that people are becoming increasingly dependent on doctors and drugs and unable to cope with personal problems unaided. This is an important issue and other commentators have taken it up. If the expectation of a problem-free life, and reliance on external help for problem-solving, possibly through drugs, becomes even more widespread, people will reach for the medicine bottle each time they are faced with difficulties. Illich argues that current thinking, encouraged by the medical practitioners, assumes that personal problems can be overcome with medical help; but many problems cannot be solved by doctors and falsely pretending that they can be, only results in concealing the problems and preventing people from finding solutions. Unfortunately for this argument, Illich goes much beyond it and suggests a total 'deprofessionalisation' of health and illness, a situation where people cope with pain and sickness without medicine. He seems to postulate an idealised hypothetical society where medicines are replaced by some other, and better, form of healing art. He is a great believer in self-reliance, but he takes it to a point with which few people would agree, advocating the abandoning of pain-killers entirely, and citing people in previous societies who dosed themselves with alcohol, or stoically bore their sufferings. Many important points made by Illich have therefore become somewhat discredited; nevertheless, at the core of his arguments is the concern, shared by many, that too much dependence on doctors and drugs is undesirable and that, especially, the consumption of psychotropic drugs for minor conditions should be watched.

Of course, dependence on medical help is not synonymous with dependence on drugs, as there are other methods of treatment. A doctor may decide that psychotherapy is more suitable than drugs; but this treatment is less extensively used because it is time-consuming, expensive, and requires special expertise.

Some general practitioners are interested in providing psychotherapy, or some form of counselling, in preference to prescribing psychotropic drugs. In Britain, Balint had a strong influence in this direction; he advocated that family doctors should set aside time for therapeutic sessions with those of their patients who go to the surgery frequently, complaining of symptoms of vague psychological origin, and needing some supportive therapy (Balint, 1957). A minority of British general practitioners, in fact, do set aside consultation time for psychotherapy.

It is a further criticism of drug use that it may conceal the underlying problem of the patient and represents a misdirection of therapeutic effort. For some patients psychotherapy may be appropriate and issuing tranquilisers may serve to conceal the fact that it is not available. It has to be borne in mind though that many patients are greatly helped by drugs even if the underlying problems are not solved. For example, if a woman's depression and sleeplessness are due to marital troubles, e.g., an alcoholic husband, then prescribing sedatives for her, while it will not get to the root cause of the difficulty may nonetheless, by enabling her to sleep at nights, help her to cope with her difficulties and perhaps lighten her depression.

Whatever treatment the patient receives, the fact that the doctor gave a diagnosis and started a treatment has social implications. The individual becomes a patient, his hitherto unorganised feelings of worry or irritability or sleeplessness have been accounted for and explained by the diagnosis and a medical legitimisation for being ill has been given. The argument against organising and legitimising vague, unspecified symptoms into illness by attaching a diagnostic label to them is that the person may abandon responsibility for his behaviour and problems, which he will then attribute to the illness, and may settle into a long-term sick role. This can happen in the case of physical illness too: the doctor may, by giving a diagnosis, confer an illness and the consequent sick-role on someone who, without it, would continue with ordinary social activities. However, the diagnosis for vague unorganised symptoms can have positive consequences; the individual whose complaints, worries or fears have appeared unreasonable and irritating to those around him, may find more sympathy and understanding after illness has been diagnosed and treatment begun.

An important consideration in the provision of treatment for minor psychiatric problems is the cost involved: in the British National Health Service the cost of psychotropic drugs has risen dramatically and accounts for a large proportion of the total drug bill. Psychotherapy provided on an individual basis is even more expensive; on financial grounds alone, an indefinite increase in this kind of treatment cannot be contemplated.

Over-Reporting and Under-Reporting

Thus, there are several reasons for the concern expressed regarding the increasing tendency of people to consult the doctor about minor psychotic symptoms: it adds to the medicalising trend, reduces ability to cope with problems, promotes dependency and is very expensive. The curious thing is that while many people go to the doctor with minor complaints, others with far more serious mental disturbances, do not. In Chapters 2 and 3 the various stages of becoming a mental patient were discussed and it was shown that people are often very reluctant to interpret their problems within a psychiatric framework; that they tend to deny, normalise and accommodate even serious psychiatric symptoms and visit the doctor as a last resort. A similar situation exists in respect of physical illness: it is often said that laymen and doctors evaluate symptoms differently. Symptoms which appear serious to the doctor would not necessarily seem serious to the layman, and vice versa. Doctors and patients have different backgrounds (one is an expert the other is a layman) and view the symptoms from different perspectives: the patient evaluates the importance of his own symptoms according to the requirements of his own life. Freidson calls this difference in perspective the 'separate worlds of experience' and it is not surprising that the evaluation of a symptom as worth taking action on or not is hardly ever a complete 'fit' between doctor and patient (Freidson, 1973).

However, in the case of mental illness there are additional considerations. The possibility that one may be losing one's mind, and going mad, is extremely frightening – one of the most frightening things that can happen to a person. Understandably, the individual concerned tends to deny this possibility, minimise the problems and avoid consulting a doctor. The analogue might be a frightening physical disease, like cancer, for which people often postpone seeking help out of fear of receiving a positive diagnosis. On the other hand, complaints of sleeplessness, or of feeling depressed or anxious are not associated with losing one's mind, and madness; these are not frightening, and consulting the doctor would not be postponed out of fear.

Another consideration is the stigma of mental illness (discussed in Chapters 3 and 4) which makes for concealment: mental illness is often kept a secret and is under-reported to professionals. People seek treatment for it if they can do so privately, without public knowledge, since the use of the psychiatric service itself is stigmatised, and there is likely to be considerable delay in consultations. By contrast, the symptoms of feeling depressed, worried or anxious are no more stigmatising than lesser physical complaints. People would go to the general practitioner with no expectation of a psychiatric diagnosis or referral to a psychiatrist; receiving a prescription for tablets from the doctor would confirm the essential similarity of their problems to physical complaints.

DISAPPROVED BEHAVIOUR AS MENTAL DISTURBANCE

Consultations and treatment for minor psychiatric complaints, then, constitute one area in which psychiatric interpretations are being expanded; another such area is the management of socially disapproved behaviour. It was pointed out previously (in Chapter 1) that behaviour which violates social norms, i.e. deviant behaviour, can be interpreted in different frameworks; it can be regarded, for example, as a crime against the law of the land, a sin against God's commands, an offence against ritual purity, a sickness. Societies vary a great deal in the categories of deviance they employ and in the emphasis they place on them; for example, in medieval Europe, an offence defined in religious terms was regarded as the most serious type of deviation.

Sociologists have argued recently that in contemporary Western societies more and more types of deviance are interpreted in a health and sickness framework and that in particular, psychiatric interpretations are increasingly used. For several types of deviant behaviour 'sickness' is now the appropriate label whereas in the past similar behaviour would have been categorised as 'sin' or 'crime'. Freidson argues that 'disapproved' behaviour is more and more coming to be given the meaning of illness requiring treatment rather than of crime requiring punishment, victimisation requiring compensation, or sin requiring patience and grace.

> As late as the nineteenth century, medicine was a relatively unimportant institution, humble before the majesty of religion

and law. But with the growth of medical science, more and more human behaviour began to seem to stem from specific 'causes' over which prayer, human choice, and will had little control. And medical discoveries allowed the successful treatment of such problems. From this core of scientific discovery grew a vague halo of authority that encouraged the wholesale extension of medical definitions of deviance into areas of behaviour previously managed by religion and law. (Freidson, 1973, p. 248)

Several examples illustrate the shift towards interpreting deviance in a psychiatric framework. Alcoholism is one such example; what was called heavy drinking in the past and was dealt with by police if the drunkard was troublesome and offensive, is now increasingly seen as alcoholism, that is, an illness, by laymen and professionals alike. (Robinson, 1976). In many countries special units have been established in the charge of psychiatrists, for the treatment of alcoholism. Homosexual behaviour is another example: in earlier times it was regarded as an illegal deviant behaviour and dealt with by law-enforcement agencies. Now, such behaviour (provided it involves consenting adults only) is legal in many Western countries and is increasingly considered to be a type of mental disturbance. Anti-social behaviour which causes harm to others is yet another example. The murderer, the violent man who beats his child or wife, the woman who steals someone else's baby, clearly belonged to the domain of the law in earlier times. Now, there is a growing tendency to regard them as mentally disturbed. As Freidson argues:

> The increasing emphasis on the label of illness, then, has been at the expense of the labels of both crime and sin and has been narrowing the limits if not weakening the jurisdiction of the traditional control institutions of religion and law. Indeed, my own suspicion is that the jurisdiction of the other institutions has been weakened absolutely because the thrust of expansion of the application of medical labels has been toward addressing (and controlling) the serious forms of deviance, leaving to the other institutions a residue of essentially trivial and narrowly technical offenses. (Freidson, 1973, p. 249)

Perhaps Freidson overstresses the situation, as many major types of deviant behaviour are dealt with by law-enforcing agencies; however, his general theme of a shift towards psychiatric definitions is a valid one. There are several reasons for this shift. There has been a change in public opinion towards more humanitarian, less harshly punitive methods of dealing with offenders. People in Western societies are shocked at the thought of punishing a thief by cutting off his hand; the harsher forms of prison sentences have been abolished as has flogging; the death penalty is rarely used and in the United States has been categorised as a cruel and unusual punishment. By and large, despite occasional calls for harsher punishment in response to some particularly repulsive crime, people like to feel that offenders are dealt with humanely, preferably by doctors or by social workers of one kind or another.

Barbara Wooton has argued that

> in the contemporary attitude towards anti-social behaviour, psychiatry and humanitarianism have marched hand in hand. Just because it is so much in keeping with the mental atmosphere of a scientifically minded age, the medical treatment of social deviants has been a most powerful, perhaps even the most powerful, reinforcement of humanitarian impulses. (Wotton, 1959, p. 206)

Another reason for the shift towards psychiatric definition is the previously mentioned availability of psychotropic drugs; these have been successfully used for a variety of conditions and, as with minor psychiatric complaints, laymen and professionals alike are anxious to take advantage of pharmaceutical achievements. A curious situation arises here; the fact that a treatment exists that can successfully change a condition or a behaviour seems to be taken as an indication that the condition or behaviour for which it is applicable, is, indeed, an illness. To quote Anthony Flew, in his critical essay: 'That some human condition could be altered by psychiatric treatment, is not sufficient reason for saying that that condition is mentally diseased' (Flew, 1973, p. 88). There are many conditions that can be altered by drugs and that are not illness in any lay or professional sense: the contraceptive pill prevents a woman from conceiving a child, but nobody would argue from this that being able to conceive is an illness. To draw the conclusion that the conditions of alcoholism, child-battering, homosexuality, or for that matter, sleepless nights, irritability or worries (as discussed previously) are psychiatric disorders, only because they can be effectively altered by psychiatric treatment, is illogical. But exactly this notion creeps in: people, learning about new medicines dealing with such problems, reinterpret those problems as illness, about which it is worth consulting a doctor.

A related point concerns the psychiatrists. They have shown an interest and willingness to take over several types of cases of deviant behaviour. They do so partly because the problems happen to be the particular interest of some of them and also because of that 'activity orientation' and commitment to help patients, previously mentioned. The fact that psychiatrists are willing to accept patients with certain types of problematic behaviour leads to the notion that the behaviour must be an 'illness' and the management of it, a 'treatment'. This is also a quite illogical notion: at the extreme it would lead to the idea that all conditions that doctors deal with are illnesses, which is manifestly false, as consideration of the doctor's function in childbirth makes apparent. But however illogical the argument, people are willing and keen to interpret conditions as illness if they think that so doing will resolve the problem with which they are grappling.

There are a number of reasons why an expansion in psychiatric interpretations of deviant behaviour gives concern to social scientists. One is the fear that once started on that path, the frontiers of psychiatry and definitions of mental disturbance can be limitlessly stretched. Not only can all the most serious types of anti-social behaviour (like major violence against the person) be regarded as signs of mental disturbance, but the more minor offences and, indeed, all types of conduct deemed as undesirable by some sections of a society. Increasing expansion of the mental disturbance concept can lead to increasing social control in the name of mental health; and to a reduction in individual freedom. Indeed, the main fear of critics of the trend is that liberty will be lost and unacceptable tastes, unpopular preferences or disfavoured views will be taken as signs of disturbance. According to Flew:

> Since everyone's health is presumptively and in itself good for him, anyone who promotes the health of someone else must be

presumed to be his benefactor; and so any opposition to the treatment which the experts prescribe as necessary in their patients' own interests can only be the outcome surely of inexpert ignorance. The wider the scope of the concept of health, the wider the scope for such not necessarily welcome beneficence. If psychological health is admitted as well as physical, then that area must be extended correspondingly. If we further proceed to construe health in general, and psychological health in particular, as positive ideals not definable in terms solely of the absence of the corresponding sorts of diseases, then 'mentally healthy' is almost bound to become a commendatory characterisation of some favoured life-style; and then the more or less forcible imposition of that life-style, being now a matter simply of health, cannot but be seen as for everyone's own good.

There is of course no general objection to forming positive ideals or to recommending favoured life-styles. The objection is to doing such in themselves perfectly proper things in covert and illicit ways. To introduce any notion of mental health here is to pretend to endow your own chosen values with the independent and final authority of objective science. More subtly, it must be to discount as merely symptomatic utterance whatever might be said in favour of alternative recommendations. (Flew, 1973, p. 48)

Of course, the fear is that it is the most powerful sections of a society which will be able successfully to define what is undesirable conduct and what is the less favoured life-style; and they will be able to control, in the name of good mental health, those who offend against their definition. Moreover, the offenders will be able to protest a great deal less if regarded as mentally disturbed. But all laymen will be in an ever weakening position if their conduct is judged in terms of standards laid down by medical experts. Freidson especially expressed concern at the strengthening of professional control over laymen, which 'Can remove from laymen the right to evaluate their own behaviour and the behaviour of their fellows – a fundamental right that is evidenced in the hard-won fight to interpret the Scriptures oneself, without regard to dogmatic authority, in religion and the right to be judged by one's peers, in law' (Freidson, 1973, p. 250).

Thus, the fears expressed concern the reduction of freedom,

the growing power of 'expert' doctors, the increase in social control and the ensuring of conformity to the norms of a powerful minority. These same fears are also the concern of anti-psychiatrists, foremost amongst them Thomas Szasz, whose views were discussed in Chapter 1. But anti-psychiatrists argue not just that the concept of mental illness has been over-extended and abused, not even that the concept is potentially wide open to increasing over-extension and abuse, but rather that it has no proper application at all, that there is no such thing as mental illness, an untenable view in the eyes of most of the workers in this field and one which creates more problems than it solves.

Concern can be more appropriately expressed over the potential dangers of the 'psychiatrisation' of problems, until the point is reached when all minor symptoms and misconducts become suitable for some form of treatment.

References

Chapter 1

Arthur, R. J. (1971) *An Introduction to Social Psychiatry*. Harmondsworth: Penguin Books.
Balt, J. (1972) *By Reason of Insanity*. London: Panther.
Barnes, M. and Berke, J. (1971) *Mary Barnes: Two Accounts of a Journey Through Madness*. London: MacGibbon and Kee.
Bateson, G., Jackson, D., Haley, J., and Weakland, J. (1956) Towards a theory of schizophrenia. *Behaviour Science*, **1**, 251–64.
Bean, P. (1979) Psychiatrists' assessments of mental illness: A comparison of some aspects of Thomas Scheff's approach to labelling theory. *The British Journal of Psychiatry*, **135**, 122–8.
Becker, H. S. (1963) *Outsiders: Studies in the Sociology of Deviance*. New York: Free Press.
Butler, J. R. (1970) Illness and the sick role. *The British Journal of Sociology*, **21**.
Clare, A. (1976) *Psychiatry in Dissent*. London: Tavistock.
Cooper, D. (1970) *Psychiatry and Anti-Psychiatry*. St. Albans: Paladin.
Coulter, J. (1973) *Approaches to Insanity: A Philosophical and Sociological Study*. London: Martin Robertson.
Flew, A. (1973) *Crime or Disease?* London: Macmillan.
Freidson, E. (1973) *Profession of Medicine: A Study of the Sociology of Applied Knowledge*. New York: Dodd and Mead.
Goffman, E. (1961) *Asylums: Essays on the Social Situation of Mental Patients and Other Inmates*. Harmondsworth: Penguin Books.
Gove, W. R. (1970) Societal reaction as an explanation of mental illness: an evaluation. *American Sociological Review*, **35**, 873–84.
Gove, W. and Fain, T. (1973) The stigma of mental hospitalisation. *Archives of General Psychiatry*. **28**, 494–500.
Hirsch, S. R. and Leff, J. P. (1975) *Abnormality in Parents of*

Schizophrenics: A review of the Literature and an Investigation of Communication Defects and Deviance. London: Oxford University Press.
Hope, K. (1976) Comments on a study of depression in women. *Sociology*, 10, 321–23.
Laing, R. D. (1959) *The Divided Self.* London: Tavistock.
Laing, R. D. (1961) *The Self and Others.* London: Tavistock.
Laing, R. D. (1967) *The Politics of Experience.* Harmondsworth: Penguin.
Laing, R. D. and Esterson, A. (1964) *Sanity, Madness and the Family.* London: Tavistock.
Lemert, E. M. (1951) *Social Pathology.* New York: McGraw-Hill.
Lidz, T., Fleck, S., and Cornelison, A. R. (1965) *Schizophrenia and the Family.* New York: International University Press.
Lemert, E. (1964) Social structure, social control and deviation In M. Clinard (ed.), *Anomie and Deviant Behavior.* New York: Free Press.
Office of Health Economics (1979) *Schizophrenia.* London: OHE.
Rosen, G. (1968) *Madness in Society.* Chicago: University Press.
Rosenhan, D. L. (1973) On being sane in insane places. *Science.* 179, 250–8.
Roth, M. (1976) Schizophrenia and the theories of Thomas Szasz. *British Journal of Psychiatry*, 129, 317–26.
Scheff, T. J. (1966) *Being Mentally Ill: A Sociological Theory.* Chicago: Aldine.
Sedgwick, P. (1973) Illness – mental and otherwise. *The Hastings Centre Studies*, 1, 19–40.
Szasz, T. (1960) The myth of mental illness. *American Psychologist*, 15, 113–18.
Szasz, T. (1961) *The Myth of Mental Illness.* New York: Harper.
Szasz, T. (1971) *The Manufacture of Madness.* London: Routledge.
Wing, J. K. (1973) *Schizophrenia: Medical and Social Models*, quoted by A. Clare: *Psychiatry in Dissent.*
Wing, J. K. (1975) (ed.), *Schizophrenia From Within.* London: National Schizophrenia Fellowship.
Wing, J. K. (1978) *Reasoning About Madness.* London: Oxford University Press.

Chapter 2

Balt, J. (1972) *By Reason of Insanity.* London: Panther.
Barnes, M. and Berke, J. (1971) *Mary Barnes.* London: McGibbon and Kee.
Bott, E. (1957) *Family and Social Network.* London: Tavistock.

Bott, E. (1971) Family and crisis. In H. Freeman (ed.), *Towards Community Mental Health*. London: Tavistock.

Cartwright, A. (1967) *Patients and Their Doctors*. London: Routledge.

Cartwright, A., Hockey, L., and Anderson, J. (1973) *Life Before Death*. London: Routledge.

Creer, C. and Wing, J. K. (1974) *Schizophrenia at Home*. London: National Schizophrenia Fellowship.

Dunnell, K. and Cartwright, A. (1972) *Medicine Takers, Prescribers and Hoarders*. London: Routledge.

Eaton, J. W. and Weil, R. J. (1968) 'The Mental Health of Hutterites'. In S. P. Spitzer and N. K. Denzin (eds). *The Mental Patient*. New York: McGraw-Hill.

Freidson, E. (1973) Profession of Medicine: *A Study of the Sociology of Applied Knowledge*. New York: Dodd and Mead.

Goffman, E. (1961) *Asylums: Essays on the Social Situation of Mental Patients and Other Inmates*. New York: Doubleday.

Hammer, M. (1968) 'Influence of Small Social Networks as Factors on Mental Hospital Admission'. In S. P. Spitzer and N. K. Denzin (eds) *The Mental Patient*. New York: McGraw-Hill.

Horwitz, A. (1977) Social Networks and Pathways to Psychiatric Treatment. *Social Forces*, **56**, 86–105.

Horwitz, A. (1978) Family, kin and friend networks in psychiatric help-seeking. *Social Science and Medicine*, **12**, 297–304.

Kadushin, C. (1968) *Why People go to Psychiatrists?* New York: Atherton.

Korsch, B., Freeman, B., Negrete, V. F. and Daws, M. (1968) Gaps in doctor–patient communication. *Pediatrics*, **42**.

Mechanic, D. (1968) *Medical Sociology*. New York: Free Press.

Mills, E. (1962) *Living With Mental Illness*. London: Routledge.

Rabkin, J. (1974) Public attitudes toward mental illness – A review of the literature. *Schizophrenia Bulletin*, **10**. 9–33.

Sampson, H., Messinger, S. L., and Towne, R. D. (1968) 'Family Processes and Becoming a Mental Patient.' In S. P. Spitzer and N. K. Denzin (eds) *The Mental Patient*. New York: McGraw-Hill.

Scheff, T. J. (1966) *Being Mentally Ill: – A Sociological Theory*. Chicago: Aldine.

Schwartz, C. (1957) Perspectives on deviance: wives' definition of their husbands' mental illness. *Psychiatry*, **20**, 275–91.

Stimson, G. and Webb, B., (1975) *Going to See the Doctor: The Consultation Process in General Practice*. London: Routledge.

Wadsworth, M., Butterfield, W. J. and Blaney, R. (1971) *Health and Sickness: The Choice of Treatment*. London: Tavistock.

Wing, J. K. ed. (1975) *Schizophrenia from Within*. London: National Schizophrenia Fellowship.

Yarrow, M. J., Schwartz, C., Murphy, H. and Deasy, L. (1955a) The psychological meaning of mental illness in the family. *Journal of Social Issues*, **11**, 12–24.

Yarrow, M., Clausen, J. A. and Robbins, P. (1955b) The social meaning of mental illness. *Journal of Social Issues*, **11**, 33–48.

Zola, I. K. (1973) Pathways to the doctor. *Social Science and Medicine*, **7**, 677–89.

Chapter 3

Balint, M. (1957) *The Doctor, His Patient and the Illness*. London: Tavistock.

Bean, P. (1979) Psychiatrists' assessments of mental illness: A comparison of some aspects of Thomas Scheff's approach to labelling theory. *The British Journal of Psychiatry*. **135**, 122–8.

Brown, G., Bone, M., Dalison, B., and Wing, J. K. (1966) *Schizophrenia and Social Care*. London: Oxford University Press.

Cumming, E., and Cumming, J. (1957) *Closed Ranks: An Experiment in Mental Health Education*. Cambridge: Harvard University Press.

Dohrenwend, B. P., and Chin-Song, E. (1967) Social status and attitudes towards psychological disorder: The problem of tolerance of deviance. *American Sociological Review*, **32**, 417–33.

Elinson, J., Padilla, E. and Perkins, M. (1967) *Public Image of Mental Health Services*. New York: Mental Health Materials Center.

Freidson, E. (1973) *Profession of Medicine: A Study of the Sociology of Applied Knowledge*. New York: Dodd and Mead.

Goffman, E. (1963) *Stigma: Notes on the Management of Spoiled Identity*. New York: Prentice Hall.

Goldberg, D. and Blackwell, B. (1970) Psychiatric illness in general practice *British Medical Journal*, **2**, 439–43.

Gove, W. R. (1970) Societal reaction as an explanation of mental illness: an evaluation. *American Sociological Review*, **35**, 873–84.

Halpert, H. P. (1969) Public acceptance of the mentally ill. *Public Health Reports*, **84**, 59–64.

Hollingshead, A. and Redlich, R. C. (1958) *Social Class and Mental Illness*. New York: John Wiley.

Holmes, D. (1968) *Changes in Attitudes about Mental Illness*. Center For Community Research, New York. (Mimeo)

Kadushin, C. (1969) *Why People Go to Psychiatrists*. New York: Atherton.

Lemert, E. M. (1951) *Social Pathology*. New York: McGraw-Hill.

Lemkau, P. V. and Crocetti, G. M. (1962) An urban population's opinion and knowledge about mental illness. *American Journal of Psychiatry*, **118**, 692–700.

Mechanic, D. (1968) 'Some Factors in Identifying and Defining Mental Illness.' In S. P. Spitzer and N. K. Denzin (eds) *The Mental Patient*. New York: McGraw-Hill.

Mills, E. (1962) *Living with Mental Illness*. London: Routledge.

Nunnally, J. (1961) *Popular Conceptions of Mental Health: Their Development and Change*. New York: Holt, Rinehart and Winston.

Parsons, T. (1951) Social structure and dynamic process: The case of modern medical practice. In T. Parsons, *The Social System*. New York: Free Press.

Parsons, T. (1958) Definitions of health and illness in the light of American values and social structure. In E. G. Jaco (ed.), *Patients, Physicians and Illness*. New York: Free Press.

Parsons, T. and Fox, R. C. (1968) Illness, therapy and the modern American family. In W. Bell and E. F. Vogel (eds.), *A Modern Introduction to the Family*. New York: Free Press.

Phillips, D. L. (1968) Rejection: a possible consequence of seeking help for mental disorders. In S. P. Spitzer and N. K. Denzin (eds.), *The Mental Patient*. New York: McGraw-Hill.

Rabkin, J. (1974) Public attitudes towards mental illness – A review of the literature. *Schizophrenia Bulletin*, 10, 9–33.

Sampson, H., Messinger, S. L. and Towne, R. D. (1968) Family processes and becoming a mental patient. In S. P. Spitzer and N. K. Denzin (eds.), *The Mental Patient*. New York: McGraw-Hill.

Scheff, T. J. (1966) *Being Mentally Ill – A Sociological Theory*. Chicago: Aldine.

Shepherd, M., Cooper, B., Brown, A. C. and Kalton, G. W. (1966) *Psychiatric Illness in General Practice*. London: Oxford University Press.

Swarte, J. (1969) in H. Freeman (ed.), *Progress in Mental Health*. London: Tavistock.

Tringo, J. L. (1970) The hierarchy of preference toward disability groups. *Journal of Special Education*, 4, 295–306.

Wing, J. K. ed. (1975) *Schizophrenia from Within*. London: National Schizophrenia Fellowship.

Yarrow, M. J., Schwartz, C., Murphy, H., and Deasy, L. (1955A) The psychological meaning of mental illness in the family. *Journal of Social Issues*, 11, 12–24.

Chapter 4

Angrist, S., Lefton, M., Dinitz, S., and Passamanick, B. (1968) *Women After Treatment: A Study of Former Mental Patients and their Neighbours*, New York: Appleton.

Bord, R. (1971) Rejection of the mentally ill: Continuities and further developments. *Social Problems*, **18**, 496–509.

Brown, G. W., Monck, E. M., Carstairs, G. M. and Wing, J. K. (1962) Influence of family life on the course of schizophrenic illness. *British Journal of Preventive and Social Medicine*, **16**, 55–68.

Brown, G. W., Bone, M., Dalison, B. and Wing, J. K. (1966) *Schizophrenia and Social Care*. London: Oxford University Press.

Brown, G. W., Birley, J. L. T. and Wing, J. K. (1972) Influence of family life on the course of schizophrenic disorders: A replication. *British Journal of Psychiatry*, **121**, 241–58.

Cumming, J., and Cumming, E. (1968) On the stigma of mental illness. In S. P. Spitzer and N. K. Denzin (eds.), *The Mental Patient*. New York: McGraw-Hill.

Freeman, H. E. and Simmons, O. G. (1968) Mental patients in the community: family settings and performance levels. In S. P. Spitzer and N. K. Denzin (eds.), *The Mental Patient*. New York: McGraw-Hill.

Goffman, E. (1963) *Stigma: Notes on the Management of Spoiled Identity*. New York: Prentice Hall.

Gove, W. R. (1970) Societal reaction as an explanation of mental illness: an evaluation. *American Sociological Review*, **35**, 873–84.

Harris, R. (1978) Why I am browned off with quantitative methodology: A comment on Brown, Birley, Wing, Vaughn and Leff. *Medical Sociology News*, **5**, 4–9.

Kirk, S. A. (1974) The impact of labelling on rejection of the mentally ill: An experimental study. *Journal of Health and Social Behaviour*, **15**, 108–17.

La Pierre, R. T. (1934) Attitudes versus actions. *Social Forces*, **13**, 230–37.

Phillips, D. L. (1966) Public identification and acceptance of the mentally ill. *American Journal of Public Health*, **56**, 755–63.

Rabkin, J. (1974) Public attitudes towards mental illness: A review of the literature. *Schizophrenia Bulletin*, **10**, 9–33.

Rutter, M. and Brown, G. W. (1966) The reliability and validity of measures of family life and relationships in families containing a psychiatric patient. *Social Psychiatry*, **1**, 38–53.

Scheff, T. J. (1966) *Being Mentally Ill: A Sociological Theory*. Chicago: Aldine.

Schroder, D. and Ehrlich, D. (1968) Rejection by mental health professionals: A possible consequence of not seeking appropriate help for emotional disorders. *Journal of Health and Social Behaviour*, **9**, 222–32.

Vaughn, C. E. and Leff, J. P. (1976) The influence of family and social factors on the course of psychiatric illness. *British Journal of Psychiatry*, **129**, 125–37.

Whatley, C. D. (1968) Social attitudes toward discharged mental patients. In S. P. Spitzer and N. K. Denzine (eds.), *The Mental Patient*. New York: McGraw-Hill.

Wing, J. K. ed. (1975) *Schizophrenia from Within*. London: National Schizophrenia Fellowship.

Yarrow, M., Clausen, J. A., and Robbins, P. (1955b) The social meaning of mental illness. *Journal of Social Issues*, **11**, 33–48.

Chapter 5

Adler, L. (1955) Patients of a state mental hospital: the outcome of their hospitalisation. In A. Rose (ed.), *Mental Health and Mental Disorder*. New York: W. Norton.

Alivisatos, G. and Lyketsos, G. (1968) A preliminary report of a research concerning the attitudes of the families of hospitalised mental patients. In S. P. Spitzer and N. K. Denzin (eds.), *The Mental Patient*. New York: McGraw-Hill.

Barrett, J., Kurionsky, J. and Gurland, B. (1972) Community tenure following emergency discharge. *Am. Journal Psychiatry*, **128**, 958–64.

Bott, E. (1971) Family and crisis. In H. Freeman (ed.), *Towards Community Mental Health*. London: Tavistock.

Brown G. W., Bone, M., Dalison, B. and Wing., J. K. (1966) *Schizophrenia and Social Care*. London: Oxford University Press.

Creer, C. and Wing, J. K. (1974) *Schizophrenia At Home*. London: National Schizophrenia Fellowship.

Davis, F. (1963) *Passage Through Crisis*. Indianapolis: Bobbs–Merrill.

Eaton, J. W., and Weil, R. J. (1968) The mental health of the Hutterites. In S. P. Spitzer and N. K. Denzin (eds.), *The Mental Patient*. New York: McGraw-Hill.

Evans, A., Bullard, D., and Solomon, M. (1961) The family as a potential resource in the rehabilitation of the chronic schizophrenic patient: a study of 60 patients and their families. *American Journal of Psychiatry*, **117**, 1075–83.

Freeman, H. E. and Simmons, O. G. (1968) Mental patients in the community – Family settings and performance levels. In S. P. Spitzer and N. K. Denzin (eds.), *The Mental Patient*. New York: McGraw-Hill.

Goffman, E. (1963) *Stigma: Notes on the Management of Spoiled Identity*. New York: Prentice Hall.

Grad, J. and Sainsbury, P. (1968) The effects that patients have on their families in a community care and a control psychiatric service – A two year follow-up. *British Journal of Psychiatry*, **114**, 265.

Miles, A. (1978) The social content of health. In Brearley P., Gibbons J., Miles A., Topliss E. and Wood, G. *The Social Context of Health Care*. London: Martin Robertson.

Miles, A. (1979) Some psycho-social consequences of multiple sclerosis: A study of group identity. *British Journal of Medical Psychology*, **1**.

Mills, E. (1962) *Living with Mental Illness*. London: Routledge.

Parsons, T. (1951) *The Social System*. New York: Free Press.

Parsons, T. (1958) Definition of health and illness in the light of American values and social structure. In E. G. Jaco (ed.), *Patients, Physicians and Illness*. New York: Free Press.

Rogler, L. H. and Hollingshead, A. B. (1965) *Trapped: Families and Schizophrenia*. New York: John Wiley.

Rutter, M. L., Quinton, D., and Yule, B. A. (1976) *Family Pathology and Disorder in the Children*. New York: Wiley.

Rutter, M. and Madge, N. (1976) *Cycles of Disadvantage*. London: Heinemann.

Shepherd, M., Cooper, B., Brown, A. C. and Kalton, G. W. (1966) *Psychiatric Illness in General Practice*. London: Oxford University Press.

Yarrow, M., Clause, J. A. and Robbins, P. (1955b) The social meaning of mental illness. *Journal of Social Issues*, **11**, 33–48.

Wing, J. K. (1977) The management of schizophrenia in the community. Lecture to the American College of Psychiatrists, Atlanta.

Chapter 6

Balint, M. (1957) *The Doctor, His Patient, and the Illness*. London: Tavistock.

Bernard, J. (1972) *The Future of Marriage*. New York: Bantam.

Boston Women's Health Collective (1971) *Our Bodies, Ourselves: A Book By and For Women*. New York: Simon and Schuster.

Brown, G. W. and Harris, T. (1978) *Social Origins of Depression: A Study of Psychiatric Disorder in Women*. London: Tavistock.

Chaiton, A., Spitzer, W. O., Roberts, R. S. and Delmore, T. (1976) The patterns of medical drug use. *Canadian Medical Association Journal*, **114**, 33.

Chesler, P. (1971) Women as psychiatric and psychotherapeutic patients. *Journal of Marriage and the Family*, **33**, 746–59.

Chesler, P. (1972) *Women and Madness*. New York: Doubleday.
Clancy, K. and Gove, W. R. (1974) Sex differences in mental illness. *American Journal of Sociology*, **80**, 205.
Cooperstock, R. (1978) Sex differences in psychotropic drug use. *Social Science and Medicine*, **12**, 3B. 179–86.
Dalton, K. (1969) *The Menstrual Cycle*. Harmondsworth: Penguin.
Dohrenwend, B. P. and Dohrenwend, B. S. (1969) *Social Status and Psychological Disorder: A Causal Inquiry*. New York: John Wiley.
Dohrenwend, B. P. and Dohrenwend, B. S. (1976) Sex differences and psychiatric disorders. *American Journal of Sociology*, **81**, 1447–54.
Dunnell, K. and Cartwright, A. (1972) *Medicine Takers, Prescribers and Hoarders*. London: Routledge.
Gavron, H. (1966) *The Captive Wife*. Harmondsworth: Penguin Books.
Gove, W. R. (1972) The relationship between sex roles, mental illness and marital status. *Social Forces*, **51**, 34–44.
Gove, W. R. (1978) Sex differences in mental illness among adult men and women. *Social Science and Medicine*. **12**, 3B. 187–98.
Gove, W. R. and Tudor, J. F. (1973) Adult sex roles and mental illness. *American Journal of Sociology*, **78**, 812–35.
Gurin, G., Veroff, J. and Feld, S., (1960) *Americans View Their Mental Health*. New York: Basic Books.
Hare, E. H. and Shaw, G. K. (1965) *Mental Health on a New Housing Estate*. London: Oxford University Press.
Hemminki, E. (1974) General practitioners' indications for psychotropic drug therapy. *Scandinavian Journal of Social Medicine*, **2**, 1.
Horwitz, A. (1977) The pathways into psychiatric treatment: some differences between men and women. *Journal of Health and Social Behaviour*, **18**, 169–78.
Komarovsky, M. (1967) *Blue Collar Marriage*. New York: Vintage Books.
Laws, J. (1971) A feminist review of marital adjustment literature. *Journal of Marriage and the Family*, **33**, 483–616.
Leeson, J., and Gray, (1978) *Women and Medicine*. London: Tavistock.
McCranie, E. W., Horowitz, A. J. and Martin, R. H. (1978) Alleged sex-role stereotyping in the assessment of women's physical complaints – a study of general practitioners. *Social Science and Medicine*, **12**, 111–16.
Mechanic, D. (1968) *Medical Sociology*. New York: Free Press.
Mechanic, D. (1978). Sex, illness behaviour and the use of health services. *Social Science and Medicine*, **12**, 3B.
Marks, I. (1969) *Fears and Phobias*. New York: Academic Press.

Mostow, E., and Newberry, P. (1975) Work role and depression in women. *American Journal of Orthopsychiatry*, **45**, 538.
Nathanson, C. A. (1975) Illness and the feminine role: a theoretical review. *Social Science and Medicine*, **9**, 57.
Oakley, A. (1972) *Sex, Gender and Society*. London: Temple Smith.
Oakley, A. (1974) *The Sociology of Housework*. London: Martin Robertson.
Phillips, D. L., and Segal, B. (1969) Sexual status and psychiatric symptoms. *American Sociological Review*, **29**, 678–87.
Prather, J. and Fidell, L. (1975) Sex differences in the content and style of medical advertisements. *Social Science and Medicine*, **9**, 23.
Rutter, M. (1970) Sex differences in children's responses to family stress. In E. J. Anthony and C. M. Koupernik (eds.) *The Child and His Family*. New York: John Wiley.
Rutter, M., and Madge, N. (1976) *Cycles of Disadvantage*. London: Heinemann.
Scheff, T. J. (1966) *Being Mentally Ill: A Sociological Theory*. Chicago: Aldine.
Shepherd, M., Cooper, B., Brown, A. C. and Kalton, G. W. (1966) *Psychiatric Illness in General Practice*. London: Oxford University Press.
Thompson, E. L. (1979) Sexual bias in drug advertisements. *Social Science and Medicine*, **13**, 187–191.
Wadsworth, M., Butterfield, W. J. and Blaney, R. (1971) *Health and Sickness: The Choice of Treatment*. London: Tavistock.
Westergaard, J. and Resler, H. (1975) *Class in a Capitalist Society*. Harmondsworth: Penguin Books.
Willmott, P. and Young, M. (1962) *Family and Class in a London Suburb*. London: Routledge.

Chapter 7

Bott, E. (1957) *Family and Social Network*. London: Tavistock.
Brenner, M. H. (1973) *Mental Illness and the Economy*. Cambridge: Harvard University Press.
Brown, G. W. and Birley, J. L. T. (1968) Crises and life changes and the onset of schizophrenia. *Journal of Health and Social Behaviour*, **9**, 203–14.
Brown, G. W., Harris, T. O. and Peto, J. (1973) Life events and psychiatric disorders: nature and causal link. *Psychological Medicine*, **3**, 159–76.
Brown, G. W., Ni Bhrolchain, M. and Harris, T. O. (1975) Social class and psychiatric disturbance among women in an urban population. *Sociology*, **9**, 225–54.

Brown, G. W., Davidson, S., Harris, T. O., Maclean, U. and Prudo, R. (1977) Psychiatric disorder in London and North Uist. *Social Science and Medicine*, **11**.

Brown, G. W. and Harris, T. (1978) *Social Origins of Depression: A Study of Psychiatric Disorder in Women*. London: Tavistock.

Birley, J. L. T. and Brown, G. W. (1970) Crises and life changes preceding the onset or relapse of acute schizophrenia. *British Journal of Psychiatry*, **116**, 322–27.

Cartwright, A. and O'Brien (1976) Social class variations in health care and in the nature of general practitioner consultations. In M. Stacey (ed.) *The Sociology of the NHS*. Sociological Review Monograph No. 22. University of Keele.

Dohrenwend, B. P. and Dohrenwend, B. S. (1969) *Social Status and Psychological Disorder: A Causal Inquiry*. New York: John Wiley.

Dohrenwend, B. P. (1975) Sociocultural and social-psychological factors in the genesis of mental disorders. *Journal of Health and Social Behaviour*, **16**, 365–92.

Dunham, H. W. (1965) Social class and schizophrenia. *American Journal of Orthopsychiatry*, **34**, 634.

Faris, R. E. L. and Dunham, H. W. (1939) *Mental Disorders in Urban Areas*. Chicago: University Press.

Goldberg, E. M. and Morrison, S. L. (1963) Schizophrenia and social class. *British Journal of Psychiatry*, **109**, 785–802.

Goldthorpe, J. H. and Hope, K. (1974) *The Social Grading of Occupations: A New Approach and Scale*. London: Oxford University Press.

Hagnell, O. (1966) *A Prospective Study of the Incidence of Mental Disorder*. Lund: Scandinavian University Books.

Hollingshead, A. and Redlich, R. C. (1958) *Social Class and Mental Illness*. New York: John Wiley.

Holmes, T. H., and Rahe, R. H. (1967) The social readjustment rating scale. *Journal of Psychosomatic Research*, **11**, 213–18.

Jarvis, E. (1855) *Report on Insanity and Idiocy in Massachusetts, by the Commission on Lunacy*. Boston: William White.

Kadushin, C. (1969) *Why People go to Psychiatrists*. New York: Atherton.

Kohn, M. L. (1979) Class, family and schizophrenia: A reformulation. In G. L. Albrecht and P. C. Higgins (eds.) *Health, Illness and Medicine*. Chicago: Rand McNally.

Komarovsky, M. (1967) *Blue Collar Marriage*. New York: Vintage Books.

Leighton, A. H. (1959) *My Name is Legion*. New York: Basic Books.

Leighton, D. C., Harding, J. S., Macklin, D. B. (1963) *The Character of Danger*. New York: Basic Books.

Leighton, D. C., Hagnell, O., and Leighton, A. H. (1971) Psychiatric disorder in a Swedish and a Canadian community: An exploratory study. *Social Science and Medicine*, **5**, 189–209.

Liem, R. and Liem, J. (1978) Social class and mental illness reconsidered: The role of economic stress and social support. *Journal of Health and Social Behaviour*, **19**, 139–56.

Mechanic, D. (1962) *Students Under Stress: A Study in the Social Psychology of Adaptation*. New York: Free Press.

Mechanic, D. (1968) *Medical Sociology*. New York: Free Press.

Myers, J. and Bean, L. (1968) *A Decade Later: A Follow-up of Social Class and Mental Illness*. New York: John Wiley.

Myers, J. (1974) Social class, life events and psychiatric symptoms: A longitudinal study. In B. S. Dohrenwend, and B. P. Dohrenwend, (eds.) *Stressful Life Events: Their Nature and Effects*. New York: Wiley.

Myers, J. (1975) Life events, social integration, and psychiatric symptomalogy. *Journal of Health and Social Behaviour*, **16**, 121–7.

Parkes, C. M. (1972) *Bereavement: Studies of Grief in Adult Life*. London: Tavistock.

Paykel, E. S. (1974) Recent life events and clinical depression. In E. K. E. Gunderson and R. D. Rahe (eds.) *Life Stress and Illness*. Illinois: Charles Thomas.

Rutter, M. L., Cox, A., Tupling, C., Berger, M. and Yule, W. (1975a) Attainment and adjustment in two geographical areas: The prevalence of psychiatric disorder. *British Journal of Psychiatry*, **126**, 493–509.

Rutter, M. L., Yule, B., Quinton, D., Rowlands, O., Yule, W. and Berger, M. (1975b) Attainment and adjustment in two geographical areas: Some factors accounting for area differences. *British Journal of Psychiatry*, **126**, 520–33.

Rutter, M. and Madge, N. (1976) *Cycles of Disadvantage*. London: Heinemann.

Schwabb, J. J. and Schwabb, M. E. (1978) *Sociocultural Roots of Mental Illness: An Epidemiologic Survey*. New York: Plenum.

Srole, L., Langner, T. S., Michael, S. T., Opler, M. K. and Rennie, T. A. C. (1962) *Mental Health in the Metropolis: The Midtown Manhattan Study*. New York: McGraw-Hill.

Turner, R. and Wagenfeld, M. (1967) Occupational mobility and schizophrenia: An assessment of social causation and social selection hypothesis. *American Sociological Review*, **32**, 104.

Westergaard, J. and Resler, H. (1976) *Class in a Capitalist Society*. Harmondsworth: Penguin Books.

Chapter 8

Balint, M. (1957) *The Doctor, His Patient and the Illness*. London: Tavistock.
Balint, M., Hunt, J., Joyce, D., Marinker, H. and Woodcock, J. (1970) *Treatment or Diagnosis? A Study of Repeat Prescriptions in General Practice*. London: Tavistock.
Balter, M. B. (1974) *New England Journal of Medicine*, **290**, 769.
Cartwright, A. (1967) *Patients and Their Doctors*. London: Routledge.
Cooperstock, R. (1978) Sex difference in psychotropic drug use. *Social Science and Medicine*, **12**, 3B, 179–86.
Dunnell, K. and Cartwright, A. (1972) *Medicine Takers, Prescribers and Hoarders*. London: Routledge.
Flew, A. (1973) *Crime or Disease?* London: MacMillan.
Freidson, E. (1973) *Profession of Medicine: A Study of the Sociology of Applied Knowledge*. New York: Dodd and Mead.
Illich, I. (1975) *Medical Nemesis*. London: Calder and Boyars.
Laurence, D. R. and Black, J. W. (1978) *The Medicine You Take: Benefits and Risks of Modern Drugs*. Fontana.
Office of Health Economics (1975) *Medicines Which Affect the Mind*. London: OHE.
Parish, P. A. (1971) The prescribing of psychotropic drugs in general practice. *Journal of the Royal College of General Practitioners*, **21**, Supplement 4.
Parish, P. A., Williams, W. M. and Elmes, P. C. (eds.) (1973) The medical use of psychotropic drugs. *The Journal of Royal College of General Practitioners*, **23**, Supplement 2.
Parsons, T. (1951) *The Social System*. New York: Free Press.
Robinson, D. (1976) *From Drinking to Alcoholism: A Sociological Commentary*. London: John Wiley.
Shepherd, M., Cooper, B., Brown, A. C., and Kalton, G. W. (1966) *Psychiatric Illness in General Practice*. London: Oxford University Press.
Stimson, G., and Webb, B. (1975) *Going to See the Doctor: The Consultation Process in General Practice*. London: Routledge.
Stimson, G. (1975) Women in a doctored world *New Society*, **32**, 265.
Wootton, B. (1959) *Social Science and Social Pathology*. London: Allen and Unwin.

Subject Index

'Accommodation' of mental
   illness, 43–9, 84, 117,
   135–6
   breakdown of, 49, 84–6
Admission to hospital, 17–19,
   80–1, 84–9
   and social class, 164–7, 188–9
Advertising, 159–61, 198
Advice-seeking, within lay
   groups, 36–9, 122
Alcoholism, 4, 30, 58, 63, 154,
   195, 203, 204
Anti-psychiatry, 5, 207
   and R. D. Laing, 9–12
   and T. Szasz, 5–9
   consequences of, 21–4
Anti-social behaviour, 4, 154,
   203

Community care, 116, 118
Concealment of mental illness,
   104–105
   by relatives, 132–4
'Conspiratorial' approach to
   mental illness, 20, 22

Depression
   and drug-advertising, 161
   help-seeking for, 52
   increase in, 195
   London study of, 176–81

self recognition of, 30
sex-distribution of, 143–4
Deviant behaviour
   as illness, 3, 4, 5
   as mental illness, 202–7
   labelling theory of, 13–14
   primary and secondary, 58–9
Deviation
   from health, 2, 4
   from usual behaviour, 27–9
Disease, notion of, 1–2, 7
Divorce, following mental
   illness, 141–2
Doctors
   accessibility of, 50–1
   and women patients, 156–9
   consulting, 52
   experience with, 51–2
   legitimising illness, 3, 5, 57,
      200
   past records of, 195
Double-bind, 10, 12
'Downward drift', 167–71
Drinking problems, *see*
   Alcoholism

Education, and attitudes, 67, 98
Employment
   and life events, 183
   of ex-patients, 101–2, 107–10
   of women, 146–7

Subject Index

Environment, and stress, 171–81
'Expressed Emotion' index, 113–14

Family
  as an influence on normal functioning, 110–14
  as cause of mental illness, 10–11, 23
  definition of, 115
  relationships, 112–14, 123–5
  strains on, 118–25

General Practitioners, 50–1, 75–8
  and differential labelling, 156–9
  and prescribing, 196–7, 199
  and psychotherapy, 199
  and 'trivial' complaints, 194
  increase in consultations with, 195–6

Health
  norms of, 2
  notion of, 7–8, 60
  of mental patients' relatives, 125–8
Help-seeking, 49–53
  and marital relationships, 38
  and marital status, 38
  and networks, 42–3
  and stigma, 82–4
  of women, 151–4
Housewives and mental illness, 146, 147, 148, 153, 180
Hutterites, 41, 139–40

Illness
  and drug-advertising, 161
  and feelings of guilt, 121
  as a social state, 1–3
  in family of mental patients, 125–8
  in theory of Thomas Szasz, 6–8
  legitimisation of, 5, 57, 200
  mental disturbance as, 65–6
  notion of, 1, 3
  social consequences of, 3, 16
Interaction stratagems, 131–3

Labelling people
  and social class, 188–91
  as mentally ill, 80–1, 92
  sex-related, 155–9
Labelling theory
  criticism of, 18–22
  of deviant behaviour, 12–14
  of mental illness, 14–18
Lay-consultations, 36–43, 122
Lay-definitions of mental illness, 26–30
  and religion, 40–1
  and social class, 39–40
Lay-recognition of mental illness, 26–33
Lay-referral system, 37, 38–41, 43, 50
Legitimisation of illness, 5, 57, 200
Life-events, 172–6
  and social class, 177–84

Madness
  stereotype of, 15–16, 63–5
  tradition of, 3–4
Marital relationships
  and accommodation of symptoms, 47
  and depression, 180–1
  and helpseeking, 38
  and recognition of mental illness, 33
  and stress for women, 148
Marital status
  and depression in women, 178

and functioning after
  discharge, 110–12
and help-seeking, 38
and rates of mental illness,
  145, 147
and recognition of mental
  illness, 32
and stress, 148–9
Mass media, 63–4
Medicalisation, 198
Medical practitioners *see*
  Doctors, General
  Practitioners, Psychiatrists
Midtown Manhattan Study, 170

National Morbidity Surveys,
  195
Neurosis
  as a label for women, 156–7
  of mothers, 127–8
  rates of, 143–4, 146, 149, 155
Normalisation, 45–6

Prescription of psychotropic
  drugs, 196–7, 198, 199
  and women, 162–3
Primary deviation, 58
Psychiatrists, 61, 79–81, 205
  and expansion of psychiatry,
    205
  and working class patients,
    189–90
  criticism of, 8–9, 12, 17–20,
    22
  referral to, 76–8
Psychotropic drugs
  advertisements of, 159–61
  availability of, 204
  consumption of, 196–7, 198
  cost of, 200
  sex differences in the use of,
    161–3

Quality of life, 193–4

Rape, 61, 63
Rates of mental illness
  and marital status, 145, 147
  and social class, 164–6
  geographical differences in,
    184–8
  sex-related differences in,
    143–5
Rejection of mental patients,
  60–3, 66, 69, 82–4, 93–7,
  98, 100–1
  and education, 67
  and social class, 67
  and the mass media, 63–4
  by relatives, 69, 140–2
Relatives of mental patients
  accommodation by, 46, 117
  and social networks, 42–3
  and stigma, 128–34
  attitudes of, 69, 134–42
  burden on, 117–24
  health of, 125–8
  reporting symptoms by, 44
  requests for hospital
    admission by, 87–8
Religion, and help-seeking, 40–1
Repeat prescriptions, 197–8
Role-congruity, 151
Rule-breaking behaviour,
  14–16, 17
Rural areas, 185–8

Schizophrenia
  and downward mobility,
    168–9, 170–1
  and life-events, 175–6
  and social class, 167
  in the theories of Laing, 9–12
  lay-recognition of, 26–7
  sex-distribution in, 143
Secondary deviation, 58–9, 91

Self-recognised problems, 26, 29–30, 35
Self-treatment, 47–8
Sex-roles, 151, 154
Sexual offences, 61, 64
Sick role, 72–3, 74, 106, 116, 136, 200
   and women, 151
   concept of, 55–60
   of discharged patients, 111–12
Sleeplessness, 30, 32, 196, 200
Social acceptability, 99
Social class
   and attitudes to mental illness, 67–8
   and depression, 176–81
   and labelling, 188–91
   and lay recognition, 39–40
   and schizophrenia, 167
   and stress, 176–84
   and rates of mental illness, 164–7
Social cohesiveness, 185–6
Social distance scales, 93–4
Social mobility, 168
Social networks, 41–3, 139–40, 152
Social norms
   and lay consultations, 37
   concerning family relationships, 125, 136
   concerning health, 2, 8
   violation of, 14
Social roles, 55, 57–9, 72
   disruption of, 31–2
   ex-patients' performance of, 106–13
Social visibility, 31
Societal Reaction theory, *see* Labelling Theory
Stigma, 3, 69–71, 74, 82–7, 88, 92–3, 97–9, 201–2
   management of, 102–6
   attached to relatives, 7, 122, 128–34, 171
Stirling County Study, 185
Stress, 172–6
   and social class, 154–5, 176–84
   and urban living, 186
   and women, 146
   on families, 118–23

Under-reporting of symptoms, 200–2
   by general practitioners, 75
   by relatives, 44
Unemployment, 182–3
   of discharged patients, 108–10
Unpredictability, 61, 62, 71, 120
Urban living and mental illness rates, 164, 184–8

Voluntary patients, 87–8
Vulnerability, 145, 149, 179–80, 184, 187

Widows, 32
Women
   and depression, 176–81
   and drug-advertisements, 159–61
   and drug-use, 161–3
   and functioning after discharge, 107, 111–12
   and medicine consumption, 150, 162
   and reporting symptoms, 150–4
   labelling of, 155–8
   mental illness rates of, 143–5
   social position of, 146–50